ASPECTS OF EDUCATIONAL
TECHNOLOGY

Aspects of Educational Technology

Volume IX
Educational Technology
for Continuous
Education

Edited for the Association for
Programmed Learning
and Educational Technology by
**Lionel Evans
and John Leedham**

General Editor:
John Leedham

Kogan Page

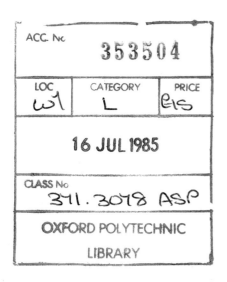
First published 1975
by Kogan Page Limited,
116a Pentonville Road, London N1 9JN
Reprinted 1977

Printed in Great Britain by
Anchor Press Ltd, Tiptree, Essex

ISBN 0 85038 291 2

Conference theme and presentation:'educational technology for continuous education'

JOHN LEEDHAM

The City University Conference of the Association, held in April 1975, was the tenth of our Conferences. The fact that this volume of 'Aspects' is the ninth refers to the omission of the second Conference publication from the list. This was the occasion when Birmingham University printed their own proceedings. It is a fortunate publishing occasion for us that on this, our tenth anniversary, Kogan Page have issued the volume. At the same time they are now publishers of our Yearbook and, from January 1976, of our Journal. It is appropriate that we should mention this, because it focuses on the fact that this Association has, for ten years, maintained its publications across the field of education and training so that we have indeed the reference literature, in depth, for continuous education.

Whilst it was not these considerations which particularly influenced Leo Evans in his definition of a theme, the European interest in 'l'Education Permanente' fell well into line with our history and development. Since the activities of the Association have always been of an evolutionary nature it was likely that the response to the invitation for papers would span a wide and engaging field of education and training. If readers care to scan the contents list they will appreciate what I mean. Any Conference capable of presenting at a professionally acceptable level, contributions ranging from 'Educational Technology in Lifelong Education' to 'Television Education among the Eskimos' or 'Scouting for Poise' is acknowledging its theme very resolutely.

It behoves me, at this point, to make some apology to contributors who may find some alteration in script. Our anxiety is to get the Proceedings to the members as soon as ever possible. Delay in rendering manuscripts has been acute this year and we have to go to press presently lacking the revised contributions from Dr Rein Buter on 'Unconventional observations on the possibility of a more general use of educational technology' and Cook and Tattersall 'Job analysis of the Naval Instructor'. I hope that it will be possible to find room for these contributions in one or other of our publications.

The Conferences of the Association have had much benefit from the contributions of Canadian Universities and Institutions. This year was no exception. The papers from Mitchell, Coldevin and Boyd, for example, feature well as continuing statements of previous work. Any hopeful researcher could do far worse than trace the contributions from Canada through the various 'Aspects of Educational Technology'. He would find a persistence of statement and achievement that in itself contributes very directly to the creation of 'educational technology'. For my part, as general editor, I welcome their contributions and express our warm thanks. Danny Langdon was a newcomer to the Conference. His accounts of his work in a correspondence college largely concerned with insurance practice led to very lively interest and much request for material. It is obvious that, in the field of 'continuing education' the elements of practical and effective instruction claim major attention. It is doubtful if any other Conference could so aptly contain such papers parallel to the philosophical abstractions necessary to examine the why and where of Educational Technology. In this respect the keynote address of Geoffrey Hubbard was welcomed by the members of Conference. As Director of the Council for Educational Technology he is better placed than most to hazard some guesses.

It is still somewhat remarkable, at least to your editor, how many papers are concerned with design and structure both of curriculum and courses. It is not implied that there is less need for such papers, rather that the fresh views and ideas which proceed from them seem never-ending. Not all, of course, are hypothetical; many quote practice very directly. The paper from Kay et al on a teaching laboratory is evidence of this.

The use that UNESCO has made of us in the past year as a reporting organization was indicated by the paper on the APLET survey of the Imaginative Uses of CCTV. The breadth of membership participation that we were able to summon for this exercise shows that APLET indeed can cover the field of continuous education.

The organization of the Conference by Leo Evans at the time when he was also functioning as Honorary Secretary deserves the appreciation and thanks which we most fully tender. He writes elsewhere in his guise as co-editor of the volume, but his own contribution on the unconventional uses of educational technology, demonstrated by what has been referred to as the first ever wine algorithm, most aptly underlined the theme of the Conference.

In the context of our ten volumes of studies, this, our most recent, will take a merited place.

Contents

List of contributors

Anderson, E W ·	Bede College, Durham
Boyd, Professor G M	Education Department, Concordia University, Montreal, Canada (currently on secondment to the National Development Programme in Computer Assisted Learning, London)
Braham, M	The Courtyard, Dartington Hall, Totnes, Devon TO9 6EJ
Brown, R N	Civil Engineering Learning Unit, Heriot-Watt University, 183 Fountainbridge, Edinburgh EH3 9RU
Burnhill, P	Stafford College of Further Education
Calder, J A	The Open University, Walton Hall, Milton Keynes MK7 6AA
Clarke, Dr W D	Department of Audiovisual Communication, BMA House, Tavistock Square, London WC1H 9JP
Coldevin, Professor G O	Concordia University, Montreal, Canada
Coombs, M J	Centre for Communication Studies, The University of Liverpool, Chatham Street, Liverpool L69 3BX
Cowan, J	Civil Engineering Learning Unit, Heriot-Watt University, 183 Fountainbridge, Edinburgh EH3 9RU
Daniel, J S	Télé Université, Quebec, Canada
El-Araby, Dr S A	AV Resources Centre, The American University in Cairo, 113 Kasr Aini Street, Cairo, Egypt
Elton, Professor L R B	Institute for Educational Technology, University of Surrey, Guildford, Surrey
Evans, L F	Centre for Educational Technology, The City University, St John Street, London EC1V 4PB
Farnes, N C	The Open University, Walton Hall, Milton Keynes MK7 6AA
Fraser, Susan	University of Keele, Keele, Staffordshire ST5 5BG
Gilmore, S	Department of Education, University of Stirling, Stirling FK9
Gould, Judith	AV Resources Centre, The American University in Cairo, 113 Kasr Aini Street, Cairo, Egypt

Hartley, Dr J	University of Keele (Department of Psychology), Keele, Staffordshire ST5 5BG
Hills, Dr P J	Institute for Educational Technology, University of Surrey, Guildford, Surrey
Hubbard, G	Council for Educational Technology, 3 Devonshire Street, London W1N 2BA
Jolly, B C	Department of Audiovisual Communication, BMA House, Tavistock Square, London WC1H 9JP
Kay, S M	Physics Department, Royal Holloway College, London
Kerr, R H, Lieutenant Commander, CF	SO Systems Development, Training Command Headquarters, Westwin, Manitoba, Canada
Langdon, D G	Director of Instructional Design, The American College of Life Underwriters, 270 Bryn Mawr Avenue, Bryn Mawr, Pennsylvania 19010, USA
Leedham, Dr J, OBE	Loughborough College of Education, Loughborough, Leicestershire
Lincoln, Mrs L	University of Surrey, Guildford, Surrey
Mackie, A	1 Brakspear Drive, Corsham, Wilts
McCormick, R	The Open University, Walton Hall, Milton Keynes MK7 6AA
Mitchell, Professor P D	Department of Education, Sir George Williams Campus, Concordia University, Montreal, Canada
O'Connell, S	University of Surrey, Institute for Educational Technology, Guildford, Surrey
Penton, S	University of Surrey, Institute for Educational Technology, Guildford, Surrey
Romiszowski, A J	47 Lissenden Mansions, Lissenden Gardens, London NW5
Turner, L P	University of Surrey, Guildford, Surrey
Turok, B	The Open University, Walton Hall, Milton Keynes MK7 6AA
Young, Margrette	University of Keele, Keele, Staffordshire ST5 5BG

(All addresses in the United Kingdom unless otherwise stated)

The host university

PROFESSOR J C LEVY, Pro-Vice Chancellor of the City University

On behalf of the Vice-Chancellor of the City University I extend a friendly and warm welcome today to all the delegates at this conference on Educational Technology for Continuous Education.

May I particularly welcome those of you who have come from abroad. I notice that a large number of countries are represented including Belgium, Canada, Egypt, France, Germany, Holland, Hungary, India, Kenya, Switzerland, Thailand and the USA. The fact that there is such a wide representation indicates, I think, an interest both in the Association and in the subject of the conference. It is certainly true that educational technology has received much serious and imaginative consideration during the past decade, leading not just to effective use of the new hardware now at our disposal, but also to new and progressive attitudes among the teaching profession as a whole.

When this solid achievement is linked, as you intend to link it in the next few days, with the idea of continuous education through life, an idea which is generally acknowledged to be a fitting target for the 70's and 80's, then interesting and constructive proceedings can confidently be anticipated.

The City University, I should stress, is entirely an appropriate venue for the conference. You are now sitting in our new lecture theatre but the City University in its former guise of Northampton Polytechnic goes back many decades and throughout that time has been concerned with continuing education. Both your chairman, Leo Evans, who is, I am pleased to see, your Honorary General Secretary, and myself have taken part in such activities here for many years past. Formerly the courses covered a very wide range of industrial and commercial subjects at degree and sub-degree level. Latterly they have included an almost equally wide range at post-experience and postgraduate level. So you are meeting essentially in a sympathetic atmosphere and indeed what are your meetings, seminars and members' marathons (not to mention the buffet-dinners and bar music hall) but themselves an exercise in continuing education?

I look forward to attending as many of the sessions as I can and from the City University I cordially wish the conference every success.

Acknowledgements

The Association for Programmed Learning and Educational Technology wishes to acknowledge the assistance given by the following organizations and individuals, who through their efforts ensured the success of the Conference:

> The City University
> The Corporation of the City of London
> Guildhall
> London Transport
> The Stock Exchange
> The Tower Theatre
> Searcy Tansley & Co Ltd
> Kogan Page Ltd
> Inter Université
> The British Council

P Aprile, P R Brown, J Chant, Mrs P M Day, Mrs W F Ghouse, D Langdon, R B Matkin, C Neville, Miss J Swann, R J Britton

Sir James Pitman KBE, Chancellor of the University of Bath, addressed the Association on the occasion of his retirement from Presidential Office. His reminder to the Association of the role of language most aptly reminded us of the distinguished contribution our retiring President has made in the wider field of education. The Association marks with great appreciation his period of Presidency.

Keynote address: perspectives for life-long education

GEOFFREY HUBBARD

WHAT IS LIFE-LONG EDUCATION?

There is no great difficulty in agreeing on a general view of the underlying concept of life-long or continuing education: that education goes on, or should go on, throughout a person's life, and should not be treated as something which is got over in the years between five and fifteen - or twenty-five - which are devoted to continuous full-time education.

And yet, what is so novel about that? This University in which we are meeting has its origins in just that world of mechanics' institutes and evening classes which have provided second chances, vocational training, retraining and cultural enrichment for so many. I'm happy too, to be able to assure you that the City University does not forget its responsibilities in this area; I enrolled a few terms back for a most enjoyable and informative series of evening lectures on Victorian Accidents.

Perhaps among the many synonyms the one I have not yet used is particularly revealing - 'recurrent education'. The new concept is, I suspect, more concerned with the need and opportunity for the individual to acquire education and training when he wants it, rather than when the education system is programmed to supply it. New concepts usually imply changed attitudes; the attitude that goes with life-long education is that education is different from the measles - having it once does not confer immunity to a further bout; a radically different attitude from that which leads to phrases like 'he completed his education at the University of Bognor Regis'.

Implicit in most discussion of life-long education is the idea also that it is a general right rather than a restricted privilege. There should be something for everyone. Now this is a somewhat curious idea, which needs to be looked at with caution. In the context of a developed country, with universal secondary education and a most varied and complex provision for further, higher, adult and informal education it is difficult to see what a universal system of life-long education would offer that is not in theory already available. The main barriers to taking advantage of these opportunities are those of sacrificing earning power, or leisure time, and of the sheer work and application involved in following a course. Professor Dahrendorf, in his Reith Lectures, (Dahrendorf, 1975) suggests that the difference is between "a catching-up with things which some have been lucky enough to get more easily the first time round" and giving people "a chance to do new things ... to return to the classroom in order to structure their experience of life and work, or to develop possibilities which their lives made them discover, to improve themselves."

Now I am not sure that this is altogether a valid distinction between old-style adult education and new-style recurrent education. I think there were always those who came back because their experience of life and work had caused them to revalue education. I think of a friend of mine who gave up his degree course thirty years ago because of his interest in political activity and who will be taking his finals at Birkbeck College this year. And the many who have their interest in the arts, sport or leisure pursuits fired by a television series and then turn to educational institutions for further and more structured assistance. It is almost tautological - since there is a straight-through route from the primary school to the top of the tree everyone who comes back to education after a break is 'catching up' - and equally everyone who studies something they don't know already is doing new things. I suspect that the crucial words Professor Dahrendorf used were 'more easily'. The straight-through route is easier in three main ways. First the guidance and counselling mechanism is geared to it - we offer those who go on into higher education much clearer and more coherent guidance than we offer to those who want to return to education; there is really no easily accessible counselling service on the very wide and confusing range of adult and further education services.

Second, the economic support arrangements are designed for the straight-through route. We all know about mandatory student grants for first degrees - we don't (for my part anyway) know half as much about how an adult seeking to renew his education might seek support.

And third, the adult has, inevitably, made it more difficult for himself. He has responsibilities, he may have family ties, he is used to a certain standard of comfort and he is out of the habit of maintaining intensive intellectual effort over a prolonged period. He can no longer face with equanimity, thanks to his experience of life and work, the student life of study bedroom or shared untidy flat, of refectory meals or pie and chips. And against this, is the alternative of trying to find study time in a home already filled with shared activities any easier? Some Open University students have faced serious difficulty over a husband or wife who feels excluded and rejected when the partner who has for so long shared their leisure time retreats in order to study.

So, my conclusion is that life-long education will come about not through the provision of new systems of education, new courses, new opportunities, but through facilitating access to, and therefore stimulating demand for, existing opportunities. And the three main steps I see as necessary are to provide an easily accessible counselling and guidance service, to simplify, extend and publicize arrangements for economic support, and to develop both the educational and economic arrangements in ways which respond to the real situation and the real needs of the adult student, not only (as in all fairness I think the educational community has always tried to do) to his educational needs, but also to his social and personal situation. If I may quote once again from Professor Dahrendorf's Reith Lectures, I would like to draw attention to

18

the passage in which he says:

"Modern society can afford a sabbatical for everybody. Short of such a rule, or perhaps to supplement it, why not give every young man and woman a voucher for, say, three years tertiary, or further, education. This right could be used up immediately after school, or later, in one lot, or scattered over a lifetime. It would offer new and relevant choices, and at a cost hardly greater than that of forcing an academic or polytechnic education down the throats of 10, 20 or even 30 per cent of all young people straight out of school."

I would strongly urge that we should work out just such a scheme - except that I would like to see it incorporate a built-in break after school of, say, two years. This suggestion is frightening to some academics, who fear that once young people are allowed to see the world outside they might choose not to come back into the cloister, or on to the treadmill. But would it be so terrible if our institutions of higher education contained only those who positively wanted to be there, rather than, as at present, large numbers carried there by momentum and inertia, or by the desire to put off as long as possible an encounter with the real world?

DO WE NEED LIFE-LONG EDUCATION?

Implicit in most discussion of life-long education is the assumption that education is a good thing and you cannot have too much of a good thing. To examine this thesis I think we need to break down life-long education into a number of component parts. First there are (i) vocational training and retraining and (ii) professional updating. The divisions are blurred; the terminology just a little snobbish - they get retrained, we get updated. But essentially this is the activity by which we keep ourselves in a position to be gainfully employed in a society changing so rapidly that a single training will no longer last a lifetime. The justification for this part of life-long education is imperative - both for a society which requires to redeploy the skills of its members and for the individual whose sense of his own worth depends on being able to hold down a good job.

The next pair of components are (iii) informal education and education for leisure and (iv) education for its own sake, as a self-justifying occupation. You may think that the distinction here is also tenuous, that informal education is the same as education for its own sake, but I think they are, or can be, very different activities. After all, a good example of informal education might be a television series on coarse fishing, and much informal education develops possibilities in connection with leisure activities. On the other hand, education for its own sake may be informal and relatively unstructured, but can well be formal and directed to very specific attainment, or to a relentlessly academic goal. The odd thing about education is that it is so thoroughly worthwhile in itself, and yet we spend so much of our time trying to find external justifications for it. Yet every now and then the student, in defiance of all our sophistry, suddenly discovers the intrinsic pleasure of learning. I think this distinction worth making because it points to a difference in justification. As regards learning for its own sake, I would unashamedly see this as a cultural activity, like running symphony orchestras and preserving great architecture. We should have as much of it as we can possibly afford; it is part of the purpose of being civilized, and the more those who wish to study for its own sake, without any other motive or any hope of recognition or reward are enabled to do so, the better our civilization will be. The justification of informal education for leisure is a little different. It is more a matter of a social requirement, a way of helping people to enjoy and explore the world about them and the time at their disposal. Its importance depends very much on how much time people have at their disposal, and it begins to occupy a more important place in our thinking as we recognize that some of us are born leisured, some attain leisure, but all too many have leisure thrust upon them - a point to which I shall return later.

A third pair of components are (v) education in social, political and economic awareness and (vi) community activities, often not overtly educational. Education in social, political and economic awareness is obviously desirable, if you believe in real democracy. It is only the up-to-date jargon for the post-Reform Bill observation that "we must educate our masters". The society we are expected to participate in is becoming more and more complicated, the answers to its problems less definite; and yet our political leaders are becoming, it seems, even more anxious that we should understand, that we should use our opportunities to take wisely the decisions that, in a more robust age, they would have taken for us!

Community activity, in its extreme form, consists of eager souls convinced that a portapak and open access television are the solution to all social and personal problems. As I mentioned, these activities are not overtly educational, yet the making of a videotaped record of a community problem, or the publishing of one of those local action group newspapers, apart from being an effective way of influencing what happens, educates those who see or read it, and those who make it. Yet this sort of education, rather more than that formally directed to improving people's understanding of the political process, is likely to be troublesome to those in positions of power.

I make this point because it seems that apart from the economic necessity of retraining, most aspects of life-long education are not prima facie likely to commend themselves to local or central government. They are of benefit to the individual, they enrich his life and leisure, they help him to understand, and be more effective in, his political and social role; they may help him to be questioning, to insist on his rights. Small wonder that governments have tended to have great schemes for industrial training, and kind words for adult education.

Yet there does seem to be a change of heart, not just in this country but in all the developed countries. I wonder why? Shall I, for a moment, forego my customary wide-eyed innocence, and be just a little bit cynical?

You see, we are facing some profound structural problems, problems which are going to affect our society radically. Professor William Gosling called his inaugural lecture at Bath University of Technology last year 'Technology at Childhood's End' (Gosling, 1974). His exposition is much simpler than the report to the Club of Rome, but the message is the same. You can't go on following an exponential curve - there has to come a turning point, and the turning point is more or less now.

William Gosling and I have a number of odd features in common, including a certain inexplicable optimism about things in general. I think we will get past the turning point; what I'm not so optimistic about is the degree of skill with which we will make the manoeuvre. It is pretty obviously going to involve whole industries being much reduced in size - those which are heavy users of raw materials and energy - and their replacement by others. Professor Gosling points to the microelectronics industry as being a major growth point. Now this transition could be smoothly planned - but I see little sign of it. So I expect the transition phase to be rough, with plenty of enforced leisure in the form of unemployment and early retirement. And this, I suggest, is why we may find an unexpected measure of support by governments for recurrent education - because education is a socially acceptable form of unemployment, and it may be badly needed over the last two decades of this century. Moreover recurrent education, with the emphasis on moving in and out, for shorter or longer spells, as seems appropriate, could very well fill the gaps and ease the transition as old industries decline and new ones take their place. But what must be realized, in good time, is that present structures, present organizations and institutions will not necessarily be able, as they stand, to provide what is needed. While the students may come forward at short notice, as a result of a social or economic upheaval, thought and provision need to be made in advance if these demands are to be met.

WHAT PART CAN EDUCATIONAL TECHNOLOGY PLAY?

Let us start with the easy bit. Wherever, for whatever educational purpose, people gather as a group to learn, educational technology has a part to play, in the provision of learning resources in all forms, and in the design of appropriate and effective learning situations.

And whenever there is a need for information, particularly for example in professional updating, the techniques we are developing for the classifying, cataloguing, storing and retrieving information for educational purposes will have an important part to play. One reflection which might serve to cut the self-important educational technologist down to size is that the really important applications of technology are almost always the applications of well-established skills to new fields, rather than the intellectually impressive development of original systems. So if our work on information and resource handling is only the modification for education of established techniques, it may not be exciting but it is probably fruitful.

But there is one field where educational technology could have a much more dramatic effect. I have commented on earlier occasions that the Open University may be far more significant in its effect on other aspects of education than in its direct effect as a teaching institution. I think this is now becoming obvious. Now life-long education, if it is to be a reality, requires that the facilities are tailored to suit both the educational and the social and personal needs of the student - that what he wants is available for him to pick up when he wants it and when he has time for it.

Don't let us leap to the grandiose obvious solution - the universal open

21

college offering all things by distant learning to all men. But let us instead look at what the Open University has demonstrated - the efficacy and practicability of the course team concept, the problems and realities of distant learning, the importance of proper tutoring and counselling services. Can we apply these lessons in the development of existing facilities to meet the needs of life-long education? I think we can; this could be an opportunity for educational technology to show that it is out of its apprenticeship, that we have learned our craft and can now make a significant contribution to dealing with a major problem.

It may be that in doing this we shall find an unexpected link with those not overtly educational community activities I referred to earlier. A really flexible and adaptable life-long learning system will have an insatiable appetite for learning material - and community groups could well be brought in as providers.

CONCLUSION

Life-long education is still an ill-defined concept - it probably relates more to changes in attitude towards recurrent education and to changes in the accessibility of currently available opportunities rather than to any completely novel provision. It will become more clearly defined under a variety of pressures, many of them non-educational. In this situation we cannot expect to predetermine its development, or even to see very far in advance the nature of the problems to be faced. What we can do is to trust in God and keep our powder dry - be ready to respond to the challenges when they come.

I realise that I have spent most of my time talking about the nature of, and the need for, life-long education and have only sketched in the part educational technology might play. But then that is what the rest of the conference - leaving on one side eating and drinking and 'Bar Music Hall' - is about. So it seems right that I should consider the question 'why', before you go on the question 'how'. 'Why' comes first - and 'why' is more important than 'how'.

REFERENCES

Dahrendorf, R (1975) 'The New Liberty'. Routledge, London
Gosling, W (1974) 'Technology at Childhood's End', University of Bath

Papers concerned with the main theme

The importance and feasibility of 'transparent' universities

GARY M BOYD

The concept of opening-up the ongoing research and scholarly work of
universities via video-computer communications systems has already been
outlined (Boyd 1973, 1974). The idea arose from earlier work attempting
to facilitate learning activities in universities by using video and computer
media. This paper is in three parts: a definition of 'transparent'
universities, a discussion of potential importance, and an outline of
factors affecting feasibility.

DEFINITION

A 'transparent' university is one where the research, criticism and creative
scholarly work of the institution is rendered 'browse-able' and accessible to
everyone within the institution, and out in society at large, via a computer-
communications library system.

   This sounds rather grandiose, and in its final forms will be; but to start
with all it requires is that researchers shall write some comments and
criterion test problems into their computer in association with whatever
research data and analysis programmes they already have there. The
comments are to make things intelligible to onlookers. The criterion problems
would be to test students and others to decide whether or not they can be
permitted to actually write in the files and run programmes on the research
data. Read-only access can be available to any student or other legitimately
interested person. But to avoid 'noise', and damage, 'write' and 'run' must
be restricted to knowledgeable folk, while 'erase' is the prerogative of the
researcher or scholar whose project the files belong to. Figure 1 portrays
these relationships diagrammatically.

   For example: Professor 'X' may be doing research on small-group dynamics
by transcribing protocols of all the communications occurring among groups of
people attempting to solve a problem. This is his data which is subjected to
key; 'chunk' (phrase) searches and sophisticated multi-factor analyses. Instead
of writing their comments in lab books the members of the research team type
them into the computer along with the data. When they run key-word or

25

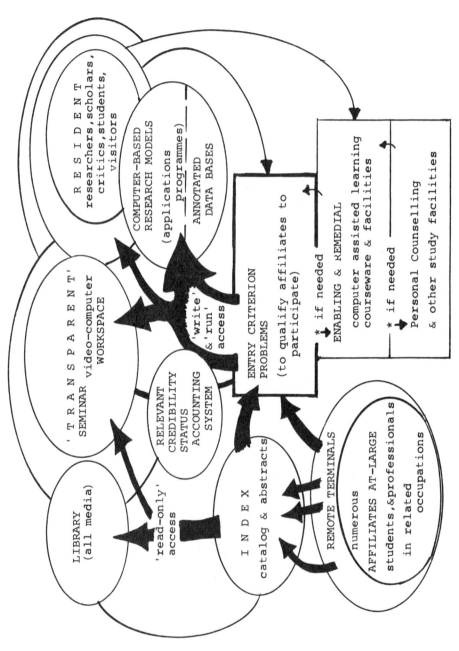

Figure 1. Major functional components of a 'transparent' university

The figure contains the following labelled elements:

RESIDENT researchers, scholars, critics, students, visitors

COMPUTER-BASED RESEARCH MODELS (applications programmes)

ANNOTATED DATA BASES

'TRANSPARENT' SEMINAR video-computer WORKSPACE

RELEVANT CREDIBILITY STATUS ACCOUNTING SYSTEM

LIBRARY (all media)

INDEX catalog & abstracts

REMOTE TERMINALS numerous AFFILIATES AT-LARGE students, & professionals in related occupations

ENTRY CRITERION PROBLEMS (to qualify affiliates to participate)

ENABLING & REMEDIAL computer assisted learning courseware & facilities

Personal Counselling & other study facilities

'write' & 'run' access

'read-only' access

* if needed

key-chunk searches they put in comments as to exactly how they are doing this. And similarly when factor analyses are run, comments on the results and methods are also typed in.

Now it becomes possible for a new member of the team to review what has been done, and run his own checks, without taking up much of anybody's time.

Moreover, social workers and teachers can dial up the files, and get an idea of what sort of research is going on and where it is leading. If they want to participate they can attempt test-questions on the computer and if they pass will be admitted to associate status with the research team via the computer. If the work they do this way proves to be of some value then they may be invited to the college laboratory as visiting workers.

If the would-be associate cannot solve the criterion problems he is referred back to appropriate tutorial modules to help him develop the required knowledge and skills to do so. He or she may also be referred to personal tutors, or to other institutions providing courses of a more elementary nature.

The central point is that this scheme for university studies is focused directly on the advanced problems, and allows all the participation any desirous person is capable of, without cluttering up the work with extra bodies.

Awareness of the opportunities available could be generated through videotaped interviews with contributing researchers to be broadcast, and made available for video-browsing in libraries, and professionals' waiting rooms.

Presently existing 'open-learning' institutions differ from a 'transparent' university in four important respects. These unique aspects of a 'transparent' university are as follows:

1. The primary emphasis is on opening up scholarship, criticism and research to public participation.

2. The secondary emphasis is on focused competence, rather than on general preparation for some vaguely conceived future career.

3. Person-to-person involvement is a privilege to be earned by more formal participation via the computer network.

4. Scholasticism, the elaboration of cultural transmissions without regard to their potential contribution to society, is likely to be ameliorated by the open scrutiny of peers and public (Krauch, 1972).

Notwithstanding the fourth point, a 'transparent' university is probably best regarded as an 'end' rather than as a 'means'. As the noted economist John Vaizey puts it: "I prefer ... to argue that the reason why we have economic

27

growth is because among other things the people need education." and "... we could diminish the sense of urgency with which people seek to acquire qualifications in the greater part of the education system." (Vaizey, 1973). Vaizey's arguments also have much bearing on the feasibility of 'transparent' universities on a large scale in the coming decades.

Having outlined what is meant by a transparent university I will now go on to discuss its importance, and subsequently the feasibility of implementations. The first question to be answered is importance to whom? Three groups of people are involved: scholar-researchers, individuals-at-large with interests in sophisticated problems, and institutions requiring facts and informed criticism in order to make major decisions.

IMPORTANCE

The main reason that the 'transparent' approach to the conduct of a university is likely to prove important to researchers and scholars is that it can probably generate a broader political base - more people will call for government support to aid research, scholarship and critical studies. The amateur astronomer, amateur biologist, amateur historian, amateur philologist, are all voters, all contributors to the climate of public opinion. Numerous worthwhile scientific and cultural programmes and projects are languishing because no pressure of public opinion is felt by funding bodies. And despite Churchill's dictum, public opinion is more than the opinion published in the 'New Scientist' and ' The Times Literary Supplement', or even the 'Daily Telegraph'.

The human imperative is: to elaborate, define, and share appetite-sustaining transmissions - and this is much more fully realizable through scholarship, research, criticism and the arts, than through purchasing consumer goods and watching mass spectacles. "The continuous pursuit of more desirable ends, is an end in itself." (Ackoff & Emery, 1972.) The importance of 'transparent' university studies to people-at-large lies in the opportunity provided to further this open-ended pursuit, which is a defining characteristic of a human being.

Secondly, widespread participation by amateur associates can involve genuine contributions to progress through the collection of research data, and the contribution of novel ideas arising from variety of experience and character. This is important to everyone.

The importance of 'transparent' research access systems to professional practitioners in government, business and the professions, is mainly in allowing them to directly apply the results of research and criticism to their daily decision-making work.

28

FEASIBILITY

Transparent universities can evolve from present-day institutions as faculty members successively conduct more and more of their research and criticism through 'transparent' computer workspaces. The techniques to do this on a small scale exist now and are being used in fact; but not as part of an overall strategy to promote open learning.

Consider three examples:

1. An NDPCAL project at Leeds University, directed by the chemistry researcher P Ayscough, involves modules which back-up and control access to a complex computer programme and data base used for research in physical chemistry. A 'test-teach' CAL package qualifies students through experience with a simplified simulated version of the actual research procedures. This in turn is backed-up for those who need the experience, by more general CAL packages to teach the planning of experiments (Ayscough, 1975). (These in turn are in a sense backed-up by other more elementary packages generated by the Leeds Computer Based Learning Project under Roger Hartley.)

2. The Institute for the Future at Stanford runs a project called 'FORUM'. Via ARPANET a common computer workspace is made directly accessible to a dozen or two professionals scattered all across the continent from Montreal to San Francisco. These people scan the file at least weekly, and enter their conjectures, refutations and points of information for each other in order to solve a major technical, business or scientific problem (depending on which FORUM task group is involved) (Johansen, 1974).

3. At Concordia University in Montreal I have been operating a 'SCRIBE' system on our CDC 6400 computer which transcribes person-to-person tutorials and enables these protocols to be edited up and indexed so as to be readily accessed by other students via computer terminals as a study aid (Boyd, 1972).

There are other indications that incremental implementation is feasible. Prof Alfred Bork at the University of California Irvine has a BROWSE system enabling faculty members at a number of campuses to keep track of and notify each other of instructional development projects. Concordia Monteal has a computer data base on research in progress covering all major projects in all faculties, which one can browse through. Neither of these index systems is directly tied to the current computer files of the projects indexed, and that is primarily what is needed to move in the direction of a 'transparent' university. Without direct connection the indices become obsolete because too much extra work is required to update them to correspond to the changes in operational status of projects and CAL courseware.

Ultimately large-scale 'transparent' universities with tens of thousands of home and office terminals to serve nearly everyone as occasional participants, will be developed to meet human aspirations and to counteract alienation. However, at the present time a large scale (or even Open University scale) 'transparent' university is not possible for several reasons:

1. The access, costing and control systems adequate to this task have not even been conceptualized. I am trying to formalize the problem of assessing the Potency, Timeliness/urgency, and Value of transmissions with respect to the needs and character of each particular participant. More conventional information retrieval problems having to do with 'precision' and 'recall' and accounting (Lancaster & Fayen, 1974) also require solution.

2. The concept or ideal of 'transparent' scholarship, criticism and research, accessible via home and library computer terminals is not yet widely disseminated. If people do not know what is possible they can hardly demand it. The purpose of this paper is to widen appreciation of this conception of a more universal university - one which, incidentally, has already been partly forseen (Brown, 1966).

3. Large-scale 'transparent' university systems are not yet feasible because computers, networks and terminals are not yet cheap enough nor good enough (Catt, 1973). Reliability, ease of use and cost have however reached levels appropriate to prototype investigations (Martin, 1973). Individual teams of research workers might quite easily set up computer and video recording equipment for their research seminars, and link these to annotated data bases as a means of access for apprentice researchers and affiliated professionals working in remote institutions.

4. A large-scale 'transparent' university network may be precluded by public antipathy to computers, to large organizations and to intellectual pursuits. It may be that a hybrid system capable of accommodating beautiful video-graphics and high-fidelity music as well as symbolic information will be the minimal combination to be publicly accepted. There is also the possibility of conducting various games and lotteries using video-computer networks and these too could lead to widespread availability of terminal-hardware and communications capable of supporting a 'transparent' university network.

5. The twin problems of ensuring that the 'transparent' university network is not filled with 'noise' and of ensuring that every worthwhile contribution is admitted is a truly formidable one. It is directly related to the allocation of grants for research and scholarship on the one hand, and directly related to examination and accreditation processes on the other. By according all participants a Credibility Reputation Status factor, on the basis of the time spent perusing their contributions by others of high status, it may be possible to allocate system resources at least sub-optimally. In a sense such credibility-status reputations among professional peers are the real basis for current resource allocations in conventional institutions.

Finally, it should be emphasized that the 'transparent' system advocated is intended as a means of bringing together people who are well enough matched to be capable to making valuable contributions to each others' work, without introducing excess noise and without wasting valuable time. The remedial and enabling tutorial materials can be developed largely by students, for other students at levels immediately beneath those the 'tutors' have attained.

The belief underlying this concept of a university is that the elaboration and transmission of knowledge and appreciation is not a privilege to be restricted, but rather is the great public enterprise where everyone should be invited and aided to make what contribution they can without regard for their age, social status, or paper credentials (Emery, 1974).

REFERENCES

Ackoff, R L and Emery, F E (1972). 'On Purposeful Systems'. Tavistock, London, pp 237 ff

Ayscough, P (1975) personal communication (but see Project report 'DP 1/06 Leeds Chemistry' from the National Development Programme in Computer Assisted Learning, 37 Mortimer St, London W1N 7RJ)

Boyd, G M (1972) 'The derivation of programmed lessons from recorded protocols'. In 'Aspects of Educational Technology VI'. (Ed) K Austwick and N D C Harris.

Boyd, G M (1973) 'Educational Technology and the recreation of the university'. 'McGill Journal of Education' Vol 8, pp 1-7.

Boyd, G M (1974) 'Educational Technology for the "transparent" university'. In Cavert, C E et al 'Proceeding First National Conference on Open Learning in Higher Education', University of Mid-America, Lincoln, Nebraska

Brown, G W et al (1966) 'EDUNET'. Wiley, New York

Catt, I (1973) 'Computer Worship'. Pitman, London, p 141

Emery, F et al (1974) 'Futures We're In'. Institute for Continuing Education, ANU Canberra

Johansen, Robert (1974) 'FORUM'. Institute for the Future, 2725 Sand Hill Rd, Menlo Park, California 94025, USA

Krauch, H (1972) 'Orakel'. In 'Computer Demokratie'. VDI Verlag, Dusseldorf

Lancaster, F W and Fayen, E G (1974) 'Information Retrieval on Line'. Wiley, New York

Martin, J (1973) 'Design of Man-computer Dialogues'. Prentice-Hall, Englewood Cliffs

Vaizey, J (1973) 'Planning higher education in the seventies'. In Bell, R E and Youngson, A J 'Present and Future in Higher Education!. Tavistock, London, pp 171-83

Scouting for poise: a search for a balanced strategy of curriculum development

R N BROWN, J COWAN

ABSTRACT

When a committed educationist sits in a field for two hours pretending to be a shop, then it is obvious that he is either conducting an experiment or going round the bend. Contrary to general opinion, John Cowan was conducting an experiment - or, to be more precise, he was taking part in an introductory simulation at a Scout Patrol Leaders' Training Course.

Having initially volunteered to teach a scout how to make a map, our educationist had fallen into the grip of a Scout Leader who saw an opportunity not to be missed. Bobby Brown recognized a man who had the experience to inject new techniques into the local Scouting scheme: and the fact that he also had access to CCTV (Bobby still insists) was irrelevant.

John Cowan was introduced to a movement where he was surprised to find that there existed the same divisions in learning which he had experienced in his career as a University Lecturer, and which he summarized as the contrast between programmed learning and open-ended activities. Bobby Brown was made aware of divisions he had only suspected. Between them they conducted a series of five experiments in the Scout Movement which convinced them that the two philosophies of instruction are complementary. They wonder if this hypothesis can be applied to education as a whole, and explore that possibility in their paper.

INTRODUCTION

The advent of educational technology has highlighted the apparent dichotomy between two strikingly diverse philosophies of instruction. On the one hand there is the firmly structured form of teaching which is an inevitable adjunct of the programmed learning approach: in complete contrast there is the open-ended, project-based type of activity, whose aims are simpler to describe than are its objectives. Instructors, teachers or lecturers have recently tended to identify themselves with one approach or the other: the few who find merit in both philosophies perhaps see their decision as a form of compromise, or as a mere blend of two contrasting strategies.

The writers, an educationist and a Scout Leader, have gradually become firm believers in a unified approach, where the union of two views is seen more positively as a marriage of two complementary partners, which interact to the advantage of both. Their grounds for this belief are based on an extended collaboration whilst training Scouts, and subsequently through training Patrol Leaders and others to train Scouts themselves.

BACKGROUND - THE EDUCATIONIST

John Cowan, having had no previous experience of training in the Scout Movement, found the two diverse philosophies of instruction firmly entrenched in their training schemes. It is easier for an outsider than it is for a Scouter to recognize that the movement has been preparing and using exemplary lists of behavioural objectives for many years and certainly since before the impact of programmed learning on the educational scheme. These thoroughly detailed and carefully structured training schemes are epitomized by most of the standard test items for various levels of badge work in the movement (Table I). Many Scout leaders would prefer every topic to be expressed in such precise terms, to enable measured standards to be adopted for each test.

Table I. Examples of badge test items

Level	Item	Full Wording
Scout Standard	4a	Explain how to use and care for a knife and axe. Use a knife to whittle a tent peg (or other object) from a piece of wood, and an axe to prepare wood for a fire.
Advanced Scout Standard	4c	Make a bivouac and sleep the night in it.
	3c	Explain the contour system and be able to give and locate an Ordnance Survey grid reference.
Chief Scout's Award	a(iv)	Make a descent on snow skis, in a reasonable style and under control, with not more than two falls, over 60 metres on a slope with a gradient of at least 15 degrees.

However, there also exists a strong school of thought which sees the aims of the movement as being best met by enjoyable activities which engender initiative, leadership and creative reaction to challenge. This intent may perhaps be described in terms of aims, but can certainly not be set out as precise objectives; and few members of this school would lament that omission. For they are anxious lest the methods of the classroom should detract from the sheer enjoyment of Scouting activities; and they are sceptical of the relevance of a structured approach to the open-ended aims which they feel are the real point of the movement.

It was with a sublime ignorance of these matters that John Cowan was foolhardy enough to immerse himself in the complexities of Scout Training. He responded to a request for assistance from parents to provide specialist badge instruction for a local Scout Troop. Having had considerable experience in land surveying, he volunteered his services in the skills of mapmaking. When this offer was accepted John decided to adopt the pre-recorded methods of instruction which he already used extensively in his work as a university lecturer.

EXPERIMENT 1

The objectives for the Mapmaker Badge are precise in all respects. So John was able to produce a series of structured packages, consisting of pre-recorded instruction immediately followed by audiotape-assisted practice sessions, leading to independent work periods with minimal supervision. The same basic scheme was used whether the work involved enlarging, drawing maps or sections, field surveying or the use of simple instruments. In each case fully detailed objective lists were prepared, issued (and used!) by course participants.

The scheme was described at a recent APLET members' exhibition, in the words of one of the younger Scouts who successfully completed the course. At that time it appeared that the significant features of the use of educational technology in planning the structured course had been the effective achievement of the objectives, together with the high level of motivation which was evident amongst the trainee mapmakers.

BACKGROUND - THE SCOUTER

Bobby Brown had been experimenting for some time, albeit unknowingly, with educational technology techniques within the Scout Movement. When the news of Experiment 1 attracted his attention, the writers' partnership was born. There followed a series of protracted coffee-drinking sessions. As their thoughts gelled, it became apparent that one of the useful outcomes of the experiment would be the reduction of calls on specialist badge instructors, who are generally unwilling to commit themselves to an extended programme of 'repeat' courses. It was also clear that a pre-recorded course, once devised, could then be re-used by the successful Scouts, to instruct their contemporaries. Consequently, when John was asked to organize a further course for the Mapmaker Badge, he decided to train and use Scout Instructors at the same time.

EXPERIMENT 2

Five Scouts from the original Mapmaker Badge course took the pre-recorded instruction and amended, augmented and updated the material during the first stages of their training as instructors. They then staffed a complete course for a new group of trainee Mapmakers, in which the discipline, enthusiasm, standard of work and display of initiative were the responsibility of the qualified Scouts throughout and were all exemplary. The original instructor quietly observed proceedings from the sidelines, and was delighted to find that he had made himself completely redundant, through the logical use of educational technology.

One other spin-off from the review of the use of pre-recorded instruction was the realization that it would be easy to produce a simple individual package to instruct Scouts in the subtleties of grid references and contours, which is a requirement of the Advanced Scout Standard Badge. Thus began the next experiment.

EXPERIMENT 3

The writers set out to show that simple self-study packages might be usefully prepared to support the leaders in Troops which were understaffed, or passing through a phase in which the boy leaders were below standard. This particular package consisted of a set of worksheets, an ordnance survey map and a pre-recorded cassette. It occupied a Scout for $1\frac{1}{2}$ to 2 hours, during which time he was called on to make frequent responses to the taped commentary. It could be followed, if so desired, by a self-administered test, to confirm competence.

When the package has been left around on display at meetings, it is seldom examined by many of those present. This happens because one of the first people to listen to the tape will generally sit on, steadily working through the programme. A number of casual observers, ranging from an eight-year-old Cub to a senior training officer from the West Indies, have succumbed in this way. So, although some Scouters have expressed considerable concern at the intrusion of what they call schoolroom methods into their movement, the writers feel that the reaction of users, and particularly of Scouts, to the package is more significant (Table II).

Table II. User reaction to mapping package

N = 9 (7 Scouts, 1 Cub*, 1 Adult)

	Strongly Disagree	Agree	No feelings either way	Disagree	Strongly Disagree
I liked learning this way	7	2	0	0	0
It was too much like school learning this way	0	1	0	4	4
I think I learnt effectively this way	8	1	0	0	0

* Most of the questions had to be explained to him

35

INTERMEDIATE DISCUSSION

Already it had become clear that there was polite but firm opposition to the use of these highly structured approaches; this reaction originated partly from suspicions of high costs coupled with the need for special equipment, but primarily from the belief that educational methods are an unsuitable basis for Scouting. The writers also noticed a slight apathy towards their experiments from Scouters who had expressed initial interest, but then showed no inclination to promote follow-up activities.

There remained only one option open in the face of these reactions - to anticipate the opposition and apathy by showing that the educational techniques were unquestionably suitable and attractive for basic everyday Scouting. Bobby and John had thought about the objections, and came to the conclusion that, although cost had immediately established itself as the greatest stumbling block, it was more relevant that their experiments had done little to date to attract those who liked their Scouting to be 'project based'. Convinced that many Scout Leaders wanted activities which required little or no previous instruction in a straight teaching form, they were spurred on to launch a low-cost activity which contained no instruction, and which used minimal equipment.

EXPERIMENT 4

Take a leaderless patrol of six or seven Scouts, divide them into three groups, hand them an old map of the Island of Mull, a taperecorder and a cassette, and then invite them to play the recorder. The commentary sends each group off on a journey round the island, giving instructions which tax their mapreading skills, and asking for checks at various intermediate points. Using a simple scoring system, the patrol accumulates a score which can be challenged the following week by another patrol. Meantime both the Patrol Leader and the Scouter are free to undertake other duties, such as the organization and supervision of parallel training or testing activities.

The recorder in the experiment was borrowed from a Scout: the cassette was secondhand, and had cost 35p originally, while the map of Mull was rescued from a dusty attic. Motivation was highly satisfactory, and the Scouts made good many gaps in their knowledge and developed several important skills. Copies of this simple kit are now being used in two other parts of Scotland by leaders who had been unconvinced of the merit of the earlier experiments. The cost of the copies was unfortunately higher than the original, as none of these leaders had a convenient stock of rejected ordnance sheets.

FURTHER DISCUSSION

It became evident after Experiment 4 that there would always be calls of 'high costs' or 'where can we get a taperecorder' - when in actual fact the sceptics were raising their objections rather than admit that they were not prepared to try out such experiments in their own situation. Having dismissed the cost problem to their own satisfaction (if to no-one else's) the writers became aware that all their experiments to date had been concerned with maps and mapreading - a very narrow field, which had traditionally presented relatively few problems to the average Scouter. Perhaps they were trying to sell him something he did not want!

Slightly disheartened, Bobby Brown turned his mind towards preparing a forthcoming Patrol Leaders' Training Course. He suddenly realized that here was an ideal opportunity to pursue their discussions in a practical context, and to enlist again the assistance, enthusiasm (and equipment) available from his new contact.

EXPERIMENT 5

It took some time to define the objectives of the Patrol Leaders' Training Course, although, in retrospect, it is probably obvious that properly trained Patrol Leaders should be able to instruct boys in each item of the Scout Standard Badge Programme, to test them on each item, and to plan and execute enjoyable patrol activities, which make use of these skills in creative open-ended situations.

Once these objectives had been established, the programme was drawn up, making full use of whichever media and methods seemed appropriate. The course began with an introductory simulation, which established motivation, exposed the individual training needs, and brought the main issues into the limelight. Micro-teaching periods then achieved their (obvious) purpose, as did the micro-testing, the use of games for specific training purposes, buzz groups, seminars, CCTV replays and practical workshops.

Minor snags could be listed, but that would give a false impression of an extremely successful weekend, during which the latent leadership potential of the boys was strikingly demonstrated and, more importantly, was harnessed to good purpose. The most striking subsequent testimony to the relevance of the educational technology approach has been the persistence with which many of the Patrol Leaders voluntarily continued to use their grubby and well-thumbed objective lists as a basis for training and testing, many months after the course might well have become a distant memory.

Those leaders who favoured activity-based Scouting were more than pleased by the format of the programme; but at the same time those who advocated the vital importance of training saw the course as an improvement over its predecessors. Was this an able compromise, a successful exercise in two-faced planning, or something rather different?

PARTICULAR CONCLUSIONS

The reader will have noted that the story which has been told so far is a somewhat characteristic description of discovery learning in action. Slowly and tentatively we have described how Bobby and John progressed on their rather unsteady way, pulled hither and thither by apparently conflicting pressures. An interesting separation in function between the two factors which influenced their progress is worthy of comment.

In each experiment, once they knew what they wanted to do, the educational technology approach led them fairly quickly to an effective solution of their problem. But in the period between experiments, when certain switches of proirities led to changes of emphasis, educational technology contributed very little to their decision-making. In these decisions the initiative was shared amongst men who found it difficult or undesirable to talk in terms of behavioural objectives, but who had a clear impression of the long-term aims which they felt worthwhile.

It was perhaps surprising to find an amiable and constructive dialogue between two such diverse schools of thought. But the final form of the last experiment demonstrated clearly that an imaginative and ambitious programme could be conceived, and then implemented efficiently, through a combined strategy which was in no way a compromise. The overall framework of each new development arose from open-ended consideration of the overall goals and aims, but the implementation of this framework was then achieved by detailed consideration of objectives, and of the best means of attaining them.

It is quite clear that training in the movement will be without purpose and incentive (and will indeed be irrelevant) unless the long-term aims of the organization are mature, challenging and apparent. But such aims cannot be realized by poorly trained boys and leaders; so the movement must stress both effective training and adventurous open-ended activities. These two aspects of planning are therefore to be seen as the twin prongs to spearhead the drive towards a worthwhile and successful programme with merit and appeal. They are not to be seen as the horns of a dilemma confronting those who determine future policy.

GENERAL DISCUSSION

The devotees of programmed learning, structured learning packages, extensive training programmes and the like are understandably concerned with the acquisition of knowledge, skills and abilities. They prepare their instruction in accordance with a pre-determined list of objectives which they have helped to draw up. Since the advent of programmed learning on the educational scene, published educational papers have therefore concentrated their emphasis on the provision of effective instruction.

But educational technology in its present form has had relatively little direct influence on the choice of course goals. In contrast, those academics who favour projects, discovery-learning, simulations and learner-directed group work, find that they cannot exercise control over specific objectives, although their activities are generally in accordance with their choice of open-ended aims, to which they give constant thought.

The writers suggest with respect (which admittedly usually implies just the opposite), that curriculum development and training programmes must always be inspired and sustained by the constant review of mature, challenging and open-ended aims; they equally appreciate that significant progress towards these aims cannot be attained unless the major share of the necessary knowledge or skills has been thoroughly imparted in a planned programme of structured learning.

The excursion into Scout Training by an educational technologist has suggested that the apparent conflict between open-ended and structured learning is perhaps a non-problem. Progress in curriculum and training development will most readily result through the integration of both viewpoints, to provide a complete strategy for future planning.

The imaginative uses of closed circuit television in the training of staff and managers

JOHN LEEDHAM

This paper reviews the report prepared for UNESCO by APLET. Although the editorship was conducted by the author of this paper, acknowledgement is immediately made to the various contributors listed below. In particular, especial assistance in the production of the paper is due to my fellow members: Eric Blackadder of Bayston Sports Equipment; Ron Clements of the Wellcome Foundation; John Fricker, Officer Commanding The Royal Army Education Corps, Beaconsfield. It is intended to video extracts from their programmes during the presentation of this paper.

UNESCO BRIEF

The following introduction explains the background to the report and the method of its implementation. The report was finally deposited in July 1974.

"The decisions made at the 17th session of UNESCO's General Conference committed the Division of Methods, Materials and Techniques to develop studies on 'Suitable methods for using the close-circuit television facilities now being installed or to be installed in the foreseeable future, in teacher training colleges in a number of developing countries, and a comparative study made of the results achieved by their use under local conditions so that they may be introduced in all training colleges'. "

UNESCO Contract 506400, 19 December 1973

"The Association for Programmed Learning and Educational Technology shall conduct a study on the use of closed circuits of television in the training of staff and managers in organizations not specially devoted to education such as Industry, Administration, Navy, Army, etc. This study of approximately eighty pages will present a selection of some representative case studies of particularly imaginative uses of CCTV."

UNESCO ESM/95/74/I/166, 10 June 1974

"Imaginative, in our understanding, refers to bringing into educational circles, ideas about the uses made of CCTV outside the formal educational constraints. By so doing, UNESCO's intention is to try to open new prospects to educators."
    The case studies submitted by the Service Officers of the Royal Army

INTRODUCTION

The Association for Programmed Learning and Educational Technology was
asked in July 1973 to conduct a limited study which would have bearing on
some significant and important experiments in the use of closed circuit
television for the training of staff and managers in the organizations not
especially devoted to the problems of education such as industry or
administration; the Army, the Navy, the Air Force. "The problem is to
know how CCTV is used and combined with specific training techniques."

After reviewing the resources available and the field to be covered, the
Association appointed Dr John Leedham, its Chairman of Publications, to
pursue the study. A work plan was implemented based on the following
considerations.

The term 'training' was judged not to be exclusive. Thus, schemes devised
for management training, for organizing staff participation in policy making,
and for increasing the potential of junior sales executives, were judged to be
equally significant with training schemes introduced to increase safety
awareness, to teach the handling of dangerous materials or weapons, or to
teach survival in an underwater environment.

The apparatus required for closed circuit television was accepted as
ranging from the simple portable pack to full 2-inch colour studio productions.

Discussion on the word 'imaginative' suggested that the employment of
closed circuit television in a given circumstance, such as role-playing at
managerial level, might or might not be imaginative, and that true definition
would only be achieved by the examination of specific case studies. For this
reason the partcipating bodies should represent a wide spectrum, but must
include organizations with real commitment and a record of successful usage.

CONTRIBUTORS

The Royal Navy	RNSETT, Portsmouth
	Inst/Commander D Cripps BSc, RN
	Inst/Commander T Austin RN
The Army	Lt Col J M Fricker BA, DipEd, RAEC
	Major D W Clary MBE, RAEC
The Royal Air Force	RAF Upwood
	F/Lt K Clarke BSc
The National Coal Board	Hobart House, Grosvenor Place, London SW1
	K Gay
The Road Transport Industry Training Board	Capitol House, Empire Way, Wembley
	N C Manley-Cooper
The Wellcome Foundation	Wellcome Building, Euston Road, London NW1
	Ronald Clements

British Petroleum   Britannic House, Moor Lane, London EC1
Roly Stafford

Insight   Fulham, London
Richard Whittington

Bayston Sports Equipment Co Ltd   Eric Blackadder DL

Their contributions were categorized as shown in Table I.

Table I.

Function or characteristic of study	Information distribution system	Cost effec- tive	Time effec- tive	Skills train- ing	Colour system	Manage- ment training
Wellcome Foundation Rolling role-play Page 20		X	X			X
Army Recruiters' course Page 82	X	X			X	X
Royal Navy Improving presentation techniques Page 29			X			X
Road Transport Board Learning saturated programme Page 35			X	X	X	
Royal Navy Photographic course Page 40			X	X		
Insight Waterbury Farrell Page 92	X			X	X	
RAF Jaguass training scheme Page 45			X	X		
Army Weapon training Page 83		X	X	X		
Army Nurse training Page 84		X	X	X		

Function or characteristic of study	Information distribution system	Cost effec- tive	Time effec- tive	Skills train- ing	Colour system	Manage- ment training
Bayston Sports Learning to play golf Page 50		X		X		
British Petroleum Novel communication systems Page 14	X		X		X	X
Insight Coca-Cola sales training Page 91	X	X			X	X
Royal Navy Revision of 16mm film Page 73	X	X			X	
RAF Rehabilitation training Page 67			X	X		
RAF Pathology study Page 70			X	X	X	
Army Immediacy Page 81		X		X		
Army Group paced instruction Page 82	X	X	X			X
Royal Navy Simulated damage control Page 63	X			X		
National Coal Board Safety campaign Page 58						X
Army Computer training Page 83		X			X	X
Insight Cassettes on tankers Page 93	X				X	

THE CATEGORIZATION

This range of inquiry included some items which were difficult to assess as imaginative unless seen in context.

The case studies vary in presentation. A suggested format was followed to some extent, but length and depth of treatment were sometimes questions of relevance to the authors rather than to the report. Topics which would appear to have considerable content were sometimes referred to quite briefly to allow for lengthier comment respecting alternative issues. This is particularly true of the submissions such as those from the Army whose paper discusses pertinently and objectively the larger issues of using CCTV and quotes case studies incidentally to support a thesis of cost effectiveness.

The categorization of the studies is arbitrary and they are identified by their common elements. The ever-present problem was, and is, the classification of studies as imaginative. An original intention to use imaginative procedures in a training programme often disappeared in practice. As is cited in the full paper 'The Imaginative use of CCTV in the Training of Staff and Managers' (Distribution Systems. Whittington) many commercial institutions employ CCTV to disseminate central policy by making a tape of a chairman or manager outlining institutional intention. Replicated on video tape machines around the country the message may stand out clearer than a circular letter, but the degree of imagination used in programme preparation and presentation would be the factor separating the picture from the letter. It was common to find that the relative newness of CCTV as an expedient masked its imaginative potential.

Each study was reviewed as to the number of centres or organizations involved, the duration of the exercise, the target population, who decided how CCTV was to be used and the method of evaluation. Typical examples are presented with this paper in order to illustrate the inquiry.

CASE STUDIES

Rolling Role-play   -   Ron Clements, The Wellcome Foundation

This paper describes a technique for involving large groups of people in a role-play situation using the absolute minimum of video equipment. The particular event described took place in Madrid at the local office of a British pharmaceutical company. Almost one hundred salesmen took part in the exercise.

Small groups were formed to discuss a particular problem, the solution to which was to be acted out in a role-play selling situation. A 'customer' and 'salesman' were nominated from each group.

Around a single television camera several role-play sales talks were set up. All the role-plays commenced at the same time and continued simultaneously. The camera 'rolled' from one role-play to another until all the groups had been covered. In this way each segment of video caught a different phase of the sale, from the opening statement to the closing of the sale.

CCTV in the Army - Lt Col J M Fricker RAEC, Major D W Clary RAEC

The Army papers stood as a complete unit to emphasize the cost-effective angle and the up-dating of instructional procedures in the Army.
Examples were quoted of the use of CCTV in:

Demonstrations, presentations and playlets

"... Videotapes are now extensively used in place of major demonstrations. They have proved most cost-effective where large numbers of people are involved in rehearsal and performance.
...In one case the use of CCTV has saved 1,130 man hours, 80 hours of vehicle time and 15 hours of civilian coach hire."

Immediacy

"The Army Recruiters' course is now CCTV based; it uses videotaped demonstrations of 'how to do it', immediate replay to highlight interviewer performance and delayed replay to allow considered assessment of students."

Group paced instruction

The Army presents several surveys of the imaginative and effective use of CCTV in its training programmes.
The Army conclude their paper as follows:

Present and Future

CCTV is now widely employed in training. Bandmasters, bomb disposal technicians, officer cadets, missile operators, nurses, recruits, Army recruiters, trainee instructors, interviewers and interviewees, lecturers and students, all benefit from the use of television. CCTV can greatly assist medical training, and it seems possible that it will have a unique application in psychiatry. It is likely to be used in recognition training and in equipment handling roles, and it can be used to bring realism into the classroom. It is used in oral training, for reconnaissance and briefings and for sports coaching.
Provided its use can be shown to be cost-effective there is reason to suppose that the application of CCTV to training will spread. Properly integrated into systems engineered courses of instruction it can help to produce optimum learning conditions by employing its unique qualities of immediacy and playback. Vision is a powerful and acquisitive sense, and television uses it to the full.
In the British Army CCTV has developed within the framework of instructional technology where emphasis is placed on the systematic design, implementation and validation of training. Within this framework it has proved an effective medium of instruction and in a period of limited manpower, complex material systems and steeply rising costs it has gone some way to increase the cost-effectiveness of training. It is a most

valuable weapon in the armoury of instructional technology and its
continuing use and development seem assured."

Use of CCTV in Skills Training - Eric Blackadder, Bayston Sports Equipment

CCTV had also been used especially in two analytical and training roles at
national level. One was that of a Rugby Union referee's course. Here a group
of referees was able to view a comparison of refereeing by a top grade referee
and one less experienced. The CCTV exposure concentrated on their
positioning to see the rules of the game, their movement around the pitch and
their ability to oversee 360° of play. A further example concerned the Royal
Life Saving Society who used Loughborough expertise to record a suitable
organized test and examination. This, in turn, was used to test examiners on
their own grasp of detail. The use of CCTV in circumstances such as these
proved valuable in providing reference points for the development of individual
training programmes based on self-assessment procedure.

One particular aspect involved the analysis of golfing techniques. The use
of CCTV was experimental in the early stages and led later to the production
of a specialist training aid.

The description of the work involved covers the use of CCTV in golf
training and as a means of developing special aids.

CCTV chain as an aids development unit

During the development of this training aid the substitution of a CCTV trolley
with a single- or two-camera aspect enabled experimentation and surmise to
be tested effectively and immediately. Whilst it might indeed be a superior
system to offer a CCTV survey of these training skills, the questions of cost
and availability rule against such a solution.

It is seen, therefore, that the specific use of CCTV to develop superior
alternative training aids can be effective. Imaginately used, economies and
motivation can obviously be achieved.

The National Coal Board

During the presentation of the paper at the City University a contribution was
made by K Gay. The study included a review of the work done with mobile
units in mine safety campaigns. The Coal Board have for long been
experienced users of CCTV along with other media in their efforts to maintain
the high level of safety in British mines. In essence, 50 pits at any one time
have special attention directed to them. CCTV vans make programmes
involving local people and local safety hazards. These programmes are shown
back in the varying circumstances of a miner's life. He is likely to see them
in the canteen, at change-over time at the pithead or in the bathrooms.

The circumstances of the programmes' creation and playback determine
that attention is paid to them. The considerable planning and outlay involved
is an indication that the Coal Board are committed to this imaginative use of
CCTV. It would be unfair however if this brief mention of their extensive study
did not indicate that the Coal Board have considerable experience in a very

wide application of their CCTV units in normal training and managerial study sessions.

SUMMARY

The range of case studies presented in this report can be viewed as representative of the imaginative uses of CCTV in the restricted field of inquiry.

The brief analysis which heads each abstract in the full report aims to give some objectivity and structure to the studies as a whole. It must be borne in mind that this is a restricted study of approximately 80 pages and the basis of the report is to furnish evidence of the imaginative uses of CCTV outside the sphere of formal education. It would be unlikely to find evaluative systems which would correspond to academic reporting; indeed it would be unfortunate, in the editor's view, if such reporting were assayed in this context.

The Association owes very grateful thanks to its independent contributors who have sustained a good deal of questioning and revision with most excellent cooperation. It is indeed a remarkable tribute to them that such a report as this can be offered after six months' compilation on an honorary basis.

The quality of imagination displayed in the case studies we submit may be suspected to vary; the study is so often a relative statement because it is a more imaginative system of training or demonstration than traditional procedures. CCTV is still new enough to some trainers for its virtue to be immediately obvious and, within their own circumstances, these advantages quickly become stereotyped. Thus it has been by no means an easy task to provide the studies; indeed it is probable that only the very experienced and large institutions are likely to have the repertoire of experimental usage from which to quote with reliable conviction.

The studies reveal that very effective work can be done and an acceptable presentation achieved using the economical $\frac{1}{2}$" range of videotape machines; indeed it is often preferentially included because of its portability and compatibility. The Army study in particular stresses the cost-effective argument for using CCTV and the argument is implied in many of the other studies. Whilst it is reasonable to expect the cost per trainee to decrease with each subsequent successful showing of a CCTV tape it is still true that the strategy of learning from packaged material needs the endorsement of a human mediator. The extent of this mediation affects the true cost. Nevertheless, in studies such as that quoted by the RAF on the 'Jaguass' training scheme the economies appear to be obvious and attractive.

Much of the advantage of CCTV rests in its distribution facility and the accounts contributed by 'Insight' suggest powerfully that the cassette network is a training technique due for considerable and early enlargement. Since cassettes embrace colour capability, their use as training and information channels is likely to find wide endorsement, especially amongst those who are just starting to use CCTV.

The case studies all demonstrate one significant feature: the introduction of

CCTV into the training of staff and management brings about considerable revision and updating of training techniques. Some studies suggest that quality and effective training can be achieved economically. The quality and effectiveness of the imaginative function is more subtle and elusive; it perhaps best arises in the reader's own mind as he peruses the case studies.

REFERENCE

Leedham, J (Ed for APLET) (1974) 'The Imaginative Use of CCTV in the Training of Staff and Managers'. Limited issue on UNESCO Licence (PUB/DA/A.74.161), APLET, London

Life-long objectives
in a college of education

E W ANDERSON

The basic idea is to construct a complete college learning system with inputs
into schools and feedback from them in the short and the long term (Figure 1).
However, there are many problems in introducing the tightly structured
concepts of educational technology into the more loosely defined system of a
college. As yet, certain parts of the system are incomplete and therefore one
course is given in some detail as an example so that the process can be seen
in practice. The fundamental concern is that students should develop
individually as people and professionally as teachers who will be able to adapt
satisfactorily to the changing conditions of life. The term 'lifelong' is therefore
taken to imply that the objectives, once achieved, should enable the teacher to
remain up-to-date and competent in his subject area and should provide him
with a range of life skills such as improved capability in decision-making.
Much of the feedback is likely to remain subjective, given the assessment
procedures at present in use, particularly in a college. This is a very broad
and ambitious aim with obvious built-in constraints for the system including
especially time and numbers of students available for any evaluation
procedure. Accurate assessment may not be possible for several years, after
which the difficulty of collecting data from more than a few former students
will be clearly acute.

1. COLLEGE AIMS AND OBJECTIVES

The starting point for the system was a formulation of a statement of the kinds
of knowledge, skills, attitudes and 'modes of personal operation' that the college
as an academic community regards as important for students to acquire or
reinforce. It was hoped that by this exercise alone, staff and students might be
assisted in achieving their aims more effectively. It was also thought that
directions for development might become more obvious and that criteria, other
than success in the final examinations, might be isolated for judging the
efficacy of college work.

   The construction of such a statement occupied one committee, consisting of
staff and students, for most of its meetings over a two-year period.
Subsequently the detail has been refined and it is hoped that this will be a
continuing process as feedback from schools and former students is increasingly
incorporated. The objectives as listed at present must result from intuition

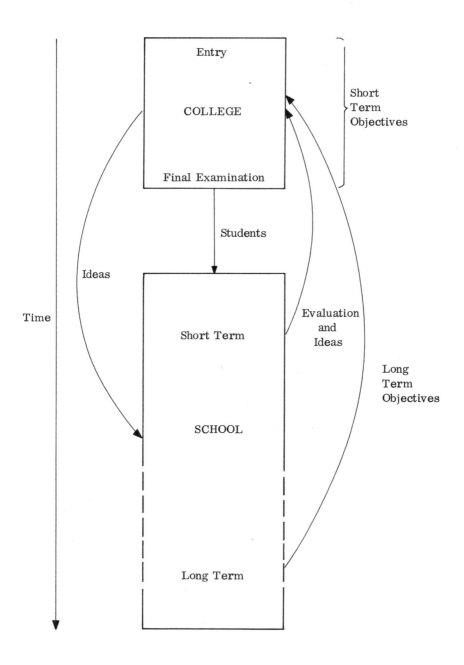

Figure 1. Basic system

and ideas and some knowledge. However, current detailed knowledge is largely limited to the college situation and will remain so until more lecturers teach part-time in schools. As a result, it was comparatively easy to produce the short-term objectives leading to the final year assessment of the student. Bearing in mind such factors as market trends and viability of courses, the college can exercise control over its own development in these areas. The long-term objectives proved far greater problems and it is particularly these which the present system is designed to identify and improve. In general, these short-term and long-term objectives can be distinguished respectively as training and operational.

With regard to their actual construction, the lower level objectives can be clearly and precisely stated with built-in standards and conditions. However, problems arise at higher levels where complete concepts or personal attitudes may be embodied. At the highest level are 'modes of personal operation', a fourth category, which includes ideas such as receptiveness, creativeness, awareness and reflection and is therefore an amalgam of the other three on a higher plane than any of them. For example, a teacher of music or poetry would aim to develop his students' receptiveness until they were able to arrive at just judgements of work in those media. This is more than an intellectual skill, which could be directly trained, as the student's whole personality is involved. Indeed, he may develop beyond his teacher's comprehension and it may be this possible increment which distinguishes this category of objective. Clearly skills, attitudes and basic knowledge are prerequisites for such development, together with self-discipline and a positive attitude.

Creativeness can also be considered on such a level, as it involves flexibility in probing the possible aspects of a complex problem, skill in weighing the alternatives and persistence in selecting and testing the appropriate solution. Through this process the final answer is a product of the student's total personality and not the result of merely mechanically applying a formula.

As a result of their greater experience of life, teachers can relate school material to real world examples more easily than children. At its highest level, this brings reality to teaching and as a basis, involves imaginative assimilation and analysis together with reflection on experience.

A fourth mode of personal operation of particular relevance to teaching results in group sensitivity. An awareness of feelings and possible responses within a community involves the subtle interplay of personalities, the 'whole' person at a deep level.

It is seen that, if objective evaluation is required, this category needs to be minutely subdivided giving a large range of low-level objectives. The result may well appear pedantic and it may suffice at least in the initial stages, to take a few examples at this level and simultaneously employ subjective evaluation of the high-level lifelong objectives. This is the procedure so far adopted in the construction of the present model.

It is with the application of lifelong objectives in course design and the evaluation at present available that the remainder of this paper is mainly concerned. Examples of college objectives within this category, and therefore basically operational, can be listed in abbreviated form using the normal classification.

Main Subject

Knowledge of the following areas:
    (a) The major concepts and the conceptual structure of the subject
    (b) The characteristic modes of thinking and inference of the subject
    (c) The relations between one's own subject and other fields of study
    (d) The bearing of one's own area of study on society
    (e) The relations between one's own area of study and world views
    (f) The mode of development of pupils in area of own subject, including types of learning experience, order and pace of conceptual development, and appropriate forms of instruction and exercises

It can be seen that these objectives form three broad groups: (a) and (b) imply subject mastery through long-term experience, (c), (d) and (e) involve life experience and (f) can only result from lengthy teaching experience. The skills and attitudes sections may be similarly grouped but the modes of personal operation each include all three aspects of experience.

Skills:
    (a) Making observations with the appropriate degree of precision, in the field of one's own subject
    (b) Drawing valid inferences from data in the field of one's own subject
    (c) Assessing validity of inferences in this field
    (d) Applying knowledge and concepts in one's own subject to unfamiliar material or situations in the field; solving problems in this field
    (e) Re-casting knowledge of one's own field in shape of questions to which the knowledge constitutes tentative answers
    (f) Planning courses for pupils
    (g) Presenting material of subject in forms suitable for pupils
    (h) Providing learning experiences for pupils in the subject and means of consolidation, including drills and tests where appropriate
    (i) Collaboration in team work
    (j) Manipulation of instruments

Attitudes:
    (a) Involvement in the subject, and expectation of continued study in it
    (b) Positive attitude to change in material and concepts of own subject
    (c) Interest in tracing wider implications of subject, particularly in its bearing on society and its relations with world views
    (d) Keen concern that pupils shall develop types of understanding and skills referred to above rather than acquire factual information alone. The factual information is important but the acquisition of understanding and skills is more important; too great an emphasis on information can obstruct the more important types of learning

Modes of personal operation:
    (a) Receptiveness towards the characteristic material of one's own field

of study

(b) Creativeness in solving problems, whether practical, intellectual or aesthetic

(c) A habit of reflecting on first-hand experience and relating it to general principles and thinking

(d) A habit of sensitiveness to the feelings and reactions of members of one's own working community

(e) An enquiring and questioning habit of mind

Principles of Education

Skills:

(a) Plan schemes of work and lesson programmes including:
    (i) devising appropriate learning situations
    (ii) relating appropriate teaching techniques
    (iii) building on pupils' interests
    (iv) making appropriate use of the environment
    (v) designing and constructing suitable materials
    (vi) using available sources of information

(b) Obtaining research results and applying to one's own professional work

(c) Applying knowledge, concepts and empirical evidence to unfamiliar educational situations, ie solving problems in these fields

Attitudes:

(a) Positive attitude to research

(b) Involvement in these subjects and expectation of continued professional study

Modes of personal operation:

(a) Creativeness in solving problems in educational spheres

(b) An enquiring and questioning habit of mind

Community Life

Skills:

(a) Performance in a variety of extra-curricular activities used in schools

(b) Performance as a member of a small group

Attitudes:

(a) Desire for effective collaboration with other people, whether congenial or not

Personal Development

Knowledge of the following areas:

(a) Self, including own personal development and own motives and values

Skills:

(a) Clarifying value issues in everyday situations

(b) Working in creative way in personal and professional life

Modes of personal operation:
(a) A habit of reflecting on first-hand experience and relating it to principles

Such a formulation of objectives is of course not unique, but the Bede College document tends to be more broadly based in its approach than others currently available. Its aim is long-term and general and it is not confined by being subject-based.

2. COURSE SELECTION AND DESIGN

Once the document of college aims and objectives had been completed, it was possible to include its use in the design of courses, distinguishing carefully between the operational and the training levels (Figure 2). The basis of a new advanced final year BEd course had already been accepted by Durham University and this provided suitable material for the exercise. Furthermore, being concerned with hydrology, it was partly lecture-room and partly field-based and therefore while there were opportunities to achieve a range of objectives, the basically factual, 'academic' nature of the subject also caused problems. The form of the examination also imposes several constraints on course design, eg:

(a) it is an essay paper
(b) the accent is on 'knowledge'
(c) skills and attitudes are incidental, possibly supportive factors
(d) fieldwork notebooks cannot be submitted
(e) practical and experimental work must all be related to 'knowledge'
(f) other aspects of personal development, etc, are also in a supportive role

Despite these, it is still vital to build in the required operational objectives.

From the outset, students from the target population were involved in the course design. They had already taken a specialist geomorphology course and were therefore motivated and familiar with the groundwork of hydrology. However, of more importance was their grading of the college objectives and their ideas on the development of what was to be the major course of their final year. Teachers were also involved at an early stage as it was envisaged that they would be concerned with part of the assessment procedure.

Six broad categories of material were identified to produce a course of sufficient academic rigour:

(a) Models and systems including their construction, classification and use: this is clearly of general application
(b) The basin hydrological cycle, concerned with processes
(c) Drainage basins, their selection, measurement and instrumentation: this category examines structure
(d) Hill slopes including theoretical modelling and surveying: this section investigates the effects of process on structure
(e) Mass movement with a consideration of measurements and links with the hydrological cycle and soil mechanics: this section together with
(f) allows the application of material, and provides a summary

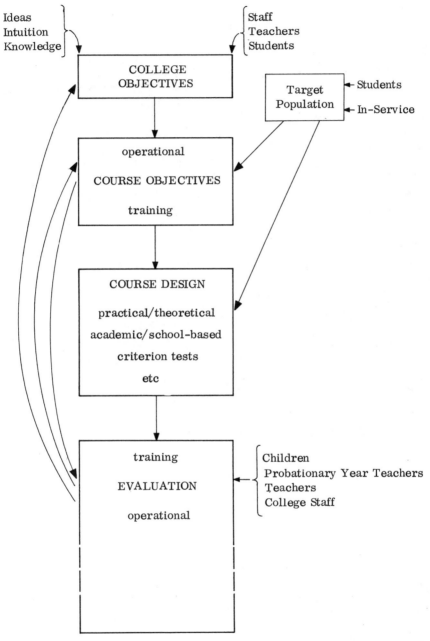

Figure 2. Procedure model

55

(f) Fluvial processes particularly in small drainage basins

A topic web was constructed for each of these and then the linkages were plotted. The overall aim was to provide detailed knowledge of one working system in which many of the parts could be measured and correlated. This should not only serve as an example with general application, but should also be capable of scaling so that it could be used at different levels in schools. Thus, the approach to each topic had to be discussed critically and fully so that it fitted into this broad pattern. The result was that certain subjects, such as the use of models, were considerably enlarged while others, including soil mechanics, were reduced. The students involved contributed significantly to the ideas on school application.

The topics were then arranged in a sequenced scalar diagram and the objectives constructed. The knowledge objectives were formulated using the college document, particularly as a guide to 'level'. The skills, attitudes and modes of personal operation sections were then consulted and found to be useful on two planes:

(a) supportive, allowing the production of enabling objectives (mainly skills)
(b) giving a series of overall aims (mainly modes)

An abbreviated version of the final course objectives is given and it can be seen how they relate in ascending level to those listed as college objectives. In most cases they are at an operational level requiring long-term evaluation.

Main Subject

Knowledge:
(a) The material: basically hydrology with aspects of soil mechanics
(b) Concepts: cycles, structures, models
(c) Problem solving, establishing linkages
(d) Scientific approach to thinking including design of experiments, statistical variability, etc
(e) Relationships with: biology, meteorology, pedology, ecology, etc
(f) Utility: the relevance of a study of water resources
(g) Perceptual development of students, eg one drainage basin - hydrological cycle relevance of scale
(h) Development of pupils

Skills:
(a) Active skills: surveying, instrumentation, measurement, experimental design, data processing, etc
(b) Methods of observational and experimental science
(c) Data collection and assessment
(d) Applications to similar problems elsewhere
(e) Using an open-ended situation
(f) Scaling the material for use in schools

Attitudes:
   (a) Care and skill in observation and recording
   (b) Continued interest in the subject at all levels
   (c) Basis on which to build as the subject develops
   (d) Acquisition of basic principles (ie, understanding)
   (e) Approach to everyday problems

Mode of personal operation:
   (a) Creativeness when faced with problems
   (b) Questioning approach
   (c) Systems approach to life
   (d) Geographical appreciation
   (e) Approach to research

These were then broken down in training and enabling objectives; the next stage of course design included:
   (a) Division of the material into topics for each lecture session
   (b) Sequencing of sessions
   (c) Listing necessary equipment and visual aids
   (d) Planning practical and fieldwork sessions
   (e) Production of a provisional course timetable
   (f) Provision of programmed material

Having completed this exercise it was possible to assess the amount of course time available for other objectives.

Relevant sections other than those concerned with main subject were then applied.

The Education section provided guidelines for construction so that the total course could be seen by the students as relevant to teaching. It also served as a reminder that specific areas which might be used directly in school could be emphasized.

Finally, the 'whole man' element was built in after consulting the sections on Community Life and Personal Development.

Examples which can be cited include:

Education

   (a) Planning scaled down and simplified versions for teaching
   (b) Develop reasoning in pupils
   (c) Encourage pupils to use basic principles
   (d) Development of imagination

Community Life

   (a) Teamwork and cooperation in the field
   (b) Seminar work
   (c) Fieldwork as an extra-curricular activity

Personal Development

   (a) Self-knowledge: application, persistence, etc
   (b) Making judgements

57

(c) Working in a creative way

(d) Approach to problems

(e) Confidence in teaching the subject

To cater for variations in the background knowledge and interests of the target population, programmed material was produced and briefly tested. To obtain a guide as to the efficacy of different types of programming, students were divided according to their record in geography into four matched groups, each group learning the same topic through a different mode. It was decided that the topic should not be part of the course out of sequence, but a geomorphological subject which could be completed in one session. An introductory study of coral reefs, their classification, distribution, and the factors controlling their development was considered to be of the correct proportions and also a topic worthy of study but infrequently learned in school. The course was taught using programmed books, algorithms, work cards and information maps. The pre-test revealed that prior knowledge was minimal and all four modes yielded post-test scores of over 85%. Closer inspection showed that work cards and information maps were slightly more effective although differences were not clearly significant. However, since these are far more easily and rapidly prepared than programmed books, they were adopted as the modes for the course. From a subjective assessment by students the only fact to emerge clearly was that they enjoyed using algorithms as they liked working through a logical sequence. Algorithms were therefore employed in problem-solving exercises.

3. EVALUATION

Immediately after the training objectives had been formulated, the final B Ed examination paper, the formal means of assessment, was set. However, this is taken at the conclusion of the training period and it was hoped that certain of the course objectives would be applicable at the operational level in schools. It is, of course, difficult to provide an initial assessment of such lifelong aims and the final evaluation cannot be made for several years. It was, however, possible to obtain some guidance from the students' own assessment of the course. As a further interim measure, criterion tests consisting of problem-solving seminars provided a useful means of examining for the longer term. These included the use of brainstorming techniques; combing, diagramming, etc, all of which are being refined and tested in a project with the Reading University School of Education. They are all small group procedures which help develop a flexible approach to problems and even allow the different approaches of the students to be classified. A further stage has included exercises on the generation of geographical ideas; linking concepts and topics by a series of the short 'memory spans' described by Edward de Bono. Essays written during some of the later seminars were evaluated by the students using six grading scales. This provided another way in which students could compare approaches to a problem. To assess many of the objectives, however, field instruction proved the most valuable. Students carried out their own hydrological measurement programme and then, using more junior students for teaching purposes, developed their own experimental designs in a small drainage basin near the college. Their final reports were assessed under the following headings:

(a) scientific method
(b) experimental design
(c) experimental procedure
(d) collation and presentation of results
(e) comparisons and correlations
(f) conclusions and discussion of model

Finally, the whole subject could be scaled down sufficiently so that students could instruct 15-year-old children from a local comprehensive school. The broad objectives are listed:

Objectives of Field Teaching (as seen by school)

(a) To obtain more fieldwork time for the children
(b) To have fieldwork in small groups with teaching available
(c) To use college expertise, equipment and transport
(d) To provide material for CSE work, etc
(e) To stimulate interest in geography

Objectives of Field Teaching (as seen by college)

(a) To obtain field teaching experience for students
(b) To allow students to take charge of groups
(c) To help students develop their own ideas on experimental design, etc, in the field
(d) To develop creativeness and a thoughtful problem-solving approach in students

This particular programme involves fortnightly field teaching trips to the school's fieldwork area in Weardale. Other assessment has involved the use of slides and 8mm films as simulated situations in which field problems can be solved.

Finally, as assessment of the course itself, each student judged the importance of the objectives on a ten-point rating scale. He then rated the coverage of each objective on a similar scale. Few objectives were considered to have been inadequately covered although certain areas, such as data processing, could clearly be enlarged. The lifelong objectives scored well although it was realized that to an extent, the demands of an academic course and the needs of schoolchildren were mutually exclusive. It is hoped that for the next class, the balance might be altered slightly towards the latter.

4. THE OPERATIONAL LEVEL

As all the college objectives were formulated to produce effective teaching, feedback must come from the classroom. It is only by receiving information at this operational level that the course and programme can be monitored and remain relevant. Therefore, an exchange scheme was instituted so that for one afternoon a week, a teacher in a local comprehensive school lectured and studied in the college while a lecturer taught in the school. The lecturer was then able to test teaching assessment procedures and keep abreast of school developments. The teacher could improve his knowledge of his subject, gain lecturing experience and introduce a few senior pupils to college life. The basic objectives for this scheme are shown:

Objectives of Exchange (as seen by school)

(a) To meet students and keep in touch with subject development
(b) To try a different type of teaching
(c) To bring children into college to have an initial look at college life
(d) To have members of the school staff trained further
(e) To help with in-service work (eg Schools Council)

Objectives of Exchange (as seen by college)

(a) To retain classroom contact
(b) To try out assessment procedures in classroom
(c) To obtain feedback on changing school requirements and procedures
(d) To monitor progress of probationary year teachers

Another aspect, following the work of Hilsum and Cane (1971) is evaluation by probationary year teachers. They compile teaching diaries, itemizing their complete working day and also listing and grading the skills involved. They also complete regular questionnaires and use the micro-techniques developed by the lecturer in the school situation. These techniques include the use of Cosford Responders for testing lesson consolidation. These allow complete class testing with immediate feedback. However, the major innovation is the micro-analysis disc which can be employed to record changes of teaching mode, etc, during the lesson. Rather than have the intrusion of an observer or even a taperecorder, it was felt that some simple measure was required which could be unobtrusively made by the teacher himself. The discs consist of circular white labels on which are inscribed the number of concentric circles required. The size of the disc is such that when it is stuck over the dial of the teacher's wrist watch, the hands protrude. Then, at any given instant, a change can be timed exactly and marked on the disc using an appropriate line for visual aids, question and answer sessions, book exercises, etc. The number of questions asked can be recorded on the centre of the disc (Figure 3). It is hoped that by using these the balance within particular types of period, depending on the age and ability of the children and the subject being taught, can be ascertained and used later for student assessment. Arrangements have already been made for the conclusions to be checked by interaction analysis and CCTV records.

There is also an 'after care' service, helping former students with course design problems and producing practical teaching papers for use in schools. The subjects for these papers are developed in college and tested

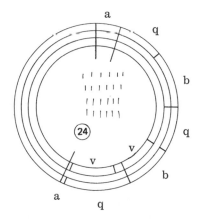

a administration

q question and answer

b work-books

v visual aid

Figure 3. Micro-analysis disc

by students during teaching practices. The most complete example so far is the graphicacy project which has been tested in two schools over a period of more than two years. This subject is taken to be the visual–spatial equivalent of numeracy, literacy and articulacy. Teachers and students were involved in the early stages of this work and it has been continuously monitored by them ever since. As a result, a paper has been published and part of the project has been incorporated into new college courses.

The direct connection of the hydrology course and field teaching with children has already been mentioned. A programme of CCTV micro-teaching sessions has also been started for probationary year teachers. The method was first used and evaluated with college students who now work with the ex-students and thus form another direct link with schools. Each student gave a five-minute presentation as a lesson introduction and this was then graded on a 0-10 scale using the following criteria:

(a) Material:
      (i) interest
      (ii) relevance
(b) Subject:
      (i) establishing need/providing motivation
      (ii) stating aims/objectives clearly
      (iii) links with previous work (if relevant)
(c) Questions:
      (i) asked correctly
      (ii) handled effectively
(d) Personal:
      (i) voice
      (ii) manner
      (iii) confidence
      (iv) enthusiasm

(e) Overall assessment:

     After the CCTV replay, the presentation was regraded and it was found that changes were commonly made leading to a greater consensus of opinion. From these lesson introductions a longer tape illustrating major teaching points is being produced.

5. IN-SERVICE

The school-based part of the system naturally leads to in-service work and the hydrology course forms part of the in-service B Ed programme. The teachers involved have been very active in helping prepare the practical aspects of the course as they are more concerned with small pieces of research than scaling down the ideas for school use. They will be acting as demonstrators during a DES course this summer which includes aspects of this programme. As the courses are improved and monitored, it is hoped that they can be used to help re-train teachers and therefore introduce new ideas into schools. The process is thus one of mutual enrichment and in fact a series of in-service courses in schools has already been arranged. A survey was made of the students to ascertain and compare the problems of in-service and Open University courses. The main finding was that the more structured approach of the latter generated a great deal of confidence and produced fewer problems. It was hoped that the type of course design described in this paper would help overcome some of the deficiencies felt by in-service students.

6. CONCLUSIONS

It can be seen that this is a broadly-based learning system involving college, schools and in-service training, with a fundamental aim of bringing the three closer together (Figure 4). As yet, it is on a small scale and feedback is only just beginning to appear. However, it is felt that by careful management and the further development of each area described, courses can be continuously improved and the college will be more effective in its lifelong objectives.

REFERENCE

Hilsum, S and Cane, B S (1971) 'The Teacher's Day'. NFER

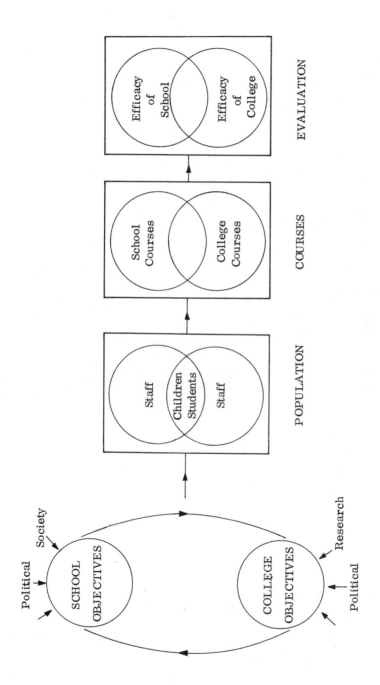

Figure 4. Working system

63

Mature students: OU and non-OU

L R B ELTON

INTRODUCTION

The subject that I have chosen is at the moment extremely topical as is evidenced by the fact that in the last four days I have collected really quite important references to it from 'The Times Higher Educational Supplement' of last Friday, the 'Observer' on Sunday and the 'Guardian' to-day. Those references are not contained in the list of references which have been handed out to you, but most of the references in this list are in fact very recent and many from the educational press because I would like you to get into a frame of mind that we are dealing here with a topic that is a real issue for debate ˘ and discussion at the moment. So what am I going to talk about? Well, I am going to start by defining what a mature student is and then outline the traditional approach that we have taken to mature students and present you with some evidence (not much evidence) on what the motivation of mature students is and some of their special features. I then want to refer to the dichotomy of Martha and Mary (see the reference to Harris and Holmes) and the special problems of working class students, which will take us to the idea of education permanente and finally - this is after all a conference on educational technology - how can educational technology help us?

WHAT IS A MATURE STUDENT?

We are all adults now in higher education from the age of eighteen onwards, and so I define a mature student as one who has had a substantial break between school and further education in the higher education sector. I have not only defined the mature student for you, I have also brought a specimen along and on my left is Mrs Jenni Thackwray, who is in fact a mature student, and is going to be my audio-visual aid for this talk. She will, I hope,be able to contribute something to our discussion after my talk, which we so often lack in our discussions, namely the view of the individual student. On the other hand there is always the danger that, once a group like us gets hold of this rare specimen, we treat him or her as representative of all of them and this would be a grave mistake. Jenni is very much herself.

WHAT IS THE TRADITIONAL APPROACH TO MATURE STUDENTS?

Adult students have enormously varied needs and this is one of the great problems of adult education. I am going to suggest to you that there are basically two ways in which we all allow adult students to study. One is to obtain an orthodox qualification in an unorthodox way, and the other is to obtain an orthodox qualification in an orthodox way. Let me explain. The unorthodox way to obtain an orthodox qualification is to take a fairly standard degree but not to take it in the normal way by attending full-time at a University or Polytechnic. This has been the time-honoured way in which the London External Degree together with correspondence courses and attendance in further education has been running for the best part of a century, and the Open University is the latest and certainly the most successful and remarkable manifestation of this particular form of education. The aims of the Open University were stated by Lord Crowther in his inaugural address. He said: "One view regards the individual human mind as a vessel of varying capacity into which is to be poured as much as it will hold of the knowledge and experience by which human society lives and moves. This is the Martha of education, and we shall have plenty of these tasks to perform. But the Mary regards the human mind as a fire that has to be set alight and blown with a divine efflatus. That we also take as our ambition." I found this quotation in an article by Harris and Holmes (Harris and Holmes, 1975) and I shall come back to it later.

Now the method which the traditional approach uses is mainly from the teacher to the student, which is indeed good for Martha. It is probably necessary for a mass approach to be of this kind because the moment you allow the student to react back in any significant way onto the teacher you get an enormous variation into the system. There is another need, which is not of a logistic kind but of a psychological kind, for this mainly teacher-to-student approach. It is to make the student feel secure. Adult students often feel very insecure in their study and a directive approach makes them more secure. So we have then here a situation which is eminently suited to the approach that the OU has developed, namely a centrally directed convergent approach to degree courses, and let me be clear, the OU has done a good deal in curriculum development to get away from the content of degree courses as well as the method of approach common in the traditional universities. But yet it is very much according to the prescription that Lord Crowther laid down for Martha. There is certainly concern about this within the OU, and Rowntree in his talk at this conference last year (Rowntree, 1975) very much pointed this out. He coined the word 'munication' being one-way traffic from the teacher to the student as opposed to 'communication' being a joint traffic to and fro.

So much for the orthodox qualification in the unorthodox way. What about the orthodox qualification in the orthodox way? This is how we treat mature students when they come to traditional universities and colleges. We do make some concessions; for instance, we do normally allow mature students with unorthodox entry requirements, and to that extent a recent plea by Walwin (Walwin, 1974), that we should do this in the University is really showing lack of knowledge. Most universities will accept mature students without the normal A-level entry. In fact we have got a good deal further in this line since Churchill, when he left the British Army and thought of going to Oxford to study, found that he had to study Greek before he could get in and remarked, "I could not contemplate toiling at Greek irregular verbs after having commanded British regular troops". We also, to some extent, allow a variation in hours of work, for instance Birkbeck College with its part-time study. This kind of approach is epitomized in the recent paper on Adult Education by the Committee of Vice-Chancellors and Principals, which is a very good and well-meaning paper in a very traditional mould (Committee of Vice-Chancellors and Principals, 1974).

It turns out that mature students in fact have significantly different needs, both in connection with their study methods and their assessment methods and not just with their entry methods and the timing of attendance. I was first hit by this when I started counselling students in study methods. I recently started a service, together with my colleague Sid O'Connell, in the University of Surrey where we offer students help with their study methods and I found that the majority of students who came to me were mature students. At the same time I had issued a questionnaire to our first-year students and asked them a number of questiona based on a questionnaire which was provisionally developed in Australia, regarding their perception of the teaching staff at a University (Elton, 1975). Now it is very interesting that the factor analysis of this showed that four of the important factors were interpersonal relations with staff, autonomous development of the student, attitude towards the scholarship of the staff and instructional needs of the student. Mature students, I found, were even less interested than young students in interpersonal relations with staff - this came as a bit of a shock to me how little students, young and old, wanted to mix socially with the staff but the mature even less than the young - but they put much greater value on their own autonomous development and on scholarship of the staff. At the same time there was no difference at all between their instructional needs and those of the less mature students, as revealed by this questionnaire. This means that they view the teaching and learning situation in a way that is different, but subtly different, from the view of young students, because on the surface it is the same, ie the instructional needs are the same. But their need for greater autonomous development and their greater respect for staff scholarship make some important differences. These were confirmed to me by a recent article by a mature student from which I want to quote later (Smith, 1975).

THE QUESTION OF MOTIVATION

Mature students by and large are motivated in a different way from 18-year-olds. Their need for a qualification, if that is their motivation, is much greater. They have less time to waste and a very large number of mature students have as their topmost motivation the need for a qualification. These are the Marthas. It makes them both docile (they want to do well in the accepted system) and worried (they are afraid they may not do well in the accepted system) and these are the students by and large I would suggest who are labelled 'excellent students' at OU Summer Schools. They are very earnest and very willing students who want to do their best in the framework set for them. At the opposite extreme are the mature students who come into education at that level because of their love of education and thirst for knowledge. This is often quite non-specific. It is not "I want to learn this subject" but "I want to learn", and for that reason particularly difficult to satisfy. I would suggest that this kind of student, who is the Mary of education, is likely to be the 'bolshy' variety at the Summer School. Obviously I have polarized here and most of us are part Martha and part Mary. Let us always be clear that when anyone establishes a dichotomy what one is really talking about is two opposite ends of a spectrum that is fairly continuous.

FEATURES OF MATURE STUDENTS

I want to divide these into three groups, and yet want to say that most students in some sense have aspects of all three. The first then is the examination-oriented group whom I already classified as the Marthas. They are highly motivated, they need security in their study and basically one gets so often the question from them, either straight or disguised, conscious or sub-conscious, 'what will I be examined on?'. This group is excellently served by what I might call the traditional Ed Tech approach: the specification of aims and objectives, the provision of materials which are designed to satisfy those aims, the provision of tests and self-tests to reassure the student that he is in fact satisfying them. Clearly the Open University has done a magnificent job in that line. In traditional universities perhaps it would be right to say that at the moment the Keller Plan is the best example of this approach. I would like to put in one caution here. It is not necessary to combine this approach with an insistence on behavioural objectives and I would refer you to a very good article which recently appeared in 'Educational Technology' (Sheehan, 1974).

The second group is the 'love of education' group. They would also like a degree because a degree is an accepted status symbol, a degree is a sign of achievement. This century is the century of the paper qualification man and woman, and nobody is really exempt from this. But their love of education conflicts with a directiveness of most degree courses and a question now arises whether we could not adapt our degree courses so that there is not a conflict in aims between the love of education and the desire for a degree of these students. I suggest that there are two main changes that are necessary compared with the traditional approach that I outlined as before, ie the OU or Keller Plan approach. The one stems from the very great importance of discussion in the life of the 'love of education' students, whether it is discussion with a tutor or, perhaps even more important, peer group learning. The second is the need for continuous assessment of some kind - and I don't mean assessing everything but on-going assessment - to replace much or all of the final assessment. Because as long as a student has to work towards an examination at the end, it is inescapable that this will colour, and colour in an unfortunate way, much of his attitudes towards his learning. Both these changes are difficult to fit into the existing image of the kind of systematic approach that I outlined before, but I would like to say that I purposely said that that was the traditional Ed Tech approach, because Educational Technologists today are not confined to the kind of approach which does not allow for the freedom of the students. Again I would like to refer you to an extremely good article in a recent issue of 'Educational Technology' (Fox, 1974) on the relationship between technology and humanism, both of which are the province of the educational technologist.

So what we have now, turning to the more specific concern of the educational technologist, is the question whether we can introduce two-way communication into teaching at a distance, because neither peer group learning nor continuous assessment is easy without the two-way communication. Well, the obvious way is of course the telephone (Williams, 1975; Short, 1974; L'Henry-Evans, 1974). I was interested when I was in Sweden recently that the technical device that is used most in teaching at a distance there is the telephone, that it is assumed that every house in Sweden has a telephone, that it is in working order and that it transmits without undue noise. These are minimal requirements and they are satisfied in Sweden. I know of at least one country much nearer home where they are frequently not. There is a paper later in the conference on the use of the telephone and also the use of the conference telephone which is an essential addition if we are to have peer group learning. It is obvious that the OU is very much alive to this problem but my worry is that it is not put high enough on the list of requirements. I think to fight for a better telephone system is more important than to fight for the fourth channel, the fourth channel being essentially a teacher-directed medium.

So far I have talked about the two groups that are the Martha and Mary. Now I want to turn to the third group which at present is not taken notice of at all. I call it the 'link-to-experience' group. Every adult student has very substantial experience of life and, so far in this country, whether in traditional universities or in the Open University, this is not integrated in any way, individual to the student, into his degree studies. Obviously, one may take a degree which is related to some previous experience that one has had, but there is no way in which the degree will be adapted to past or ongoing experience, far less will that experience be allowed to be counted for what the Americans call for credit, as part of your degree requirement. The only course of this kind that I know of in this country is the Lancaster School of Independent Studies degree (University of Lancaster Prospectus, 1975-6), where it is possible to take part of the degree through a student directed curriculum, ie the student evolves his own curriculum in the light of his experience. There is considerable experience in the United States in this area and I recently came across a rather interesting booklet 'How to go through the University of Massachusetts on your own terms' (Mollner, 1972) which lists fifty different ways in which in one single university in the United States a student can influence his own course. Some of them are as trivial and well known to us as options in courses, but many go far beyond that and, in particular, one is the 'University without Walls' where it is actually an essential part that the student must have ongoing life experience and that this is counted as part of his credits.

MARTHA AND MARY

In any teaching and learning system the student has something to contribute. However, in an adult system it becomes absolutely crucial. The student has many experiences which his teacher does not have and which are extremely relevant. Here I would like to quote from the article by Smith (Smith, 1975): "Many of the lecturers appeared to be living in a small world that was closed even to ideas. Students were often treated as incomplete people - children in fact - and children who couldn't possibly add anything to the subject being studied." It is interesting that he in fact was taking a postgraduate course in Engineering, and he is a practising engineer. Harris and Holmes (Harris and Holmes, 1975), in discussing the work of the OU, say that "the teaching system fails to recognize that adults have something to offer to the educational experience they have decided to undergo. Milton Keynes simply dispenses knowledge to all, using principles which see students' everyday lives as producing only 'noise' within the system." This is from two people who used to work for the OU but don't any more. However, there are similar quotations from within the OU (Wilkins, 1975; Northedge, 1975): "The general assumption is that the student is a stranger in a new-found land and that the best way to find his way is by asking an officially approved OU guide." And, on the subject of discussion group teaching and learning, "the OU cannot afford to place great demands on the skill, the time, or the tolerance of students or staff since group discussions will inevitably be regarded as a relatively low priority aspect of the OU teaching system". Let me be quite clear, this is not an indictment of the OU. If at all, it is an indictment of the OU for not doing a great deal better than traditional universities, because it is an indictment of all universities in much the same way, and perhaps I should remind you here of what Geoffrey Hubbard said earlier in this conference, that in the long run it is possible that the greatest contribution that the OU can make to education in this country is the way that it influences traditional universities rather than the way that it teaches its own students.

THE WORKING CLASS STUDENT

Next let me turn to the special problems of the working class student. He is very often in the Martha category and needs a professional qualification, but even more often than not this is not at degree level but at sub-degree level. He has a gap between where he is and where the degree starts, and this is as true of a traditional university as of the Open University. This is, I am sure, one of the main reasons why there is still such a shortage of adult working class students in the Open University population. But there is also the Mary of the working class student, the one that wants a general education, the one that perhaps, if he is lucky, gets a Trade Union Scholarship to Ruskin College. Now can the OU meet this demand? This really was the question which Crowther set himself and again I quote Harris and Holmes (Harris and Holmes, 1975): "A wide ranging liberal academic curriculum like the one at the OU has a greater potential for becoming meaningful to working class students than a narrow vocationalism. But that potential can only be realized if the form of communication allows for a bridge to develop between everyday working class culture and academic knowledge." There is a real problem here in this gap between us middle-class educators and the working class student, and this becomes important when we now turn to education permanente.

EDUCATION PERMANENTE

Let me start here with professional training and re-training. This is likely to be the major component of such education for many years to come. Short courses of a vocational kind are frequent. What we do not have at all yet in this country but which is getting very common in Europe at least as a talking point, if not already in existence, is paid educational leave. A report on paid educational leave in Sweden, Germany and France came out only last week (Charnley, 1975). Well, could we achieve educational leave? Houghton, who is acting secretary for the Association of Recurrent Education and works for the Open University, suggests (Houghton, 1975) that "if, as has already happened in Australia, one of our more powerful unions threatened to strike for paid educational leave and the consequent educational facilities, then one has little doubt that such facilities would be provided." Is that all that is necessary? What are the implications of education permanente through paid educational leave and full-time study? Well, the OU clearly is not the right place for that because, once you have full-time study, the students might as well travel to the place of learning and have more individually designed courses. But the OU experience will be enormously valuable to us in traditional universities, once we have such courses. There are some very serious problems about the paid educational leave because if industry pays for it, it wants its 'tit-for-tat'. We may not all agree with Illich but at least we ought to listen to him (Illich and Verne, 1975): "Popular education movements, mesmerised by the financial resources offered them by the permanent education legislators agree to submit to the rules of the financial inspectors, to the criteria of the legal administrators and to the selection of the purveyors of knowledge." Indeed, Charnley (Charnley, 1975) quotes with approval the American system where the educational system and the industrial system are closely linked. There are very considerable dangers in such a situation.

The second aspect of education permanente is general education. When I was in Sweden recently, they pointed out to me that to them education is no longer a social service, it is a consumer good, and they suggested that the present decline of popularity of education amongst students is simply a reflection of the general recession. We are buying less refrigerators and we are buying less education. It will go up again when, as we hope, the trade cycle reverses. But if it is a consumer good then we ought to seriously consider providing what the consumer wants and that very often goes against the academic's idea of a discipline. The consumer very often wants very general education, not necessarily three years, not necessarily tightly packaged, not necessarily depth but breadth. This becomes even more serious when we turn to this most revolutionary of proposals for adult education, namely, life-experience credits. This requires a radical change in our attitude towards "what is degree work?" Obviously it is going to be difficult to assess what the life experience of a nurse who has walked the wards, and is walking the wards, is in connection with a course she is taking in advanced nursing. But it is important. It is getting very common in America, and a recent report (Hill, 1975) from the American situation suggests: "Faculty tend to resist the use of life experience grades partly because they feel threatened by them. But it is a fallacy to suppose that teachers may lose their jobs if too many students are receiving life experience credits instead of 'sitting in class', as adults coming back to college tend to be interested in cross-disciplinary subjects and generate new topics like pollution, social change and black and white women in American society."

Well, I think Frances Hill has been terribly naive. The reason why we academics feel threatened by this kind of course is not because we fear we would be out of a job - we are quite good at looking after ourselves from that point of view - it is that these students will bring in experiences that are very strange to us. They will threaten us by coming from what even we call the 'real world' and we will be even more threatened if they suggest that we should put on new courses on black and white women in American society. So we are going to be threatened, but if we are not going to admit this and then accept the threat and turn it to our advantage, we are going to fail as academics because the University must interact with the community if it is to remain relevant to the community of the future. The University has always had both these roles, conservation of what is best in a community and innovation, often influenced by the community. It will broaden our outlook, and how much better it would have been for the teachers of Mr Smith if they had listened to his practical experience as an engineer.

CONCLUSION

What I suggest is this. That the Open University is very well suited, and traditional universities are moderately well suited, to the needs of students whose primary aim is to obtain a qualification. Neither provides much for the student who loves education, although traditional universities probably have more openings here because of their greater flexibility. Neither has begun to enable a student to integrate life experience into his study.

How can educational technology help? Well, I suggest that there are at least four ways in which we ought to be able to help in this process. First is the analysis of aims, which is eminently suited to us. What is it that the mature students really want? These aims will not be uniform. Next, what methods of assessment are best suited to the various aims that these students have? It is clear that mature students have very diverse aims, which will require diverse methods, and this will require a great deal of individualization. This can only be done by providing materials that can be used for individualized study. Then I suggest that, on the technical plane, the problem of the two-way communication system is one that we ought to solve. This is as important in the traditional university as in the Open University, because the telephone is a quick and cheap method of communication, even if you happen to be on the same campus or if, as a mature student often would be, he only visits the campus occasionally. Finally, my conclusion is that the development of degree studies for the Marys in adult education is something that I believe that the traditional universities are intrinsically better equipped for than the Open University, but that the Open University has, I hope, given the traditional universities the necessary jolt to look at this problem.

REFERENCES

Charnley, A (1975) 'Paid Educational Leave'. Hart-Davis Educational, London

Committee of Vice-Chancellors and Principals (1974) 'Adult Education'. Report A5/4/3/CIRC/74/57

Elton, R L B (1975) 'Student Perception of University Lecturers', unpublished. Based on Magin, D 'Evaluating the Role Performance of University Lecturers'. 'University Quarterly', 28, 84, 1973

Fox, G Thomas Jr and Vere De Vault, M (1974) 'Technology and humanism in the classroom: Frontiers of educational practice'. 'Educational Technology', 14, 7

Harris, D and Holmes, J (1975) 'Open to Martha, closed to Mary'. 'Times Educational Supplement', 14.2.75

L'Henry-Evans, Odette (1974) 'Teaching by telephone: Some practical observations'. 'Teaching at a distance', No 1, p 67

Hill, Frances (1975) 'Life credits attracting more mature students'. 'Times Higher Educational Supplement', 21.3.75

Houghton, V (1975) 'Recurrent education'. Letter in 'Times Higher Educational Supplement', 21.3.75

Illich, I and Verne, E (1975) 'Imprisoned in the global classroom'. 'Times Educational Supplement', 21.3.75

Mollner, T (1972) 'How to go through the University of Massachusetts on your own terms'. University of Massachusetts, Amherst

Northedge, Andrew (1975) 'Learning through discussion in the Open University'. 'Teaching at a distance', No 2, p 10

Rowntree, D 'Two styles of communication and their implications for learning'. In 'Aspects of Educational Technology', Vol VIII, p 281 (ed) Baggaley, J, Jamieson, G H and Marchant, H. Pitman, London

Sheehan, T J (November 1974) 'Why the cool reception to behavioural objectives in the university?' 'Educational Technology', p 54

Short, J (1974) 'Teaching by telephone: the problems of teaching without the visual channel'. 'Teaching at a distance', No 1, p 61

Smith, R (1975) 'Portrait of the student as an old man'. 'Education Guardian', 28.1.75

University of Lancaster, School of Independent Studies Prospectus 1975-6

Walwin, J (1974) 'Admit adults without A-level to university'. 'Times Higher Educational Supplement', 6.12.74

Wilkins, Roger (1975) 'Cooperative learning in discussion groups'. 'Teaching at a distance', No 2, p 7

Williams E (1975) 'The application of interactive telecommunications systems to education'. In 'Aspects of Educational Technology, Vol VIII, p 294 (ed) Baggaley, J, Jamieson, G H and Marchant, H. Pitman, London

A proposed system for mass continuing education*

N C FARNES, R McCORMICK, J A CALDER

SUMMARY

Proposed in this paper is a comprehensive system for mass continuing education. This will inevitably require radical methods to attract in the educationally disadvantaged. Some of the problems and pointers are considered to see how such a system might operate in practice. Evidence supporting the need for the kind of provision outlined in this report is given in the Appendix.

1. Radical methods are proposed to attract in the educationally disadvantaged.
2. Three types of provision are identified:

   (a) learner-based provision
   (b) provision based on monitored demand
   (c) provision initiated from outside bodies or from the centre

3. Methods of delivery appropriate to each type of provision involve:

   (a) Individuals requesting resources to meet their own educational needs at all levels.
   (b) Tutors actively seeking out people's needs and obtaining resources to meet these needs.
   (c) Packages of materials assembled on the basis of monitored demands and delivered, on request, to learners or tutors.
   (d) Cooperative arrangements with other organizations.
   (e) the Open University undergraduate model for course delivery.

4. A Resource Management System is required involving:

   (a) A computerized resource catalogue containing information on local and national resources and resources held by (b) below.
   (b) A multi-media resource centre.

5. The OU has assets that makes it well suited to setting up and running a comprehensive programme for continuing education.

---

* The system is proposed by the authors and is not an official Open University proposal.

INTRODUCTION

We must explain the origins of this proposal. The OU with its multi-media learning system based on a central course production, a delivery system and regional support networks is an undoubted success in terms of number of applicants. Despite this, the OU is failing to reach many sections of the community, not just because they have not heard of it, but because we are only offering a limited amount of the possible types of educational provision - undergraduate courses. The OU Charter* says that the University should promote the educational well-being of the community generally and hence the University is setting up a high level Planning Committee to consider a wider educational provision.

This means that our proposal is no mere academic exercise but an attempt to spell out a system to provide for mass continuing education. In that context we felt it necessary to present it to a wider audience in the hope of refining it and indeed changing it completely.

THE PROPOSED SYSTEM

1. Continuing Education

We take it as axiomatic that adults at various times in their lives have needs that can be met or partially met through education. However, the majority of adults do not participate in adult education. In the past, participation in adult education has widened rather than closed the gap of educational advantage between those who were reasonably successful at school and the majority who were not. Many of the latter found school a humiliating experience and left convinced that they were incapable of benefiting from education and a fear of anything associated with it. So even if the offerings of adult education could help them meet their needs it is unlikely that they would consider enrolling.

The concept of continuing education is essential for giving coherence to a wide range of offerings that will be required to meet people's different and changing educational needs during their lives. Only a full continuing education programme is flexible enough to meet these needs as they arise at various stages of a person's life.

If this programme is to make a significant contribution to the educational well-being of the community generally it must attract those who do not as yet participate in any form of adult education. This will require an approach radically different from the traditional one of putting on courses and then waiting for students to enrol. Those who take advantage of the current provision will no doubt welcome the opportunity to participate in a more comprehensive programme of continuing education but, by definition, they are already to some extent provided for.

---

* This is taken from the Open University Charter, April 1969: "The objects of the University . . . shall be to provide education of University and professional standards for its students and to promote the educational well-being of the community generally."

Three broad types of provision within a programme for continuing education are identified below. We expect people to take advantage of these different types of provision, and of different offerings within a particular type, at various stages of their lives.

The general principle of the system is based on the Open University model, in that there is a centre with a regional network. However, it differs from the OU in that the centre not only initiates the provision of learning material, but also receives initiatives from learners and others. Thus we have classified the types depending on who initiates the provision of learning materials.

1.1 Learner-Based Provision

Here the request for materials comes from individual learners to the centre. The centre responds individually with one-off packages made up of those items requested. The request will come from the learner and a package will be sent direct to him (like a public library or a mail-order firm). Such a package, for example, might contain multi-media materials related to a particular problem, project or situation faced by an individual or group, or simply a book list.

The request can also come from a tutor (see Sections 2 and 3). The items requested will be based on his assessment of what is required to meet an individual's or a group's needs. They may well be decided on by discussion, but the tutor orders and receives the materials which are dispatched as a one-off package. Packages or materials might be related to a programme of study, or a series of meetings.

The request procedure is discussed in Section 3.

1.2 Provision Based on Monitored Demand

The demands arising from the above provision will be monitored by the centre and will provide the basis for making an assessment of future demands. Where it is thought likely that the demands for similar one-off packages will continue the centre will mass-produce a package, perhaps with an additional specially prepared study guide, and the availability of this package will be publicized. Mass-produced packages can then be requested by individuals, by tutors or become incorporated into larger packages. The availability of a package will save time for learners and for the centre in selecting each item. Such packages might be related to concerns of the home and family, employment, trade unions, housing, consumers, hobbies, the environment, social issues, etc.

1.3 Provision Initiated from Outside Bodies or the Centre

Materials will be offered in response to initiatives from sources other than from the learners or tutors. We distinguish the following sources:
The professions and other agencies responsible for occupational needs, eg banking, social work, teacher training, accountancy, electronics, etc. They may be materials related to pre-professional qualifying courses or to

post-professional course, ie conversion or up-dating courses. The materials provided and the way they are used will be flexible. For example, only small packages might be provided and distributed by the agencies themselves, the materials might be used by local colleges or materials might be offered by the OU as in its current post-experience programme.

Organizations such as national clubs, societies, etc, eg Ramblers Association, the AA, Help the Aged, National Association of Community Associations, etc. As for the above, such offerings would be flexible in size and manner of usage. All the materials would be freely available as packages.

Within the Centre, eg the academic faculties. These materials will include undergraduate and postgraduate courses, that may be subject-centred, problem-centred, innovatory, cultural, academic, etc. The materials will be assembled and produced on the initiative of central staff. Possibly in anticipation of a need or interest arising from changes in government legislation, developments in industry, technology, politics, art, etc. These materials, in whole or in part, will be freely available to anyone, not just those registered for a degree.

The balance between the different types of provision is a matter for study, but it is likely that initially the learner-based provision should command most of the resources. (For costings see Section 3.3.)

2. Methods of Delivery

It is essential to be flexible about:

(a) the materials offered; these will vary from individual items, eg pamphlets, books, information documents, source material, measuring equipment, educational games, films, tapes; packages of items to a group of packages (modules) or a large package (eg a full course); and

(b) the methods by which the materials will be delivered; these will range, from at one end of a continuum, the learner-based provision - where individual items of materials are sent to individuals directly - to the OU undergraduate model of course production and presentation at the other end of the continuum; here large packages of the same materials are sent to large numbers of individuals.

Also along this continuum are the possibilities for many kinds of cooperative schemes for the production and delivery of materials, eg with LEAs, colleges, professional societies, institutes of adult education, WEA, BBC, national clubs and organizations, publishers, libraries, museums, etc.

The details of how each kind of provision might be offered are considered below.

2.1 Learner-Based Provision

The learners serviced by this provision will range from educationally disadvantaged adults to PhD students. There is no difficulty in conceiving how the relatively small numbers of PhD students might use this provision; the difficulties arise in attracting in educationally disadvantaged adults. For them it is not sufficient to be able to respond flexibly - we have to adopt a more

77

active approach. This approach should be modelled on the community development projects run by certain local authorities who are currently employing community education workers with special responsibilities for adult education. (Examples are shown in Appendix, Section 2.3.)

Community education workers will need to be employed as part-time tutors in the continuing education system and will correspond to tutor/counsellors in the OU undergraduate programme but with different roles. They will be responsible for seeking out needs, helping individuals and the community to articulate their needs and for obtaining learning resources to meet these needs. They will be in contact with other tutors in the region and with the centre. In their region they can meet to compare notes and discuss needs and resources. The part-time tutors and the full-time staff tutors can collect information on local resources (people, places and things) that can be passed on to the centre. The centre can coordinate and catalogue the resources available in each region. Also at the centre multi-media materials will be collected and produced and these will be catalogued as well (see Section 3).

The part-time tutor with his knowledge of local and central resources, and in discussions with individuals, could organize a range of materials to meet their needs. These materials would be obtained from the centre on loan, and by taking advantage of local resources. Where appropriate the tutor might suggest certain packages of materials. Work with these materials would lead to solving problems and might lead to the creation of a product, eg adventure playground, community centre, artwork, film, radio programme, tape/slide presentation, (of which an example is given in Appendix, Section 2.2.2.). The completion of the product can be recorded by the tutor and this record can be held by the individual or individuals who created the product. They could use it how they wished - eg present it to a possible employer as evidence of a particular kind of experience. The product would thus become a 'reviewable item' and such a concept would be useful in dealing with accreditation. However, a more far-reaching aspect of the reviewable item is the possibility that it could be entered into the resource centre for others to use.

The important characteristic of these materials is that they are related to changing and improving conditions of life through self-help and cooperative action. The materials provide practical knowledge that has immediate relevance for what are often intellectually demanding problems. They can also lead learners onto problems of a related but more general nature taking them beyond their existing horizons. Furthermore, success with these materials might lead learners to more demanding materials and if their interests are in this direction, towards a degree programme.

2.2 Provision Based on Monitored Demand

The demands for resources from the 'grass roots' can be monitored by resource advisors working at · the centre . This information can be used for assembling multi-media packages of related material and offered perhaps with broadcast support to those who express an interest. In this way these packages would be <u>responsive</u> and arise out of expressed needs. They could be assembled on a one-off basis but it will be more economic to mass-produce packages where there is a sufficiently clear and large demand for related materials. Where there is not a clear demand, then individual items can be loaned. Thus the mass-produced packages will have been automatically market-researched before they are offered.

The packages could be loosely structured multi-media materials. In addition they might contain a study guide or suggestions on how to organize the information to make decisions. They can be worked by individuals or by groups - with or without the help of the tutor; and may lead to the production of reviewable items. An offering along these lines could be called 'a course', but as adult educators have found, there are considerable advantages in not emphasizing the formal educational aspects of such an offering.

2.3 Provision Initiated by Outside Bodies and the Centre

The advantage of cooperative arrangements with outside bodies for the production and delivery of materials is that they often have their own methods for contacting potential students and providing their own means of delivery to their own members. Many organizations have a national, regional and local structure through which members are kept informed and activities are coordinated. They can make the successful completion of certain courses a condition for membership and give their official recognition of courses for various purposes. Often they are able to provide facilities for meetings, viewing films and running courses.

These bodies might take advantage of existing materials and request these as individual items, packages or as a selected group of packages and deliver them themselves. On the other hand, they might contribute to the production of new materials that are then made available to their members through a common delivery system.

The Open University has its own clientele and is able to produce and deliver materials to them. On obtaining their degrees many of these students will want to take further courses. The faculties might offer specially prepared postgraduate materials or they might recommend certain existing materials and provide book lists, etc. These could be obtained from the resource centre. Alternatively, the students might pursue their own studies and by taking advantage of the learner-based provision request their own materials.

2.4 Examples

The following examples illustrate how the provision described above might be used.

Mrs A lives in a tenement block; she left school at 15, worked in a clothing factory for 3 years and then married. She has a young child - who is constantly seeking attention, is unable to play on its own and says very little. It is quite likely that she is not aware that there is anything unusual about her child; she might feel, however, that things are getting on top of her and find it increasingly difficult to cope. A talk with a sympathetic health visitor could lead her to realize that perhaps there are problems about how she relates to her child. But how can she find out how to improve her relationship? The health visitor can offer advice and guidance but is not in a position to undertake the involved task of teaching the mother how to interact with her child.

Now it is conceivable but very unlikely that a local WEA class on child development just happened to be open to enrolment at that moment. And, providing she could schedule the time and find someone to look after her child, she could sign on and attend. This is unlikely, and in any case much too passive an approach. Sending the child to a nearby playgroup would not help her to relate to the child; but the health visitor might suggest that she visits the playgroup and talks to the playleader about how children can be encouraged to play, what toys and games are available and how to talk to children.

Let us suppose the mother does this and returns from the playgroup impressed by the materials there and with the helpful way the playleader questions the children about what they are doing. Suppose also that the health visitor is employed part-time as a tutor and has access to a wide range of resources. In discussion with the mother they decide that some of the materials used in the playgroup might interest the child. In addition to these materials there are simple work cards suggesting how the mother might participate. Also the tutor is able to obtain a disc with a commentary and recordings of mothers and children talking, and points out that there are a series of BBC TV programmes about children's play currently being broadcast. The mother becomes involved in playing games and discussing these with her child, she becomes increasingly confident in her ability to make progress with the child and to cope with the additional materials. She feels the need for more materials and wants to know more about child development. The tutor suggests she obtains a ready-assembled package that contains educational toys, work cards, workshop materials, magazine-type articles and some more discs. This package is one of a series designed for children of various ages and has adjunct material for the mother.

The tutor has helped other mothers in the locality obtain similar materials and she suggests that two or three mothers meet to carry out workshops with their children and to view and discuss films on various aspects of child development. The tutor is able to borrow films and projection equipment and to show the films in the mothers' homes. The tutor suggests that the mothers visit a local home for disturbed children and talk to the staff. She also knows a developmental psychologist in the area who is willing to talk to the mothers.

After some time many of the mothers are pleased with what they have learnt and obtain satisfaction from their developing relationship with their children. They understand the crucial role of the mother in helping their children develop and they are able to carry this out. For the time being they do not require any new materials.

However, some of the mothers have become increasingly interested in particular aspects of their child's progress and obtain materials related to their varied interests. Other mothers have become concerned with other quite different problems - for example, how to relate to their husbands or with opportunities for women who wish to return to work.

A few mothers, inspired by their success with increasingly more demanding materials, decide to enrol for a home-based multi-media course on child development. This might be a short course involving 30 hours of study with perhaps some written work.

Following this, one of the mothers wishes to take a single course out of the OU undergraduate programme. Success with this course leads her into the degree programme. After obtaining a degree, a diploma in child care qualifies her to work as a local authority playgroup organizer - and of course, as a part-time tutor in the continuing education programme.

Mr B leaves school and takes a job in a car factory; he is dissatisfied with his job, he meets a tutor in a working man's club. Through discussion the tutor obtains information describing jobs, a do-it-yourself vocational guidance kit, and some material that helps to organize and weigh up the pros and cons of a difficult decision (see BBC course 'Living Decisions in Family and Community'). He makes a good choice, the new job turns out to have promotion possibilities, he takes a pre-professional course (a supervisor's course). He becomes involved with trade union work - and takes a Shop Steward's course; finding this unsatisfying he takes a course on industrial relations from the undergraduate programme. His success with this course encourages him to register for a degree, taking mainly social sciences. After gaining a degree he takes a pre-professional course so that he can qualify as a probation officer and starts a new career. On occasions he orders packages on house improvements, running an allotment, local government, etc. He takes a pre-retirement course and becomes interested in the Arts. In retirement he takes undergraduate courses in Arts.

These are admittedly only illustrations. However, they illustrate a number of features:

(a) First the system is _responsive_ to individuals' needs when they arise and whatever they are.
(b) The initiative for requesting materials lies with the learner and/or the tutor.
(c) The materials are multi-media, flexible and can be delivered to the learner's home.
(d) The materials are related to real and immediate needs and are oriented towards changing and improving the quality of life through self-help.
(e) There is a range of provision for individual items to complete courses.
(f) The tutor has an active role in helping learners to articulate their needs and obtain appropriate materials.

What might such a system look like?

3. The System Required

Figure 1 gives an outline of the system required to run and service the continuing education programme. The scale of the system will be large - much larger than the current operation of the OU. Currently the OU services a relatively small number of students with large quantities of material - the new offerings are likely to service considerably larger numbers of learners with smaller quantities of more varied materials. This will involve new physical resources as well as a structure of appropriately staffed units, departments and regions.

3.1 Physical Resources

A major facility forms the centre-piece of the system for continuing education. This is a computer-based <u>Resource Management System</u> which will service all the different provisions. It will be made up of two parts: (1) a computerized resource catalogue; (2) a multi-media resource centre. These will be described before we consider the organization of support staff who will be required to run this system, and the costs.

<u>Computerized resource catalogue</u>. The system for continuing education will make a large and varied range of resources available to a large number of people. The resources will include people, places and things that are available to learners; they may be local or national or may be held by the resource centre. Information about the nature and location of these resources will be stored in a computerized resource catalogue. In the regions full-time and part-time staff will seek out and negotiate access to resources. Information about these resources will be sent to the centre and entered into the catalogue. At the centre resource advisors will be responsible for collecting and cataloguing resources that are held by the resource centre and are made available to learners or tutors. Links to the National Lending Libraries' catalogue and others would be established. Information can be obtained from the catalogue in a number of ways:

1. Multi-access terminals in the regions: users who would be either learners or tutors could use terminals located in the regions (ie in local centres) to make resource inquiries. In a simple interactive language an inquirer could formulate requests by responding to questions that make his request more specific. Items located by the computer could be printed up and the inquirer could indicate whether these were likely to be suitable - if not he could set the computer searching in another direction, and so on. In this way inquirers could learn to explore the available resources in order to find those specifically related to their needs.

2. Machine-read inquiry forms: forms on which information can be coded with pencilled marks and which can be read by a machine (as for OU computer-marked assignments) could be used by inquirers requesting information. A multiple-choice algorithm might be used to help inquirers formulate their requests. Alternatively, inquirers might work from a catalogue guide in order to indicate which items they were interested in. The reply could be printed up and automatically mailed to the inquirer.

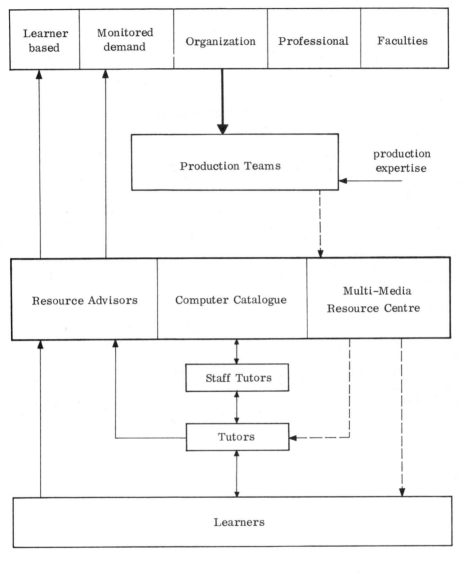

Learner based	Monitored demand	Organization	Professional	Faculties

Production Teams

production expertise

Resource Advisors	Computer Catalogue	Multi-Media Resource Centre

Staff Tutors

Tutors

Learners

- - - - ▶ flow of materials

———▶ flow of information

━━━▶ movement of people

Figure 1. The structure of the continuing education system.

83

3. Letter or telephone: inquirers could write or phone resource advisors who could suitably 'translate' the inquiry and follow up items in the resource catalogue (using terminals themselves). The information could be printed up with recommended items marked with an asterisk by the resource advisor and sent to the inquirer.

The information provided in response to these inquiries can be used in various ways:

1. Information about resources held by the resource centre can be fed directly to the centre where the requested items can be collected and packaged, and mailed directly to the inquirer.

2. Information about local resources can be sent via a terminal or a computer-printed letter to the inquirer who can then make his own arrangements to contract the local resources.

3. All inquiries and information provided will be automatically collated and monitored by the resource advisors who will be looking for unmet needs and for popular items. In particular they will be looking for popular groups of items for the possibilities of mass-producing a package.

4. Information on the total numbers of each item sent out can be compared with the number of items held by the centre (and the items returned if they are returnable) to inform an inquirer of the availability of an item. More importantly, this information can be used in applying stock-control procedures for ordering replacement items.

5. The information can be used to monitor the activities of tutors and for a system of levying fees from learners perhaps based on the number and cost of items requested.

6. The information might be used to create an adaptive catalogue where those items most often requested together can receive a high association index. This can provide a basis for informing inquiriers of one or more items that are most often requested with a particular item.

Multi-media resource centre. The system for continuing education proposed here is heavily dependent on a large multi-media resource centre. The centre will have to respond to a large number of requests for a wide variety of materials, eg pamphlets, articles, books, films, tapes, discs, apparatus, home experimental kits, educational games, packages, course materials, etc. It would spend much of its time serving individual requests for perhaps a few items, or a package of items. Less time would need to be spent on bulk orders for packages and course materials (eg for mailing out an undergraduate course). All requests to the resource centre will be routed via the computer and much of the work of the centre would be automated; possibly along the lines of large mail-order businesses and Boston Spa (the national mail-order book and periodical library, which incidentally relies on reproducing requested articles).

Resource advisors and other subject-matter experts will be responsible for purchasing or producing new material, up-dating or discarding obsolete material.

The returnable materials would also be received, checked and stored by the resource centre which would pass the information back to the catalogue.

3.2 Staff Resources

In addition to the resource management system the following staff would be appointed to various units, departments and regions.

Central staffing:

1. Resource advisors. These will be experts on a variety of subjects, not only academic but also others, eg social security, house repairs. Resource advisors will be employed in the resource management system. They will be responsible for:
   (a) organizing and up-dating the resource catalogue;
   (b) servicing requests and recommending resources where the automatic system cannot cope;
   (c) coordinating the purchasing of materials;
   (d) monitoring the requests for information and materials;
   (e) identifying the need for packages.
2. Learner-based provision. The staff in this department will be people with experience in community, social and other work that enables them to understand in particular the needs of the educationally disadvantaged. They will work closely with the resource advisors and be responsible for preparing, purchasing and adapting materials to meet the needs of the educationally disadvantaged. (Students studying independently on academic subjects will be the concern of other departments.)
3. Provision based on monitored demand. The staff will be similar to those in 2 above. They will receive information from the resource advisors concerning the monitored demand for groups of items and be responsible for designing and assembling a suitable package. They might prepare additional study guide material to accompany each package.
4. Provision for outside organizations. Staff employed in this department will work in cooperation with outside organizations in the selection and preparation of material. They would be, of course, suitably qualified at whatever level and subject for which they were preparing materials.
5. Profession and vocational provision. As for 4 above.
6. The faculties. At present there are already many people in the OU who wish to make their expertise available to a wider public and are prepared to adapt their knowledge to meet the particular needs of learners. Faculty members could be seconded to other departments to do this. Others in the faculties may wish to contribute to undergraduate and postgraduate materials.

There will be no falling off in demand for the courses and materials offered in the OU undergraduate programme. The learner-based provision should feed towards the undergraduate programme many individuals who would not otherwise become involved. The continuing education provision generally is likely to stimulate demand for professional undergraduate and postgraduate offerings.

In addition, there is a serious need for academics whose interests involve the organization and reorganization of knowledge. This is an important contribution to making knowledge accessible to people. Improving the

85

organization of information in the resource catalogue will require fundamental studies on the organization of knowledge. This will be an academically challenging task.

Also experts in particular areas will be called on to act as resource advisors and respond to inquiries about suitable resources for individuals or groups who have problems or interests in the area. Postgraduate students will need to have materials selected and recommended for them.

Regional staffing:

1. Tutors. The most important and largest requirement is for tutors to service the learner-based provision. This makes demands quite different from the current OU undergraduate and postgraduate courses. The tutors will be employed in the regions and will have to work very much on their own initiative. They will be responsible for:

   (a) contacting people, particularly the educationally disadvantaged;
   (b) encouraging them to become involved;
   (c) supplying them with appropriate materials;
   (d) seeking out and passing on information about local resources to the regional centre.

   The tutors may be community or social workers employed part-time, or they might be suitable students in the continuing education programme gaining credit for their work as a tutor. Outside tutors and teachers in existing institutions will also be able to request materials from the resource centre and use them in their own classes.

2. Staff tutors. These will be employed full-time as team leaders and be responsible for:

   (a) selecting, organizing, advising and training part-time tutors;
   (b) collecting, checking and passing to the centre resource information;
   (c) finding local educational resources and negotiating access to them.

3.3 Cost

The costings below are presented to give a rough idea of what we think would be a realistic scale of investment. Obviously more sophisticated costings would need to be undertaken before any request for funds was made. The Learner-based and Monitored demand provision would represent the major cost. If we start from a figure of one million students taking advantage of this provision at a given time, let us assume that each individual spends 1 year in 5 involved with the provision (or one-fifth of any unit of time). This means that in 5 years, 5 million people will take advantage of the offering.

Let's say one tutor is assigned to 50 active students. (We have already said that the demands on the tutor will be different from existing tutors in the OU and the ratio of 1:50 may have to be revised.) This will require 20,000 part-time tutors. If they are paid £300 per year this will cost £6 million per year. Full-time staff tutors supervising up to 50 part-time tutors each, will mean that we require 400 staff tutors. If the average salary is £3500 this will cost £1.4 million per year plus, say, £1.4 million as overheads.

For this provision central staff numbers are difficult to estimate, but if we include support staff we can crudely assume that the costs will be the same as for the staff tutors. The cost of setting up and running the Computer-based resource catalogue and the Multi-media resource centre are also difficult to estimate, but let us say £5 million per annum. This brings the total to £16.6 million per annum. In other words costing less than £17 per student to the taxpayers. The fees (if any) paid by the student will have to be considered separately.

The Organization-based provision would be largely self-financing, with perhaps a subsidy of up to £2 million. With 50,000 students taking advantage of this provision each year this would cost £40 per student.

The OU undergraduate and postgraduate provision would continue, hopefully with expanded student numbers, at already known costs - say approximately £15 million.

These total costs per year are:

Learner-based and Monitored demand provision	£16.6 m
Organization-based provision	£ 2.0 m
Undergraduate and postgraduate	£15.0 m
	£33.6 m

Total student numbers per year:

Learner-based and Monitored demand provision	1,000,000
Organization-based provision	50,000
Undergraduates and postgraduates	50,000
	1,100,000

Cost per student - £30 per year (to the taxpayers). Fees will have to be considered separately.

4. What the OU can Offer

The OU is in a unique position to make a major initiative in this area. Even though the system for continuing education will eventually involve many other bodies and organizations the importance of the OU's potential ability to go-it-alone on a national scale should not be overlooked. The success in the undergraduate programme established this. In making the initiative the subsequent negotiations with LEAs, colleges, adult education institutes, libraries, community and social worker organizations, etc, are more likely to be successful.

In proposing a Development Council for Adult Education the Russell Report says:

"One of the endemic problems of a comprehensive service will be its sheer size. As unmet needs are uncovered, the resources of local communities will sometimes prove inadequate. Recourse should therefore be had to forms of teaching-at-a-distance that allow for national coverage. The Open University has evolved a multi-media system, based on specifically prepared teaching materials which provides such a service at university level, but there will be many other demands at other levels and in non-

87

academic subjects. It will be necessary for some central body
to establish contact with agencies already at work in these
fields, including commercial agencies. It will need to initiate
studies of materials available or likely to become available
for adult education and to collect information about their use."
Para 162, p 54.

The proposed programme will involve a vast extension of the current OU
activities; experience to date makes the OU particularly well suited to
carrying out the programme and becoming the 'central body' referred to by
Russell.

The following are the OU's main assets that make it suitable for this role:

(a) a favourable public image and academic credibility;
(b) the only educational institution that comes anywhere near being able
to operate on the required scale;
(c) experience in the design, production and management of multi-media
materials;
(d) the means of delivering these materials into people's homes;
(e) experience in designing and operating open learning systems gained
from launching the undergraduate programme and subsequent
operations;
(f) experience in designing and operating a computer-managed learning
system;
(g) experience in designing and operating a regional tutorial/counselling
support system.

Furthermore, those associated with drafting the Charter of the OU and
many others clearly expect it to contribute in this area. The OU should
therefore put forward a comprehensive system for mass continuing education.

5. Practical Issues and Problems

The foregoing proposal raises many questions concerning the feasibility of its
operation. Some of these are outlined below, covering: the computer-based
resource management; the community education worker/tutor; the operation
of the system as a whole.

5.1 Computer-Based Resource Management

The computer catalogue and the multi-media resource centre form a
computer-based resource management system and this would lead to at least
three major areas of difficulty.
1. The knowledge span of the material is potentially infinite, covering
techniques for relaxing through the chemistry of cooking or beer brewing, to
the Marxist theory or particle physics.

Take, for example, the case of the mother and her child outlined in Section
2.4; here knowledge about child development, a child's play, playgroups,
children's conversation and language development were involved. In addition
these 'subjects' (which need not be thought of as purely knowledge-based but

could be process- or action-oriented) can be viewed from the conception of a mother, a playgroup leader or a child psychologist.

All this has to be catalogued in terms of 'subject' areas, concepts, problems, etc, and then used as a basis to access the various resources. The implications for work on such areas as the structures of knowledge, and the development of suitable descriptors to access them, are enormous. In fact this whole issue poses the greatest problem for the system. It may be necessary to choose a limited number of areas to develop the catalogue around. These could be areas of social problems or need, eg housing, health, etc.
2. The multi-media resources will mean that a whole variety of types of resources will need storing and cataloguing: books, articles, book lists, films, filmstrips, slides, tapes, discs, names and addresses. This poses nowhere near such a problem as the previous aspect, and such work is already taking place in Britain.
3. The problem of access to the catalogue and resources is linked to the above two aspects, and includes the following:

(a) There will need to be a conversation between tutors or students and the computer system, to find out what it can offer to suit their needs. Some sort of 'interrogation' could take place in which a tutor investigates the catalogue. It could, of course, be a two-way interrogation with the computer trying to find out the tutor's needs. For example, the computer may present images of certain files and ask the tutor to specify which one is of interest - here the need for the descriptors comes in.

(b) If a tutor or student requests a resource from the centre then a retrieval and mailing system will have to be established. This can follow the lines of a mail-order firm.

(c) Many students will be producing items of use to others and of which the resource centre has no comparable item. The student can thus enter the item into the system. The resource advisors would, of course, be responsible for this entry and in fact the item could be held as a tangible resource, for instance, a report or a tape-slide presentation, or as a name and address of the person to which inquiries could be directed (in the case, say, of no tangible item being available).

5.2 Community Education Worker/Tutor

There are four major problems for this person: the building up of a local resource catalogue; the updating of this catalogue with the central one; the contacts he will make to develop learning opportunities; the responsibility for his employment.
1. Local resource catalogue. How will the tutor go about building up a local catalogue in terms of people, artifacts, books, buildings, etc? Will he wait for requests from learners and go out and look for the resources, or build them up in anticipation? What use can he make of local libraries, teachers' centres, schools, history societies, etc? (see Appendix, Section 2.4).
2. Updating central catalogue. Will he have direct access to the computer files and be allowed to update and add to them; or will he make up a dummy

file, which the resource advisors then sort through and from this update the main file?

3. Contacts. How will he go about his work, in making contacts with people and developing learning opportunities? Where will be his areas of communication - pubs, community centres, shopping centres, chat clubs, WI, etc? (Some evidence is shown in Appendix, Section 2.2.1.) How will he liaise with the other workers, ie health visitors, social workers, etc?

4. Employing agencies. Is it possible, in terms of these agencies, to have someone with a responsibility for community work and education? Will the health visitors, etc, be able to take on an educational role or will there be problems of professional ethics, ie using information in one context for another? Interagency groups are developing in which needs identified by one group of professionals can be passed on to be dealt with by another. The ultimate development of this would be an 'interagency person' rather than group. However, it is the liaison between the community education worker and the other workers (health visitors, etc) that will determine the way individual roles develop.

5.3 The Whole Operation

There are a whole host of problems that will arise, and only three are considered here:

1. How will the monitoring operation be carried out? What variables will it monitor - just the sheer number of requests, or will judgements as to 'quality' be made? How will rationalization take place? Much of these will be answered only after trying to operate such a system.

2. What forms could the packages thus produced take? How flexible can they be, eg can a package serve a mother who just wants a background understanding of her child's development, and a group of mothers wanting to have workshops on child development and the place of play?

3. How imaginately can the contents of such packages be - in terms of, say, whether games and simulation experimental kits, or printed material, is used. It must be remembered that conventional didactic presentations, whether by face-to-face contact or by printed text, may be reminiscent of school days happily left behind.

APPENDIX

Notes on developments in areas related to the kind of provision outlined in this report.

1. Internationally

1.1 Laws requiring industry to set aside money for workers to take time off and re-train exist in France and Holland. Britain is considering a scheme along the lines of a modified Industrial Training Levy.

1.2 The notion of a sabbatical year for workers has been floated in Australia and elsewhere.

1.3 Overseas' versions of the OU (in places like Pakistan, Mexico, Iran, Israel, Alberta, Canada, Quebec, USA) have broadened the vision and included non-undergraduate provisions. In some cases they have ignored an undergraduate provision.

1.4 OECD, the EEC and the Council of Europe have produced many publications and are actively involved in developing the concept of continuing education.

2. Nationally

2.1 BBC has various types of offerings:

(a) For Colleges of Further Education - 'Engineering Craft Studies'; 'Parents and Children'.
(b) Vocational and Professional Interests - 'Job Prospects for Adults'; 'Going Solo'.
(c) Home and Leisure - 'For Senior Citizens'; 'Roof Over Your Head'; 'Football'; 'Stranger Abroad'; 'Model Making'.
(d) Community and Contemporary Affairs - 'Living Decisions in Family and Community'; 'Planning and the People'; 'The Environment'; 'Conflict in the Middle East'; 'Economics of the Real World'.
(e) Arts and Science - 'The English Novel Abroad'; 'Music and the Spirits'; 'Aspects of Psychology'.
(f) Languages - French, Russian, Spanish, etc.
(g) Films - in the above six areas.

Some examples of the involvement with other institutions are shown below (for the Bethnal Green Adult Education Institute). In addition, the BBC has recently joined with the TUC in a venture to help educate union members and workers in general, using multi-media learning materials.

2.2 Traditional adult education providers (institutes and university departments of extra-mural studies).

The traditional adult education institutes are not solely engaged in classroom teaching of the familiar non-vocational leisure-time

91

activities. There is now a spectrum of provisions, a few examples of which are outlined below.

2.2.1 Bethnal Green Institute (ILEA)
There are four basic types of provision: (a) the traditional leisure activity classes; (b) a community service programme; (c) educational TV and radio; (d) use of 'outreach workers' or 'community orientated lecturers'.

(a) Traditional leisure activity classes: this is familiar to most people and an extract from their timetable of classes illustrates their activities: "Dressmaking, keep fit, photography, sub-aqua swimming, table tennis, weight training, woodwork and polishing, art, ballroom dancing, cine and film making, introducing London, metalwork and model engineering, motor car maintenance, pigeons, radio, television and domestic electricity, shoe repairing, swimming."

(b) Community service programme: this is aimed at helping people take part in their own community. Courses in such things as 'Citizens' Welfare Rights' can develop from a series of classes on 'tenants' rights, rent legislation, social security', etc to support local groups of 'advocates' who can then help local people. Special provision for the immigrant community also exists.

(c) Educational TV and radio: this programme of courses is based on BBC, ITV and closed-circuit TV programmes. There are several levels of involvement open to students: student only watches/listens to programmes and buys appropriate publication; student watches/listens to programmes at home and takes part in group discussions; study groups watch the programmes at the institute and discuss and enlarge upon them. The latter two fall within the institutes' programmes of courses, and it produces an associated text where it is not already available.

(d) Outreach Workers: their task is to 'go out and identify ways in which their centres (adult education institutes) can better serve local community interest'. In other words, they attempt to make their centres more responsive to the local community, and try to articulate community interests.

At a recent conference on adult education John Brown, principal of the Bethnal Green Institute, outlined how these outreach workers had attempted to contact the Asian community in the local area. The standard procedure of advertisements and posters had failed to elicit any response from this community.

By making direct contact with the community it was found that the Asians wanted English classes, but given by people from their own community. Informal groups were started up outside the centre. Eventually, some of these groups moved into the centre and became, in fact, part of the standard offering of courses, ie the institute had taken up the community's response.

2.2.2 Liverpool Neighbourhood.

The Institute of Extension Studies at Liverpool University set up neighbourhood classes; one class managed to get the job of producing a report on crime in Liverpool which was requested by the Lord Mayor's Committee. A social worker had managed to convince the Committee that they might just as well give it to such a group.

The group, in conjunction with a tutor and working to a deadline, produced a 40-page report giving a community response to the reasons for crime. This contained all the conventional ideas which sociological analysis would turn up, but the group did not have any formal teaching in this area.

In addition, they produced a tape/slide presentation, which contained interviews of young people, as well as a commentary on the problem of crime.

2.2.3 Lee Park, Portsmouth.

Two community education workers from Southampton University went to a post-war estate to find out the needs of this community and see what they could do to satisfy these needs. The estate was isolated from Portsmouth by poor bus facilities and in addition it had poor social facilities.

The workers spent six months talking to residents and then launched a publicity campaign to attract people to an adult education centre based in a school. They set up a course on welfare rights and a law advisory service, both of which were served by the University's Law Department. In addition, they set up a playschool and an adventure playground.

Other activities that followed included: a newspaper; group for single-parent families; literacy scheme; discussion groups. The latter groups developed from a 'chance to talk' group for women and it provided a creche. An extra-mural tutor was assigned to a group and their formal achievements included: an education course involving study reading, field work and written work, a politics group with activities as for the education course. Informal achievements included: visits to theatre, skating, attendance at political meetings, a local petition.

2.3 Community development work.

Action groups who require specialized help or knowledge often request it in fields which help them to articulate their views and consequently to bring pressure to bear. For example, a group of residents in three roads in Coventry were threatened with a development plan that involved the demolition of the houses they lived in. With the help of community development workers, a planner and a public health inspector they conducted extensive surveys, compiled data and published their plan. The plan proposed that the area be made a General Improvement Area and this was submitted to the Council who accepted the proposal outright.

Workers in this field, who were approached on the subject of a provision such as this report suggests, were very enthusiastic.

Note the advertisement in the Brighton area:

"Brighton Area
YOUTH AND COMMUNITY WORKERS
(A) the primary duty of this post is to be the Warden of the Prior House Youth and Community Centre and to act as Team Leader to the team of (at present) three in this central area of Brighton. A general responsibility for overseeing the development of community work in the neighbourhood is also involved.
(B) to join a team of five in the Moulsecoomb district of Brighton, with the primary duty of acting as Assistant Warden of the purpose-built Youth Centre which is also being developed for other community purposes. The opportunity for general neighbourhood work and adventure playground experience is also available.
(C) to be the second member of a team being established in the Patcham area of Brighton under the team leader who is designated District Further Education Principal. The primary duty of this post is to be responsible for the Youth Club meeting in the youth wing of a secondary school, and, as the youth specialist in the team, to advise Voluntary Youth Groups in the area. The appointee will also assist the Principal with non-vocational adult/community educational work and deputise when necessary."

2.4   Community schools and resource centres.
There is an increasing interest in both of these areas, often as a joint venture. There is an example on the doorstep of the OU - The Stantonbury campus - which could develop as a central influence in the community.

Note the advertisement in the Cumbria area:

"Cumbria County Council
COMMUNITY RESOURCE CENTRE
The Centre will be located in Cleator Moor and will provide support services, information and ideas for community groups engaged in social action and community self-help. Resources at present available include secretarial and reprographic services, an information bank, video- and audio-visual equipment and minibus. There is also access

to other facilities in West Cumbria. Initially the Centre will operate closely with the Community Development Project Team but it is anticipated that an independent management structure will be developed involving user groups. The person appointed will be expected to develop and promote the facilities of the Resource Centre, make them easily available to community groups and to provide a flow of ideas and useful information."

2.5   Industrial field.
Apart from the training programmes in various industries the unions have an extensive network of correspondence education. In addition, unions collaborate with the WEA on evening and weekend courses concerned with general industrial problems and issues.

2.6   Within the OU, Ken Jones (Staff Tutor) has pioneered some work with the sort of people whom the OU has generally failed to reach.

The tentative implication of these developments is that there is a need for a provision which is both responsive and on a national scale. Throughout the world there is a move towards the mass continuing education concept, and Britain should be part of this. Within Britain the notion of a learner-based provision is not catered for on any scale by present institutions, so the OU can contribute particularly well in this area; rather than concentrating on duplicating existing provision.

The idea of continuous education

MARK BRAHAM

1. THE IDEA OF CONTINUOUS EDUCATION (PRELUDE)

The idea of continuous education is, simply enough, the idea that education should be continuous, subject to neither a restricted period in a person's life, nor to a limited range of institutions. As such the idea is normative or prescriptive, indicating not that education is necessarily a continuous affair, as some would argue, but rather that it ought to be. We find, therefore, that there is some sort of obligation that is attached to the idea of continuous education that calls for justification.

Several kinds of justification can be invoked to support the idea of continuous education, although whether they are all adequate is a very open question. For example, one may want to justify the idea on the grounds that continuous education provides for the acquisition of information and skills and for the achievement of knowledge that leads to improved, if not to increased, employment opportunities. Or, one may want to point to the supposed extensive leisure time that some twenty years ago it was assumed would now be available to untold millions of people by virtue of industrial automation, thus providing ample time for the increase of one's 'personal culture'. Or one can note that there have always been considerable numbers of people who have been, and are, interested in increasing their fund of learning quite apart from how much leisure time is available, so that for them the idea of continuous education is but a confirmation of their belief in the desirability of being informed, skilful and knowledgeable.

To some extent or another the interests of people in acquiring or furthering education opportunities have been served by various kinds of institutions such as the Folk High Schools first established in Scandinavia, later to spread across much of Europe, the Chattaqua Movement in the United States, the Workers' Educational Association in this country, and a range of adult certificate, degree and non-certificate and non-degree programmes in evening and summer schools, colleges and universities in many nations. And of course one turns to the Open University as one of the most notable advances in increasing educational opportunities for the older student in this century.

Without attempting to enter into a discussion of the justification of all the foregoing, it can be suggested that each is an expression of something far deeper than an ideological support fof the idea of continuous education, for each is an expression of an all-pervasive tendency that appears at every level of life, including human life, for what we may call 'optimal self-organization'. It is this tendency to optimal self-organization as it appears among humans that has given rise to the need for education, and it is this tendency unfulfilled and unsatisfied that calls for continuous education.

From this perspective the discussion takes a slight shift in emphasis. The immediate concern is, then, less with the technical and institutional provisions for what one way wish to call continuous education than it is with casting the idea of continuous education itself in the perspective of the optimal self-organization of human life from its incipient beginnings in infancy to its potential and sometimes actual full flowering in middle and later adulthood.

2. OPTIMAL SELF-ORGANIZATION

This phrase, 'optimal self-organization', is perhaps inelegant, but it is not, I think, without meaning. By 'optimal' we may understand that state of the individual living unit in which it is able to manifest its form and fulfil its functions within the conditions of its milieu with the least possible expenditure of energy (the 'principle of least effort'). As such it expresses itself both as genotype and phenotype to the fullest extent possible. Thus, to use E S Russell's phrase, one notes that there is a 'directiveness of organic activities', a 'goal-directedness' or 'tele-finality' that is at work:

> "If in a living normal animal structural and functional relations,
> either external or internal are disturbed, activities will usually
> be set in train that are directive towards restoring structural
> and functioning norms, or to establishing new norms which are
> adapted to the altered circumstances." (Russell, 1945)

Every form of life, therefore, not only tends towards the fulfilment of its potentialities, in the sense that tadpoles tend towards the actualization of their potentiality to become frogs; acorns to become oaks; ducklings to become ducks, and human infants to become adult members of their species, but each also acts in such a way as to achieve the most satisfactory conditions for its existence. In this sense, every form of life is self-interested, not as a matter of intention, but simply because of the biological necessity to survive as an individual and act as an agent for the perpetuation of the species.

But, before the moralist begins to object and raise the spectre of self-interestedness as selfishness, one must also add that the self-interest implied here or in our terms, optimal self-organization, involves both reciprocity and extension. There is reciprocity, for no unit of life can act without affecting, positively or negatively, other lives within its milieu and often a whole chain of lives that extends well beyond its milieu. Hence optimization cannot be carried out at the expense of the whole 'web-of-life' within which every individual exists, for if it were, then the very life forms upon which any individual or species depends for its own continuity would be destroyed, and with it, the individual life or species concerned. Even the current ecological concern amongst humans is a recognition of boundaries within which human attempts at self-optimization must work if the human species itself is not to be endangered.

There is extension in the matter of optimization for as each living unit is able to develop its potentialities it becomes an additive and contributive factor to its milieu, bestowing overall survival benefits upon others. Thus foraging animals provide nutrients to the soils, which in turn provide directly or indirectly sustenance for vast numbers of other lives, whether these are micro- or macro-organisms. Or turning directly to the human dimension, the development of human technique, technology, arts and sciences on the part of individuals has added not only to the survival of populations but to their spread and the development of all that we call 'culture' which in turn provides an information base for the increase of complexity and development of human consciousness. Of course we shall have to say more about the human dimension for whilst humans clearly have the power of wreaking havoc and destruction at-large in pursuit of their own self-optimization, this is apparently not the case at the infra-human levels of life.

Placing all of this in a more philosophical perspective, however, optimal self-organization involves in the long term actions that support the optimization of others, a point well noted in existentialist literature where one finds insistence upon the importance of 'being-for-others' rather than for oneself, but such being is not a negation of oneself but the fulfilment of one's potentialities for creative and contributive action.

Now, the idea of optimal self-organization involves the idea of a 'self', an active agent. Unless we are to suggest that every unit of life is but an automaton managed from without we must infer intrinsic forces within each living unit that guide behaviour. Whilst many of these forces are still clouded in mystery, we do use terms such as 'instinct', 'motivation' and particularly at the human level, 'intention' to indicate the bases of action. And we can recognize, with the biologist Agar, the existence of hierarchies of control centres such as plexi, which in the higher chordates are capped by the brain or 'central agent':

> "The locus of the Central Agent concerned with the behaviour of the animal as a whole is the brain, especially the cortex in higher animals ... Like all the other agents of the body, the central agent is a nexus of processes..." (Agar, 1953)

If these processes are not being managed from without, as is the case with machine systems, then perhaps they are managed from within. To turn to, as Teilhard (1969) has put it, 'the within of things' indicates to be sure that there are intrinsic mechanisms at work which determine the life of the organism, such as the role of the nucleus within the individual cell, or the roles of various other organs and their parts within each organism. We may modify the environment and provide various kinds of situations - or stimuli - but we recognize the idiosyncratic nature of behaviour as we wait for, and then seek to measure and even 'shape' responses. So, we speak of the 'self' as a mark of the individual's tendency to act on and for its own behalf. But as we do so we recognize no absolute autonomy or isolation from outer pressures and actions but degrees of 'selfhood' along a continuum from external or 'exonomous' control in which environmental factors play a dominant part to autonomous control in which the individual, most significantly at the human level, has become conscious of his own powers and potentialities and seeks to fulfil the catechism of the lines: 'I am the master of my fate; I am the captain of my soul...'

Given the fact of self (or of 'self-ness') and the tendency towards optimal behaviour, the third term that we have used, 'organization' comes into play. To organize is to establish patterns of functional inter-connectedness or relations among disparate and previously unrelated elements. The individual organism above that of the single cell comes into existence not fully formed and functioning, but rather begins as an essentially amorphous and poorly differentiated zygote that must then rapidly differentiate internally and follow up this differentiation of parts with the establishment of patterns of internal connections or communication enabling, as a result, each part to contribute to the formation of the eventual whole. As the establishment of internal patterns of relations proceeds this in turn becomes the basis of the individual's structure which in turn acts as a matrix for the integration of its total activities. Thus, says Sinnott:

> "An organism is an organized system, each part or quality
> so related to all the rest that in its growth the individual marches
> on through a series of specific steps to a specific end or
> culmination, maintaining throughout its course a delicately
> balanced state of form and function which tends to restore
> itself if altered." (Sinnott, 1961)

Herbert Spencer has spoken of this as "the dynamic integration of diversity" (Spencer, 1880).

Not only does the individual living unit organize itself as a part of its general growth and development, but its behaviour is organized so as to facilitate this growth and development, and at the same time it organizes its milieu for its own particular purposes, as any observer of insect colonies, or of animal and human behaviour, can attest.

Thus we may say that throughout the order of nature every unit of life is self-organizing, elaborating, modifying and developing a behavioural programme that is directed to the single end of achieving an optimal state within its milieu and, if necessary, changing its milieu in order to achieve its requirements.

3. OPTIMAL SELF-ORGANIZATION AND EDUCATION

There are many who will object to this naturalistic and somewhat anthropological presentation, seeing in it a departure from the primary matter of continuous education. But rather than having departed, the attempt here is to focus on the very root of our concern. To repeat an earlier point, it is the tendency for optimal self-organization as it appears among humans that has given rise to the need for education, and it is this tendency unfulfilled and unsatisfied that calls for continuous education.

Whilst our concern is properly with human self-organization, much of the foregoing, it is clear, has referred to self-organization in nature, and legitimately so, for humans are as much a part of the order of nature as is any other species and manifest as do all other forms of life what Maslow has called "a press for fuller and fuller being" (Maslow, 1962). What is significant is that this 'press' takes on particular characteristics at the human level of life and it is these characteristics which give rise to the need for education.

Every unit of life, including the human, requires a programme to guide its development. For present purposes a programme may be understood to be a generally sequential arrangement of information whose function is to elicit particular kinds of activity. In this sense a musical score or a set of laboratory protocols are nearer to the meaning we require than, let us say, a concert programme that is designed to inform, but not to change the behaviour of, an audience. As we cannot indicate any self-created and thus self-programmed units of life outside of theological concepts of deity or of an Aristotelian 'Prime Mover', we have to look beyond the individual for the source of its (or his) programme. One can accept, of course, that the environment within which each living unit is immersed continually broadcasts information (the collective information broadcast by every inorganic and organic unit) which in turn acts as a modifier of, as well as a stimulus to, individual behaviour. One can also think in species terms of adaptations acquired as a response to environmental conditions, but in both cases we are returned to the individual as a programmed and broadcasting unit.

What we find, as we press the matter further, is that every individual comes into existence with a basic programme derived from information that has been genetically transmitted in the course of reproduction, inscribed presumably upon DNA/RNA. We may therefore speak of genetic information transfer as a result of which each living unit is able to manifest that form and fulfil those functions that are in keeping with its species within a given ecological niche. At the same time, because of incomplete genetic self-copying of molecules, sufficient inexactitude in information transfer exists to allow for variability and thus individuality of type. Moreover, genetic information transfer means that each individual is born 'pre-wired', so to speak, with the overall patterning of its behaviours largely predetermined. Consequently its self-organization works essentially as an agency for the elaboration of an historical programme subject, apparently, to Darwinian-type modifications.

Now, before advocates of human distinctiveness rise to its defence, let us make it quite clear that it is here, precisely at this point, where human life departs from the infra-human, for among humans genetic information transfer largely concerns the nature and course of physical - or more accurately - neuro-physiological development, and except for that neuro-physiological substrata that provides for cortical structure, it has apparently little reference to the significantly human characteristics of emotional and mental (or affective and cognitive) behaviour. Thus, if one follows a curve from simplicity to increasing complexity of form, function and behaviour, from single-celled organisms up through the human level of life, one finds a gradual decrease in genetic information transfer, and in the same sense an increasing incompleteness of pre-programming or instinct. This incompleteness is marked particularly by the extension of infancy so that by the time one reaches the human level, considered from an evolutionary aspect, one finds the greatest prolongation of infancy and thus dependence upon adult assistance.

Where genetic information transfer is lacking, extra-genetic information transfer is required, for without it the human infant could not long survive. Although there is a basic neuro-physiological 'unfolding' as the physical form and its functions follows an ontogenetic course already laid down in the germ plasm, the human infant, at birth, is incapable of self-feeding beyond an instinctual ability to suck. Whilst heart and lungs may well move to an ancient rhythm not of one's own choosing and the biochemical processes that energize and maintain and regulate the body are grounded in a species programme that rests well below the thresholds of consciousness, choice, selectivity and discrimination are constant requirements beyond the processes of sheer physicality. Where there is no overall behavioural programme one must be constructed, and where its information is not genetically supplied, it must be acquired. To live, one must be informed. And, to premeditate the rest of this discussion, where instinctual self-organization is inadequate, intentional self-organization is required.

The acquisition of information and its translation into a programme is signified by the term 'learning' and we may say, I think correctly, that learning takes up where instinct has left off in the course of human phylogenesis. Learning compensates for our deficient genetic information processing and characterizes that extra-genetic information processing that is most distinctively human. Hence, there is real meaning in the idea that to live one must learn.

But all learning is not necessarily conducive to optimal living, or in terms of earlier points, to optimal self-organization. It is entirely possible for humans to learn to restrict, to distort and even to destroy their own lives. Thus it is not learning per se that is required, but self-optimizing learning, and this suggests the need for a criterion for purposes of demarcation between those learnings that are conducive to optimal human self-organization and those that are not. It is here, we may suggest, that the term 'education' finds its application.

We must go further. Not only do we have to distinguish between educative and non-educative learning, focussing on the matter of information acquisition and utilization, but we must also make a similar distinction between educative and non-educative information transmission. Information, of course, is constantly being transmitted but whilst much of the transmission is random, having no specific target, there is also that transmission that is intentional and is designed to inform and affect others, and often in particular ways. This is particularly the case with the transmissions of adults to the young. Apart from the matter of propaganda which is information transmitted in such a way as to persuade people to change their views (believing that they are, in fact, the instigators of their changed beliefs and attitudes) there is also that intentional transmission of information designed to elicit changes in behaviour that we call 'teaching', 'instruction' and 'training' (with the recognition that there are distinctions to be made among these).

Because there is no necessary connection between information that is

101

intentionally transmitted to an individual and his optimal self-organization; because, in fact, it is entirely possible to teach, instruct and train in ways that are restrictive, distortive and even destructive, we must recognize the need for demarcation here as well. If, therefore, we are to be interested in the optimal self-organization of persons, then our interest is in educative rather than non-mis, or anti-educative learning and teaching.

4. FOUR TASKS FOR EDUCATION

An examination of the place of education of human life suggests, therefore, that its role is to provide for the optimal self-organization of individual, and by extension, species life as a consequence of the inadequacy of genetic information transfer, and that this role can be broken down into at least four major developmental tasks. These are:

(a) to provide for environmental adaptation;
(b) to provide for environmental participation;
(c) to provide for creative environmental contribution;
(d) to provide for constructive environmental transformation.

The term 'environment' is used here to designate the individual's external milieu, human and non-human, within which at any time 'he lives and moves and has his being'.

(a) The Task of Environmental Adaptation

By 'adaptation' we may understand the 'fittingness' of the individual to his surroundings. More explicitly one may say that that individual is better adapted than another who functions in his milieu with the greatest rapport, or harmony. We use such phrases as 'settling down', or 'fitting in', when referring to an individual's adaptive behaviour.

The human infant, similarly to the young of other species, is born as a dependent being who must adapt to his surroundings. His difference, already indicated, lies in his instinctual incompleteness, and in the extensive period required for maturation processes on one hand (the development to an implicit 'end-term' of neuro-physiological development, for example) and for learning, on the other, before he can become capable of self-support in his milieu.

The child's earliest activities are basically concerned with his survival in the post-uterine state and with the differentiation and integration of his total organic system. His body needs to assimilate new food; to accommodate itself to a host of micro-organisms, and as affectation and cognition he must also develop adaptive responses on these levels.

Whilst the child's adaptive behaviours begin below the threshold of cognition, lacking any intentional intervention on his part, by his first year of life his activities begin to show considerable self-determination. During the first four or five years of his life, the child, under the direction and guidance of parents of the immediate - and where existing, extended - family, learns how to eat, to dress, to speak and understand the local language, and to know and to respond to the expectations of an increasing number of people. He begins, in sum, to adapt to and to acquire his culture.

Whilst it is common to speak of this period of a child's learning in terms of 'education' we should do so with the recognition that his learning is, for the most part, informally carried out. While there is certainly some intentional organization of the child's learning through, for example, the approval and disapproval of behaviour, this organization is not necessarily clearly conceived or grounded in particularly justifiable concepts of child growth and development, except perhaps where professional assistance has been employed.

(b) The Task of Environmental Participation

By 'participation' (within an educational context) we may understand the individual's engagement in activities that, for the most part, are conducive to the maintenance of his group, and in the human context, his culture. Whilst adaptation continues to be a concern for the individual, at least until the parameters of his environment (phenomenally rather than geographically speaking) have become stablized, it is far from all there is to his life. Adaptation, we might suggest, is primarily ego- or auto-centric for it concerns essentially the individual's need to survive, something which, of course, is not limited to the period of early childhood particularly in these days of constant travel and transfer to new locales. Participation, however, within which adaptation must be included, is essentially socio- or allo-centric as it concerns the individual's engagement in an increasingly objective world of social as well as of material events.

It is probably not too much to say that from about the age of five, children the world over are placed under increasing pressure, not only to continue their adaptive learning, but also to participate in group and communal activities. For this purpose the organization of a child's learning becomes far more intentional and systematic; it becomes more formally pedagogical.

Under hunting, fishing and even more complex agrarian styles of life, daughters are generally relegated to household duties under the tutelage of the women, while sons undertake designated chores under the tutelage of the men. In industrial societies the complexity of adult tasks (accompanied in many cases by child-labour legislation) has transferred the child's learning from direct participation in the work of the community to a period of specialized instruction in the institution of the school. It is here that the child is expected to acquire the basic competencies in requisite fields before he is permitted to engage directly in an occupation.

It is in this institutionalizing of the teaching-learning situation that the critical factor of the child's separation from the community of work appears. Schooling, rather than enabling the child to engage in and develop his understanding of his community, for the most part restricts him to the confines of the school. Little 'bridging' work between the school and community experience seems to be evident in industrial societies except in the form of 'field trips' and to this extent the task of environmental participation as an educative goal has hardly been realized. Dewey, the followers of the 'progressive movement' and, more recently, the 'de-schoolers' have all displayed what may be taken to be justifiable concern over this matter. And to cap the point, I think we may say from the standpoint of education viewed continuously, that discontinuity, rather than continuity, has already entered the scene.

Whether the learning is to be provided through schooling (as is the case in industrial societies) or through direct participation in the adult world of work (as is often the case still in agrarian societies) the child is expected to acquire gradually a body of lore, method, rule and ritual that in some cases has been transmitted from generation to generation, and in others represents recent innovations. Whatever its source, the community, rightly or wrongly, regards this information as essential for its survival. Any extensive failure to provide the young in a given society with such information means the inevitability of that society's decline. There is evidence for this, for example, in the deterioration of the North American Indian and Eskimo social life, and in the paucity of North American Black culture owing to the historic separation of the Negro from his African heritage and the restrictions placed upon his development in exile.

In the life of what we may call simple communities there exists what might be termed a 'toti-potency' of roles. In this, other than for sex-differentiated activities, each member of the community is expected to be capable to carrying out a wide variety of tasks. As communal complexity increases, however, task competency tends to demand increasing specialization, or in biological language a 'functional specificity' of behaviour. As a consequence, increasing task specialization has meant an increase in the kind and extent of instruction such that in technologically advanced societies a few years of pre-adolescent schooling, once deemed sufficient, is now regarded as inadequate to prepare the younger members for participation in the work of their culture.

Schooling therefore continues, not only through adolescence but, for many, into the first and second decades of adulthood. To this we must now add the increasing interest in and practice of 'adult', or now 'continuous' education for those who wish to acquire or advance their educational opportunities well into, if not throughout, their adult years.

(c) The Task of Creative Environmental Contribution

Thus far, education has been considered in its adaptive and participatory roles, that is to say, as that form of information processing - of transmission and acquisition - that enables instinctually deficient humans to organize their behaviours to enable them to find their place within their milieu and thus at least meet the basic requirements for their individual survival, and further to gradually take on the responsibilities of agents in the continuity and development of their own group, and thus of the species at large. In this, education is seen, not as a matter of social whim, fiat or legislation, but as having a naturalistic sanction, that of the continuity of nature at the human level.

But there is more to be considered. The evolution of human life on the psycho-social rather than on the biological levels (for our biological evolution may well have ceased or slowed down sufficiently since the advent of our own type homo homo sapiens to expect little further in this regard) like that of nature in general is twofold. It is both general and specific. General evolution

104

concerns the continuity of life through successive levels or stages of complexity; specific evolution concerns the amplification of general evolution into adaptive specializations that have functional efficacy within a given space-time locus. Once a mode of behaviour becomes adaptively specialized it tends towards self-maintenance and this tendency tends to become dominant over pressures for continuity unless conditions are such that dysfunctionality and decline are immanent.

As there is no instinctual programme to shift a culture out of its adaptive specializations back into the stream of general psycho-social, or cultural, evolution, the recognition of both the actual or impending stasis and of evolutionary possibilities rests with the membership of any given social group. This recognition, however, comes not of its own accord but as a result of the awareness of individuals. If their learning has been such as to canalize their thought and action into purely adaptive and participatory modes we then find that the possibilities for innovation and thus for personal development and cultural evolution are restricted. This again returns us to the much earlier point that the optimal self-organization of the individual, by extension, is contributive to the environment, and this in human terms must also be seen in the context of culture. This means then that the idea of creativity takes on a central role in our thinking about education.

The position, then, is that a culture's evolution rests upon the continuing development of its members. Their development rests on their ability to harness those tendencies and powers that can take them beyond the status quo. As, however, such recognition and harnessing of such tendencies is learned, the problem is implicitly educational. The difficulty is that our pedagogical institutions - and it is a serious question as to whether they should all and always be regarded as educational institutions - for the time that they have existed and to the extent that they do exist have more or less concentrated on the tasks of shaping the young for adaptive and participatory roles and have disvalued those activities that might be creative and innovative. Thus, the creative individuals in our societies are liable to have succeeded despite, rather than because of, our general pedagogical institutions. While the facts of individual successes, despite our educational deficiencies, cannot be denied, the possibilities of providing for a wider base of creative contributions to the culture through intentional educational provisions cannot be overlooked.

Now, by 'creative contribution' we may understand the application of novel responses to continuing or new circumstances such that these responses becomepart of the general fabric of the culture and according to some measure (which we cannot possibly develop here) provide for an improvement over what constitutes a normal pattern of thought and action, or in some way indicates possibilities for the future.

This implies, then, that there is more to creativity than merely a spontaneously novel response to a situation, for such a response is but the indication of possibilities. Creativity emerges as a vital factor when it becomes organized and directed towards the solution of problems and to the elaboration of new possibilities for human arrangements whether we are dealing with artistic, literary, philosophical, scientific, political, legal, technical or other features of life. For a creative idea to be contributive it must be grounded in a recognition of the societal or environmental conditions to which (and within which) it is to be applied.

Such objectivity is scarcely possible in childhood. Only in rare cases do we expect to find intentionally culturally contributive activity emerging much before middle and later adolescence, by which time the majority of youth have left school to take up jobs, and those who are able to continue their schooling are concentrating on how to meet establishment criteria in order to proceed to post-secondary institutions. Whilst the impulse to innovate and create is certainly available and requires supporting throughout childhood, we must turn to adolescent education as the stage for guiding talent for creative contributions.

(d) The Task of Constructive Environmental Transformation

Whilst the creative contributions of individuals add to and enrich the cultural environment (as well as the environment at-large if one takes the idea of creative agriculture, horticulture and animal husbandry into account), they tend, on the whole, to find acceptance insofar as they are not in conflict with, or at least are not perceived as a threat to, the life-style of the culture and to the vested interests of dominant individuals or groups. If, however, the prevailing cultural structure cannot, or will not, accept further creative contributions we then find individual pressures building up towards social transformation on the one hand, and 'establishment' pressures being exerted for the maintenance of the status quo on the other. If the pressures for transformation are sufficiently strong, then a period of cultural conflict is inevitable until either stasis or transformation succeeds.

It should be clear that all pressures towards cultural transformation are not necessarily constructive. Where the impetus is for 'negative' freedom from restraint without a 'positive' orientation towards clearly conceived goods we are not in a position to speak, except perhaps after the fact, of constructive transformation. Destructive transformation is always a possibility.

As our concern is for the optimization of life it is in accordance with the idea of successive cultural transformations, for every cultural state, no matter how successful it may be at a given point in time, or in a given epoch, signifies but a stage in, not the termination of, the course of human development. The problem, and it is by no means slight, is that unless the members of a culture have been prepared to be constructively transformative we are liable to find ourselves caught up in change for the sake of change and not for justifiably conceived purposes.

But where is the needed preparation to be obtained? Clearly, whilst an orientation for openness and creativity belongs to childhood, the child's adaptive needs, his concern for identity and for acquiring his culture, on the one hand, and the culture's need to assure its continuity, on the other, through the adaptiveness of its young, means that this is not the stage for concentrating on social transformation.

In adolescence we find but the 'birth' of objective and reflective thought. It is hardly likely that we will find, or can expect to find, the intellectual proficiency that is required for the awareness of prevailing conditions, for the rational search for alternatives, and for a concern with the possible consequences of actions at this stage.

It appears then, that the task of assisting individuals to become constructive transformers of their culture belongs to adult life. Translated into the formal terms of schooling this suggests that the responsibility of colleges, of universities, and of those concerned with continuous education is to enable culturally aware and sensitive men and women to achieve the knowledge and to develop the expertise that can help transform their culture for the benefit of all. Lacking this preparation cultural transformation will continue to rest on the activities of particular pressure groups, unplanned social conflict and the hope that the right leaders will emerge at the right time true to the Messianic tradition. As this discussion is neither one of value theory nor of curriculum design the twin problems of determing 'desirable goals' and the appropriate curriculum content cannot be dealt with here.

To summarize the education implications of the tasks outlined thus far: adaptation, participation, creative contribution and constructive transformation, whilst not in the least espousing mutually exclusive practices that are restricted to particular educational levels, it is suggested that the emphases, or central tendencies, might be as follows:

(a) Environmental adaptation. Early childhood education (comprising the sensory-motor and pre-operational periods of thought) (Piaget and Inhelder, 1969);

(b) Environmental participation. Middle and later childhood education (comprising the period of concrete operational thought) (ibid);

(c) Creative environmental contribution. Adolescent education (comprising the first period of formal thought) (ibid);

(d) Constructive transformation of the environment. Adult (ie post-adolescent) education.

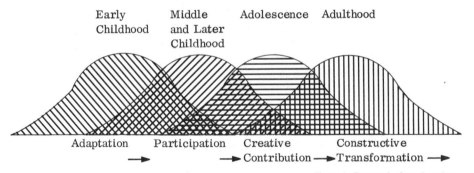

Figure 1. Four tasks for education

5. THE IDEA OF CONTINUOUS EDUCATION (SEQUEL)

The idea of continuous education, then, is that education should be seen in continuous perspective, seen as a dynamic affair that provides for the evocation and elaboration of human consciousness as long as ability and willingness exist. Education is not, therefore, seen as a terminal matter, although there may very well be a termination to specific kinds of learning, but it is seen as a means - perhaps the means - through which the individual can constantly renew himself and, by extension, a culture can be constantly renewed.

Where education is seen as a terminal affair, limited to an age group and restricted in terms of a given institutional style, we have not only the restriction and limitation of individual consciousness but the restriction and limitation of the culture as well. As, however, there are constant pressures for growth and development that are rooted in the organic tendency for optimal self-organization, conflict between the forces of stasis and the pressures for growth and development are inevitable. Hence, we look not only to education being the right of children and youth, but as a necessity for all persons of every age, for as long as they have the ability and willingness to learn. Thus one sees the importance of provisions for the widest possible base of the population to have educational opportunities, and for the availability of programmes and facilities for life-long learning. One cannot but advocate the encouragement of youth to seek to continue their education, and at the same time seek provisions for adult learning, not only where leisure time permits, but through business, industry and state-supported release time for those engaged in occupations to have regular 'study leave' (one can envisage this for every fourth year to allow for keeping up with the increasing generation of new information and knowledge in the various domains of inquiry rather than being restricted to the sabbatical leave arrangements usually restricted to privileged academics). And of course because of the high cost of constructing specialized facilities one recognizes the importance of the widest use of educational technology through radio, television, audiovisual cassette systems for home use and telephone computer terminal facilities that are hooked up to centralized computer information processing and resource centres.

To propose continuous education, therefore, is not, at least in my judgement, to propose an elaboration of our general pedagogical civil servantry and its extension for adult use. It is, instead, to propose the formulation of theories, programmes and practices that are in keeping with the human need for optimal self-organization with particular reference to the emotional and mental dimensions of life. What is of importance here is the recognition that whilst there are recognizable limits to human physiological development - we use the term 'maturity' to indicate this - there are no recognizable limits to our emotional and mental development. There are no instinctual forces moving on to an already determined 'end-term' which enable us to say of one person or another that he or she has reached his or her limit, for we do not know what the 'upper limits' to human development - or let us call it 'human consciousness' - are. Yet, if we turn back to our general patterns of schooling we find that not only do the vast majority of people in the world have little schooling, but that the schooling that exists does not particularly encourage the development of consciousness in the areas of what we may call 'creative feeling' and 'reflective thought' particularly as these refer to one's potential contribution to and reconstruction of culture. And given that the vast majority of people leave school in adolescence to take up routine employment which gives little opportunity to further these aspects of consciousness we find our adult populations largely 'locked in' to the kinds of feeling and thought that is engendered in primary and secondary schooling. This in turn restricts the evolution of culture at-large.

REFERENCES

Agar, W E (1953) 'A Contribution to the Theory of the Living Organism'. Melbourne University Press, Carlton, Australia, 2nd revised edition, pp 7-8

Maslow, A (1962) 'Towards a Psychology of Being'. D Van Nostrand Co, Princeton, N J

cf Piaget, J and Inhelder, B (1969) 'The Psychology of the Child'. translated by H Weaver, Basic Books, New York

Russell, E S (1945) 'The Directiveness of Organic Activity'. Cambridge University Press, Cambridge, p 44

Sinnott, E W (1961) 'Cell and Psyche'. Harper, New York, p 22

Spencer, H (1880) 'First Principles'. A L Burt Co, New York, 4th edition, p 283

Teilhard de Chardin, P (1969) 'The Phenomenon of Man'. Collins, London

Consumer-orientated programmed learning in adult education

ALAN MACKIE

PROGRAMMED LEARNING: A DEFINITION

If the early protagonists of programmed learning were at fault in the way they promoted what appeared to be a promising new pedagogic science (and at fault to the extent that they might well have had second thoughts about what they said), it was in giving the impression that all the problems had been solved, the techniques finally determined and all that was required was the large-scale creation of the learning programmes themselves.

To maintain that the problems were all solved was to preclude the possibility of development.

It seems a more reasonable view that here we have a technique - or a range of techniques - that are sufficiently promising to merit further investigation and possible development. But one soon runs into a kind of creed incorporating phrases like, 'small steps', 'logical sequence', 'active response', 'immediate feedback', 'own pace', and so on.

They are most ill-defined terms but at the same time are traditionally very narrowly interpreted and mesh together to form an entity which makes progress only with great difficulty.

I propose to talk about the programmed learning activities at the City of Bath Technical College, particularly in relation to the Learning by Appointment Centre. But as the general tenor of the paper is that such centres could provide a modest but possibly significant contribution to the development of programmed learning techniques and applications, it seems necessary to go back (and possibly a little beyond) first principles to determine a set of ground rules and definitions that have the required degree of flexibility.

In plain language, programmed learning is about putting instruction in store - in a can for subsequent use and re-use, and why it may be useful to do this.

More explicitly - A learning programme is a schedule of instructions and learning activities stores in permanent physical form and employing appropriate educational strategies and tactics. I would want to add, but not insist upon ... and such that criteria relating to the attainment of its objectives at all stages and (b) related decision options regarding possible courses of action and (c) the courses of action themselves, are predetermined.

BASIC PRINCIPLES AND FEATURES

1. We cannot teach (and the learner cannot learn) all aspects of a particular discipline simultaneously. Since we cannot teach the entire content of a subject 'at-a-stroke' we therefore need to present the topic a bit at a time: in discrete amounts of appropriate size. 'Appropriate size' here supersedes 'small' as in 'small steps'. What is of an appropriate size depends on the demands of the subject, and on the target population. Further, the word 'appropriate' is at least as precise as the word 'small'. 'Step' is discarded because it was never clear whether it referred to the student's response effort or was a unit of presentation such as a number of lines.

2. There is no single ideal ordering or structure for the presentation of learning items - but some structures are manifestly better than others. It is better, for example, to learn to walk before one attempts to run. In general it is better to deal with elementary or component skills before moving on to the compound skills which require them.

3. For a learner to successfully execute activity A it is necessary for him to have an opportunity of executing activity A. If we want the student to be able to solve simple equations he must at some point have the opportunity to do so. If we want him to speak French he must have the opportunity of speaking French.

4. For a student to execute an activity A which requires the execution of sub-skills A1, A2, A3 - the student must be able to execute sub-skills A1, A2, A3 ... If we want him to be able to solve simple equations he must be able to add 'like terms', and so on. The list of sub-skills A1, A2, A3 ... is to include any combination of sub-skills that the task requires. The requirement, then, for active responses arises directly from the requirements of the task. It will not be met by any response. It has little to do with the kind of required responses we see in programmes on any subject one cares to name, which appear to be teaching one how to spell.

5. Persistent genuine success favours the student's continuing with the schedule, if only because persistent failure will (rightly) lead him to the conclusion that he is not deriving much benefit from the programme. I insert the word 'genuine' as a reference back to the notion of the relevant active response. If the response requirements are irrelevant a sequence of successful responses may still leave the student rightly feeling he has derived little benefit from the programme. More positively, success favours the student's continuing with the schedule because he is then in the process of achieving what he set out to achieve.

6. If the learner is to assess his own response, then to do this as objectively as is possible the programme should furnish him with a model response. To effect the comparison, these items - the student's and the model response - need to be temporally or spatially adjacent. It would appear that the matching operation is most relevant to the student when he has just made the response. (Remembering, of course, that responses will range in size: for example, in a typing programme required responses will range from typing a letter of the alphabet to typing a paragraph.)

7. There is no fundamental property of stored instruction that requires that

111

it should be confined to individualized learning. This is a matter of design. The storing of learning schedules can, by design and frequently anyway, permit the possibility of individualized learning - and this remains the most important branch of programmed learning. Group learning programmes may well deploy different tactics. A group response might be discussing a question posed by the programme. These possibilities arise particularly in the field of audio-visual programming.

8. An individually presented programme will allow the student to proceed at a pace which is at least independent of other students' rates of working. The influence of the programme (reflecting the way it has been written, its mode, the competence of the programme writer) on the rate of working in an absolute sense, is such that the term 'own pace' has little value.

9. To access and present stored learning schedules, and to deploy appropriate strategies, it may be necessary to use presentation devices or machines.

10. It is a fundamental property of stored learning schedules that they can be checked for accuracy and be tested and amended. If there is a feature of programmed learning that permits of a genuinely scientific approach it is this one. Schedules can be tested and refined systematically to ensure pedagogic quality control.

11. We shall require of any programme, as of any other course, that it states for whom it is intended, and its objectives. Though I would add (the heresy) that a particular action may qualify as a good stratagem even when we have no available means of knowing that we have achieved our goals. Actually exposing someone to music might be such a case when our goal is that the student will appreciate music.

12. We shall require of any programme that it has been validated and meets its objectives. With the reservation that validation figures do not constitute a guarantee of terminal performance, and that sub-validation (of the technical accuracy of the content, and the general strategy) by an expert provides sufficient grounds for the course to be made available or not. This is necessary if programmes are to be tested under the actual conditions in which they are to be used.

THE LEARNING BY APPOINTMENT CENTRE AT BATH

The Learning by Appointment Centre at the City of Bath Technical College is a programmed learning resources centre serving the general public, college students and schoolchildren. It is open 12 hours a day, Monday to Friday, for most of the year. Adults enrol for programmed courses on payment of a fee. College students require the signature of a tutor, and schoolchildren attend on the signature of their head teacher. The courses available are mainly commercially produced courses in a variety of subjects; but with the decline in the number of programmed learning companies the Centre will depend increasingly on programmed materials developed in the College Programmed Learning Unit, or from similar establishments.

All Centre students attend at times convenient to them, on an appointment basis. They can also enrol at any time of the year. This is one aspect of the system which may be described as consumer oriented. We quite frequently get students who must obtain (say) the greatest possible command of French in a month because of some new job situation.

Each student is shown how to operate the presentation devices by a Centre Assistant who also arranges that the programme is ready for him at the appropriate frame on his arrival. The appointment system is a necessary administrative device but we believe it is also useful in helping the student to persist with the programme.

The majority of Centre students (about 60%) are adults, and in fact the Centre operates within the Department of Adult Education. This partly reflects the state of the art, in that 'Adult Education' in the Further Education Colleges is concerned with non-vocational work. Programmed courses that lead to professional qualifications do not exist, nor is it suggested that they are required - though useful pogrammes are available that might complement vocational courses or assist a person in his work (for example on 'sales training' or 'stocktaking'). Of the adult students about 50% attend to study a foreign language (including English as a second language). Mathematics and Statistics are also fairly popular areas of study and ones where the Centre is well served with programmes. There is growing interest in new programmes in the commercial area, including Typing and Pitman Script.

Some tutorial support is available in certain subjects. For example, the computer programming course in Fortran developed in the College has tutorials built into its schedule. At the tutorial, the student has a chance to run the computer programmes he has been set in the learning programme. In the main, however, students study the programmes without further assistance, except where they attend to complement a class course. This must be the case in minority subject areas - for example in Dutch where no specialist help is available. What is then a critical issue for the longer courses is not so much whether they will meet their objectives, given that the students complete them, but providing the programme would do this, will the student attending at his own volition derive sufficient benefit from the programme in relation to the effort he puts in, to persist with it to completion? Many papers have been published demonstrating that particular programmes meet their objectives, but usually the students are 'captive' or have agreed to cooperate in a validation exercise.

Thus the Centre acts as a test-bed where particular programmes and presentation media stand or fall according to their level of acceptability to students.

The old chestnut about a linear versus a branching approach, it was once suggested, would be resolved by time. All that has been resolved is that this is a question at the tactical level and that either tactic has its merits; and particular subject areas are more appropriate to one than to the other.

What does seem important is what one can only describe as the 'aura' surrounding a particular device or approach. Some of the primitive teaching machines with their tiny windows and not very reliable wind-on systems completely lack the right kind of aura. In the market-place the packaging counts. I recall a student not wishing to enrol for the Fortran course mentioned earlier, when he discovered that the visual element (it is an audio-visual course) was presented as typed material in a ring binder. The medium was not inappropriate as much of the visual material consisted of computer programme segments. Arguably the student needed to be instructed in the matter. However, the programme has since been converted to tape/filmstrip form. This permits visual as well as audio elements, which are to be encountered later, to be concealed. And the student had a point; the tape/filmstrip version would appear to have greater acceptability than the tape/book version.

Programmes are produced for the learner, and it is right that the students should have direct access to them. Yet one would also like to see these techniques in use in the classroom; and the Centre has a role to play in this respect.

Consider the possible situation where a course is made available at the Centre and proves to be successful in terms of being popular and in winning the approval of the students. A teacher in the College who has responsibility for that subject is bound to take note of this and think in terms of using the material, or something like it, in the classroom situation. In fact this has already occurred in connection with some programmes.

Also, where a course comes to enjoy high demand it becomes possible in view of the numbers of students involved to think in terms of their being a kind of 'serial' class even though they attend on different occasions. A large enough population for a particular subject would justify the appointment of a tutor in that subject, who would see each student at intervals of several appointments (say, every fifth time he attends) but would be able to give the student more individual attention and time when he does see him. The literacy scheme outlined below has something of this character.

The appointment system makes it possible to use plant to a maximum degree. One individual unit can be used by as many as 60 students in a week for one hour per student. The programme itself may quite typically have a working life of ten years. (We have programmes, for example, on calculus, that are ten years old but continue to be very useful to students and will continue to be so until the celluloid finally rips and the programmes cannot be replaced, or are superseded by new ones.) Thus, if programmed learning needs to 'trade up' and provide better, and therefore possibly more expensive, equipment and programmes it may be used most economically in a 'continuous' appointment situation rather than in a class.

AN ADULT LITERACY CENTRE

With the impending National Adult Literacy campaign it was appropriate that John Manley, Head of Adult Education at Bath, and I should examine the possible role the Centre might have to play in this area. The concept of an Adult Literacy Centre emerged which would have the following characteristics: (1) It would be such that to attend the Centre would not of itself indicate any particular learning difficulty. (2) It would provide free access for the student to the best available learning materials 12 hours a day. (3) All students would be referred to an adult literacy specialist who would assess the students' requirements and monitor their progress. (4) it would make use of trained voluntary tutors who would assist students on a one-to-one basis.

The Learning by Appointment Centre provides an established administrative base through which to operate such a system. Adults already attend the Centre for different reasons. The experience of the staff in handling sophisticated equipment would permit the use of technically advanced audio-visual systems such as the EDL 'Learning 100' Adult Literacy scheme even when the specialist tutor was not present.

The Centre would certainly store the forthcoming BBC television and radio programmes for the students and voluntary tutors to use at their convenience.

THE IDENTITY OF AV PRESENTATION SYSTEMS

Perhaps the most promising development for the programme writer in the last two decades of programmed learning is the advent of the audiocassette. Manufacturers of primitive teaching machines went to great trouble and expense to produce machines that would conceal what was coming next - and particularly the model response. In a great many instances it is possible to use the audiotape to do this and in a very natural way. The model response is concealed by virtue of the simple fact that it occurs later. The importance of the audio channel has surely been underestimated - particularly when one considers to what extent teachers depend in their teaching on the spoken word. Further, it is not possible for a student to follow a written explanation about a diagram and keep his eyes fixed on the diagram. In contrast, audio exposition will permit the student to keep his attention on the diagram and direct his sight to particular points.

The full potential of combined audio and visual presentation has not been realized in programmed learning terms. But there appears to be an emergent identity of audio-visual presentation devices. The cassette tape provides for audio exposition and a time base for scheduling visual changes and automatic stops, and indeed the whole learning experience. With the automatic programme stop facility the reality about pace may be stated by a programme writer thus: 'I will present this material at what I think is an appropriate pace but when I want you to do something I will stop the tape so that you can do it at your pace. I stop the tape, you start it.'

AN AUDIO-VISUAL BRANCHING DEVICE

Those moderately (but perhaps sufficiently) adaptive presentation devices known as 'branching machines' are usually visual only.

An audio-visual version would, on the face of it, require an audio frame corresponding to each visual frame. This would appear to be quite a difficult piece of engineering. Apart from that, what would be achieved by arranging the two channels to be isomorphic in this way? It is better to examine the character of the branching requirement and what contribution each channel could make.

Multiple choice items need to be seen to be judged, in order for the student to make the selection. Remedial instruction (frequently about the visual component of a frame) could be stored on the audio channel. Main sequence frames would be audio and visual, remedial frames audio only (staying with the visual frame where the question occurs). Again, there is no simple way of doing this at present.

What can be done with the traditional branching mode using cassette tape support? One possibility is that the instructional statements themselves can be stored on the tape. Another is that revision audiotapes could pulse one through the correct answer sequence. And in fact there are many possible variations.

The Programmed Learning Unit at Bath commissioned the construction of a response unit which would plug into a slide projector and permit the selection of up to seven slides in each direction, from any slide position. It has three selector buttons which are used separately or in combination giving the required seven moves. It works like a binary adder: (A = 1, B = 2, C = 4, AB = 3, AC = 5, BC = 6, ABC = 7).

There is an activating 'go' button and another button which changes direction of movement. An experimental lesson on Highway Code signs is being developed to explore the machine. This uses normal tape/slide mode to initially state what each sign means (taking five at a time) and then goes into traditional visual branching mode testing the signs, and re-teaching if necessary. It then reverts to tape/slide mode, and the cycle is repeated.

Another application to be explored is the use of the machine to present algorithms one box at a time. (It is very easy to lose one's place in an algorithm.) For example, one supplies an algorithm in slide form on how to solve equations. Supporting tapes would talk or pulse the student through it a few times using particular examples. After that, the student could continue to work through a list of examples using the algorithm repeatedly until he could dispense with its support.

This has the (perhaps dubious) merit for the programme writer that user-time may actually exceed programme-writing time. It is a branching technique where the object is for the student to come to know the branching structure itself by repeatedly moving through its different routes. One could present the whole map (the chart of the algorithm) when the student is familiar with its corners and turnings.

PRODUCING PROGRAMMES

What has proved to be a successful way of producing programmed courses at Bath is for a subject specialist to supply the content and general approach in permanent (ie recorded) form sufficient to teach the programmer, given that he can spend enough time at it and consult the specialist.

The programmer then converts this material to audio and visual scripts to be checked by the specialist.

It is worth doing only when the subject is reasonably stable. Given this, the creation of programmes towards making a significant contribution to the programme bank becomes less daunting as the programmes accumulate.

CONCLUSIONS

A question very much in the programmed learning tradition is this: under what circumstances will we consider programmed learning in general to have succeeded?

The answer suggested here is that it will have succeeded when, as with any good teacher, it gathers unto itself a student following.

The student is the consumer and will be the final arbiter. Existing techniques achieve a high level of student acceptability. Learning by Appointment Centres, given they have built-in developmental facilities, would furnish an environment where such techniques could continue to evolve.

Operational research models applicable to educational technology for life-long learning

P DAVID MITCHELL

ABSTRACT

Educational decisions and operations lack the precision and control of a laboratory, involve many variables simultaneously, and usually include several - often conflicting - objectives. Improving the effectiveness of lifelong education demands another research approach. Operational research provides just such an approach. Its integrating concepts combine with cybernetics to form a powerful conceptual and experimental tool for investigating the nature and control of complex systems. Such systems abound in education, ranging from the individual to the supra-national level.

The systems methodology of operational research provides some standard models of direct interest to educational technology where seemingly diverse phenomena can be described by a single mathematical or computer model. Decision theory, the bottleneck problem of too great demand for immediate access to resources, the economizing function of linear programming, the multi-stage problem-solving approach of dynamic programming, and the transition or choice-directed Markovian process are introduced. Finally, computer simulation of educational processes and systems can provide knowledge about long-term effects of decisions and permit theory testing. An Appendix describes a curriculum for Educational Systems Analysis.

INTRODUCTION

The purpose of this paper and the research that underlies it is to identify and introduce several planning and decision-taking technologies for practitioners of educational technology in an age of lifelong learning. Not concerned with specific problems or detailed solutions, it examines classes of problems that are common to operational research in complex systems. Educational technologists seem unaware of various recurrent phenomena in the problems and systems they study, phenomena that appear to be operative across system levels. Theoretical understanding of such recurrent processes is valuable whether we are concerned with designing and managing a national education system, a small learning resources centre, educational materials production, or other educational system.

LIFELONG EDUCATION

No longer a catchword phrase reflecting social romanticism, the prospect of lifelong education has been catapulted into the realm of possibility and necessity by scientific and technological advances. Lifelong learning is a functional necessity for most people (indeed it is part of our biosocial heritage), though the degree and intensity vary widely. To adapt to the capital-intensive industrial era and then to a post-industrial, labour-intensive, low-energy, and high-equity economy may be the lot of industrial nations. To be required to cope with predicted crises (shortages of food, fuel or clean environment; social unrest) may become universal.

Man is the only animal who provides for the intentional organization of educational experiences which prepare his young both to appropriate their culture and to contribute to it. The more highly industrialized his society, or the more it aspires to become so, the more pressing the demand for educational instruments for shaping it. More than half the world's children are not in school and the demand for education has been rising. This forces us to refurbish our ideas about how to implement educational aspirations, as well as to augment existing educational manpower. Perhaps more important is that school costs (in both affluent and penurious nations) are rising even more rapidly than enrolments or national incomes. We face an inevitable conclusion, "Les faits s'imposent donc avec une évidence irréfutable: aucune pays au monde n'a les moyens d'assurer par l'école seule l'éducation dont sa population a besoin" (Gerin-Lajoie, 1971).

Most individuals in the world are deprived of access to stored human experience - ideas, knowledge, skills and opportunities to acquire them. Such deprivation (because no-one can afford to provide them) should be morally repugnant to the humanistic educational technologist. To make matters worse, only those persons and nations who develop educational autonomy are likely to avoid self-destructive activities. Adaptation calls for continuous education of all members of society. Thus education (as the optimal organization of personal and social development) implies continuity from its genesis at a parent's knee to death. This functional necessity is not limited to institutions organized to provide instruction (Mitchell, 1971).

Schools alone cannot satisfy educational needs. More and more, serious discussions of education find the concept of éducation permanente suited to societies where changeover in knowledge and skills is rapid. Not simply an extension of school into one's working life, it is a 'conquest of life' in which conditions of study, work and living become interlocked in a most intimate fashion. Education permanente incorporates two aims, the development of society as a whole and personal development. Together they force us to transcend the propaedeutic intervention which commonly occurs in school in order to produce an educational ecology (ie an environment that is at once educational, free of compulsion, and available as an essential right) which supports the 'educative society'. Changing from dedication to efficiency of specific activities, to dedication to the effectiveness of human existence reflects less a change in educational technology than in priorities. Superior technological approaches make it possible (Mitchell, 1973a).

THE SCOPE OF EDUCATIONAL TECHNOLOGY

Educational technology embraces a fivefold conceptual mosaic of core meanings: Psychotechnology; Information and Communications Technology; Organizational Technology; Systems Technology; and Educational Planning (cf Mitchell, 1973b). Educational technology has become an area of study and practice concerned with all aspects of the organization of educational systems and procedures whereby resources are allocated to achieve specified and potentially replicable educational outcomes. It is an intellectual and practical pursuit, not a stable product. The practitioner asks: How must education be organized so that the maximum benefits of personal and cultural development can be enjoyed for each expenditure of effort and resources? - a basic educational question and one open to continued philosophical analysis, objective research and pragmatic compromise. As a problem-solver, one's methods, techniques and tools, as well as one's knowledge and values, are derived from many spheres of activity.

It is pointless to debate whether educational technologists are too concerned with the interface between the individual and the structure or content of a subject. Education is conceptualized as occurring within a set of systems within systems which range from one person to mankind's collective intentional organization of educational opportunities. Educational technology stands as a bridge between educational requirements and resources, between theory and practice, between a just, educative environment and cultural evolution. And intellectual technologies such as systems analysis, which translate desired outcomes into plans for an operational system, can build such bridges as readily on the scale of national educational requirements as in organizing instructional subsystems. What matters is that all relevant knowledge and skill be directed to the task of producing good decisions and more effective solutions to applied or theoretical problems. We must not prejudge the best approach to a particular decision.

EDUCATIONAL SYSTEMS RESEARCH

Educational research typically is represented as a scientific investigation of events considered important to education. An important purpose is to provide theoretical and practical knowledge about human behaviour which can be used to make education more effective. Emphasis is placed on problems associated with producing changes in a person's capability and a concern with refining our scientific understanding of instructional processes. Experimental investigations permit testing of presumed relationships in a restricted setting. We need another approach to deal with lifelong education.

Applied educational decisions and systems development or management lack the precision and control of a laboratory, involve many variables simultaneously, and usually include several - often conflicting - objectives. Further, we need solutions to operational problems qualitatively different from that of the classroom. Improving the effectiveness of education may be achieved not simply by improving instruction but by addressing molar questions that subsume an interrelated pattern of many variables. Nowhere is this more necessary than in considering lifelong learning, through interplay with myriad educational opportunities (eg schooling, social and community organizations, vocation-related activities, public media). How can the educational technologist cope?

In order to avoid misleading discussion we shall not consider unplanned or unanalysed educational opportunities (eg conversation, personal investigations, visits to museum or theatre) which can be exceedingly important for personal development. However, operational research is applicable to investigating such complex problems in order to guide the policy and actions of educational planners. Here we examine tools applicable to common problems.

System analysis is little more than a fashionable term to describe the employment of scientific knowledge, methods, techniques and tools to solve complex planning problems involving the direction and management, or allocation, of resources (men, materials, money, time) to achieve desired outcomes. Operational research is distinguished from traditional educational research by its emphasis on system analysis of ongoing operations at a molar level. Phenomena can be investigated holistically in all their multidisciplinary aspects. Description, analysis, explanation and prediction of system behaviour using OR theories and procedures provides a scientific basis for solving problems involving a complex of interrelated entities. It does so in the best interest of the organization as a whole and its clients. Systems research supplements educational research.

OR transcends traditional disciplinary boundaries in its focus on the function and structure of a system to obtain information to guide policy and operational decisions. To describe a process or complex of interrelated entities typically requires construction of some kind of representation or model of it. We can predict and compare outcomes of alternative strategies or explanations which might obtain with the real system by conducting experiments on the model. OR has produced a number of theories and models that describe recurrent processes which exist in a wide variety of systems. Seemingly diverse phenomena can be described by mathematical or computer models that portray key structural and functional factors. The disciplinary characteristics of the system are unimportant to OR theory.

Identification of classes of educational problems in terms of their amenability to systemic analysis has hardly begun. But the impact for future practice of educational technology is sure to be profound. No matter what one's sphere of operation several OR models have the promise of educational application. Here is an introductory description with, however, no attempt to set forth quantitative and computer procedures. Reference is made to relevant sources for specific techniques.

DECISION THEORY

The essence of educational technology research and development is that: the practitioner has a problem with a desired outcome (perhaps several); there are at least two courses of action possible; the decision occurs in a context; and a state of doubt exists over the best activity to select. Some of the variables can be controlled by his decision, others cannot (though they may be controlled by another person). Decision theory permits one to solve a simple problem by constructing a model (based on a verbal problem formulation). The model might be physical, graphic, statistical or algebraic. Analysis of the model permits decision-taking to proceed and the solution thus derived is tested and implemented. The aim is to select the most attractive course of action (Beer, 1966; Plane and Kochenberger, 1972).

Simple, especially repetitive, decisions can be taken easily using a decision table, decision tree or simple algorithm. The efficiency of a course of action is the probability that the action will yield the intended outcome. The relative value of any outcome may be determined by a relatively simple procedure outlined by Churchman (1961).

A decision-theoretic analysis of instruction aims to provide an optimal instructional strategy (Atkinson, 1972). However, in some cases it may be more appropriate to consider nature and other people as competitive decision-takers rather than passive systems. Here game theory might be the more helpful conceptual framework even though this is as yet impractical for planning lifelong education (Thierauf and Grosse, 1970).

QUEUEING THEORY

Although operational research has yielded many techniques to facilitate decision-taking under conditions of uncertainty, one model is salient. The bottleneck problem - too great a demand for immediate access to educational resources - pertains to information retrieval, educational channel capacity, idle production facilities or students arriving at a self-instruction centre. These recurrent waiting-line processes are explained by a queueing model which provides an optimal number of service facilities to keep waiting times within acceptable limits. Queueing theory is especially useful when we must design and manage many similar services (eg self-instruction systems; institutions) in which the same procedure can be used to analyse each planning problem even though specific details vary from one installation to another. It is indispensable if we must plan a system to cope with predicted demands for service by recommending the number and capacity of very costly facilities (cf Plane and Kochenberger, 1972; Thierauf and Grosse, 1970; Wagner, 1972)

A queueing problem involves balancing the costs involved in a system which could have too much waiting time on the part of users (input) or service system (idle process time). With a shortage, or inefficient use, of facilities, a queue of arrivals builds up - a familiar process. But a queue of idle or wasted time on the part of the server (process) occurs with insufficient input demand.

Education systems are replete with illustrations of queues. The educational cost is difficult to estimate but lost opportunities can be identified. How can we determine the optimal organization of educational services or facilities to provide acceptable service at an acceptable cost? Redfearn (1973) shows an application of queueing theory as a course design tool, given fixed service capacity. But how can we determine what is needed?

First we must recognize that a queueing system consists of the processing system and the queue of arrivals. Suppose a learning centre is expected to serve 100 persons who may come at any time during a 15-hour day and each will use a self-instruction facility for an average of 20 minutes (depending on remedial sequences or early departure). How many self-instruction units will we require? To answer this we might wish to know the average length of the waiting line, the average waiting time, the per cent of time the queue holds one, two, etc persons, the longest waiting time or per cent utilization of the service. Intuitively each unit could handle up to 45 users per day (3 per hour x 15 hours) so three units handling up to 135 users seems adequate. But application of queueing theory, using a simple approximation technique, shows that a problem could arise. Suppose the arrival rate AR is 7/hour and service rate (with three units) SR is 9/hour. The average length of the queue, QL, is approximated by $QL = \frac{AR}{SR-AR} = \frac{7}{2} = 3.5$. The maximum time waiting, $WT = \frac{AR}{SR(SR-AR)}$ or $\frac{7}{18}$ hr or 23 minutes. How many clients are likely to wait that long for a 20-minute programme, especially if this is a service to out-of-school users? If we try four units, expected QL is 1.4 and WT is 7 minutes; five units reduces QL to 0.88 and WT to 3.5 minutes. Armed with capital and operating costs we could now decide the best capacity for this system. A similar approach could suggest the number of channels required for ETV on demand.

It should be noted that this crude approximation assumes random arrival rate and random service time and approximates a multi-channel service by a single server. Other assumptions require different approaches. Newell (1971) provides some useful approximations for queueing problems while McMillan and Gonzalez (1973) focus on computer simulations of the system. The latter approach gives more accurate information and is worth the effort in many situations. But even a crude approximation is better than an unfulfilled wish.

In applying queueing theory, variations in arrival and service rates by time of day (eg typical vs peak demand) can be taken into account as can unexpected events (breakdowns, budget changes). Further, self-aggravating queueing situations can be turned into self-improving situations by minor technological or organizational changes (eg scheduling users or service, providing an alternative to unproductive waiting time). Finally, most queueing systems consist of multi-channel, multi-phase components, varying priority rules and other complexities. Though these prohibit analytical models they can be studied using computer simulation models. Often a single measure of managerial effectiveness may emerge which otherwise remains elusive. For instance, problems of decentralizing vs pooling facilities may be analysed in this way.

MARKOVIAN PROCESSES

Many systems can be described by discrete variables because the result of a decision or change in system state is not continuous (eg a behavioural objective is met or it is not; a student chooses one learning system over another). Often we want to know how a system makes a transition from one state to another or to forecast future system states. Markov analysis provides a way of analysing the current state of a system to calculate the probability of particular transitions and rates of progress through a sequence of states. The term, Markov process, refers to a mathematically definable sequence of system states in which the state of a system at some point in time does not uniquely determine subsequent system states. Rather the present state determines only the probability of future developments (Kemeny and Snell, 1960; Thierauf and Grosse, 1970).

Suppose that a person can be found in any of several courses or learning centres; that students may remain or switch allegiance from one centre to another (due to resources, policies or advertising); and, finally, that a representative sample of students yields data on the probability that a person will remain with the centre initially used. Preparing a matrix of transition probabilities enables one to forecast the number of students in each centre in the future or to analyse the effects of changing system procedures. Similarly, one can analyse learning as a process whereby some capability state undergoes transformation to a new state (eg from not learned to learned). One might do this to investigate the effect of alternative instructional strategies.

Individual rates of progress through instructional systems can be predicted by treating the sequence of instructional operations as a Markov chain process. It is possible tp predict the number of students at various places or stages in a continuous education system, the number completing their studies and those who will drop out. By knowing what to expect in the future the educational planner is in a position to do something to avoid undesirable outcomes.

LINEAR PROGRAMMING

Linear programming is a mathematical tool for allocating scarce resources to competing demands for them. It helps one to find the best value for the total outcome of one's decisions while simultaneously satisfying several requirements imposed by the situation. Thus one might allocate production facilities to alternative educational materials or allocate personnel to tasks so as to maximize effectiveness of the system. Similarly, given a set of educational objectives and alternative systems or ways in which students might prepare to meet them, it is possible to formulate an idealized way to assign students to learning activities in order to maximize learning (subject to available facilities and learning rates). The measure of effectiveness to be maximized or minimized could be cost, profit (if you market your product or service), research grants, or any quantifiable measure of educational effectiveness. The statement that denotes the objective as a function of controllable and uncontrollable variables is termed the objective function. (cf Thierauf and Grosse, 1970; Wagner, 1972.)

Linear programming's usefulness reflects its ability to help economize. The objective function assumes proportionality (eg a production centre produces twice as much in two time units as in one) which may not hold in practice. Although many feasible solutions can exist for a LP problem, the aim of LP is to find that unique solution that satisfies the constraints and maximizes the value of the solution to the decision-taker.

There are essentially three ways to go about linear programming; graphically, analytically, or with a standard computer programme. For a simple problem a graphic solution is easy. Suppose you must prepare modules for a learning centre that has a limited capacity for media 1 and 2. Course objectives fall into two broad categories, A (evaluation and synthesis) and B (memorization). Research has shown that, in a given time, media 1 enables six students to achieve an A or 15 to achieve a B objective, while media 2 helps 12 to achieve an A or 5 a B. What is the optimal assignment of objectives and media to maximize the value of this system, given that class A is considered twice as important as B? A graphic solution is illustrated in Figure 1. (For more complex problems, requiring more than two dimensions, use a computer.)

DYNAMIC PROGRAMMING

Some problems must be broken down into a series of smaller problems (decomposition) and the solution of the original problem is synthesized from the solutions to the sub-problems (composition). Dynamic programming is such a multi-stage, problem-solving approach. It solves for a stochastic series of sequential decisions with the outcome of each depending on the previous decision in the series. It is essentially an extention of the LP concept (which assumes a static system with one transition to a new state) dealing with uncertainty. The 'decisions' included in the structure of a DP problem are opportunities to change the values of state variables in a probabilistic manner; each decision is to change the state and maximize the value of the subsequent outcome (Nemhauser, 1966; Wagner, 1972).

Teaching is essentially an adaptive multi-stage decision process, so DP may be a useful analytic tool for the researcher (Groen and Atkinson, 1966). Since the instructional designer often must apportion the kinds and amounts of adaptation requirements between the instructional system and the student, DP is a useful concept to consider; the paucity of applications makes this an area ripe for research.

SIMULATION

An educational system or decision problem can often be investigated by recreating the effects on the system of relevant inputs through time. A simulation is a procedural model which expresses a dynamic relationship between variables in precise terms (eg in the form of a flow chart, set of decision tables or algorithms). By carrying out the sequence of operations on variables and parameters of the model with assigned values we can predict what might happen in the real system including long-term effects of decisions. Thus simulation involves features of both classical experimentation and formal analysis in a way that provides great flexibility for educational technology. Usually a simulation is processed on a computer where one can rapidly test hypotheses concerning theoretical questions and practical problems. Simulation models, eg of different queueing systems and decision processes, can be investigated using fairly standard procedures (cf Barton, 1970;

	OUTPUT	
	Hours/ Student A B	Total Time (hours)
INPUT M 1	$\frac{1}{6}$ $\frac{1}{15}$	1
(resources used) M 2	$\frac{1}{12}$ $\frac{1}{5}$	1

Problem: Maximize 2A + B

Subject to the constraints

$$\frac{1A}{6} + \frac{1B}{15} \leq 1$$

$$\frac{1A}{12} + \frac{1B}{5} \leq 1$$

$$A \geq 0 \quad B \geq 0$$

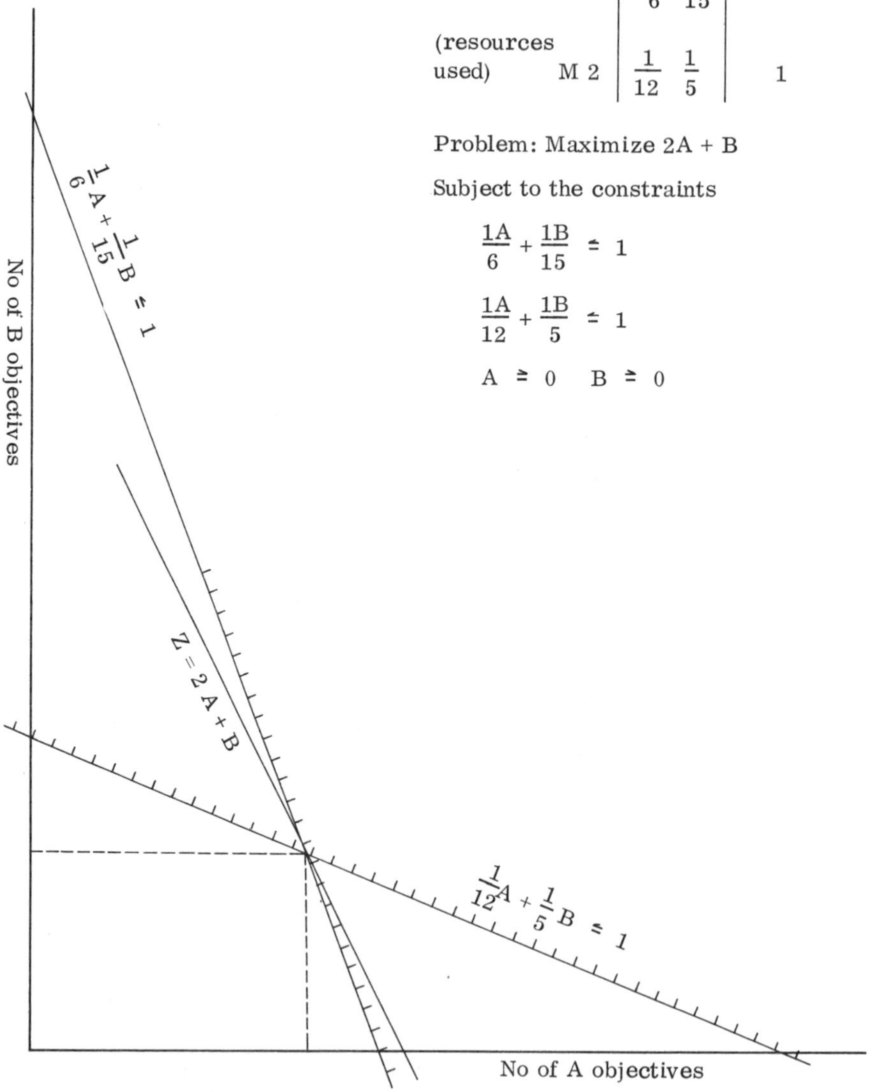

Figure 1. Summary of solution to linear programming problem

126

McMillan and Gonzalez, 1973; Naylor et al, 1966). Simulation models for policy-decisions in éducation permanente are possible. We could even produce a model of the global society to present to mankind the probable effects of present and proposed activities, and to generate and describe alternative courses of action (Mitchell, 1972). This might bring into existence new arrangements to foster lifelong education.

Some simulations are useful not for studying the system but for investigating the decision processes of educational managers whose normal behaviour in interplay with the system is difficult to analyse. Thus a computer simulation of a classroom with 30 students (Mitchell, 1973c) can be used to study instructional planning by teacher trainees or to compare such decisions with those of experienced teachers. Operational gaming denotes simulations of this sort. Games have pedagogical uses too, since they can stimulate both understanding and interest in participants (Barton, 1970).

CONCLUSION

An imbalance of judgement seems inevitable between those who have been fed mainly a diet of convergent instructional design principles (with concomitant emphasis on objective, mechanistic ordering of efficient instructional systems which may subordinate persons to the process) and those nurtured in the creative or humanistic realm (with its emphasis on aesthetic rationality, search for truth, personal freedom, or concern with the ultimate purpose and meaning of human life). This is complicated by the inability of one man to be expert in all the disciplinary approaches inherent in educational technology. Systems thinking can unite these opposing tensions by providing a common perspective on problems of communication and control (cybernetics), the rigour of scientific and technological research, and the scientific language of quantitative methods (cf Appendix; Ackoff, 1969). Nonetheless we must beware lest we yield, unwittingly, to societal pressures to measure educational activities and human dignity largely in terms of utility. The means-ends language of contemporary techniques distracts us from a vision of man as a temporal being in dynamic equilibrium with the rest of nature. The professional Weltanschauung of the educational technologist surely must transcend technocratic distortions if optimal education is to be achieved.

Changing from dedication to the efficiency of specific educational systems to the effectiveness of human existence leads one beyond technology (in essentially the way a metalanguage permits discussion of another language from a wider perspective). In the concept of éducation permanente we have a framework that transcends the preparatory intervention of school. Educational technologists who function within this broad perspective may find opportunities to bring into existence alternative arrangements to improve the allocation of financial, material and human resources to optimize personal and cultural development - to become agents in the evolution of man.

REFERENCES

Ackoff, R L (1969) 'Systems, organizations, and interdisciplinary research'. In 'Systems Thinking'. (Ed) F E Emery. Penguin, Harmondsworth

Atkinson, R C (1972) 'Ingredients for a theory of instruction'. 'American Psychologist' October 1972, p 921

Barton, R F (1970) 'A Primer of Simulation and Gaming'. Prentice-Hall, Englewood Cliffs

Beer, S (1966) 'Decision and Control'. Wiley, New York

Churchman, C W (1961) 'Prediction and Optimal Decision, Philosophical Issues of a Science of Values' Prentice-Hall, Englewood Cliffs

Gerin-Lajoie, P (1971) 'S'associer pour innover', paper presented to l'Institut de coopération internationale de l'Université d'Ottawa, Ottawa, Canada, 22 September 1971

Groen, G J and Atkinson, R C (1966) 'Models for optimizing the learning Process'. 'Psychological Bulletin' Vol 66, p 309

Kemeny, J G and Snell, J L (1960) 'Finite Markov Chains'. Van Nostrand, Princeton

McMillan, C and Gonzalez, R F (1973) 'Systems Analysis, A Computer Approach to Decision Models'. Irwin-Dorsey, Georgetown, Ontario

Mitchell, P D (1971) 'The professional development of educational technologists'. In 'Aspects of Educational Technology V'. (Ed) D Packham, A Cleary and T Mayes. Pitman, London

Mitchell, P D (1972) 'Systematic research for educational development'. 'Cybernetes: International Journal of Cybernetics and Systems' Vol 1, p 215

Mitchell, P D (1973a) 'Educational technology for lifelong learning'. Paper presented to International Symposium on Lifelong Learning in an Age of Technology, Turin, Italy, September 1973

Mitchell, P D (1973b) 'Technology for educational change'. 'Programmed Learning and Educational Technology'. Vol 10, p 315

Mitchell, P D (1973c) 'Computer simulation of a classroom'. In 'Aspects of Educational Technology VII'. (Ed) R Budgett and J Leedham. Pitman, London

Naylor, T H, Balintfy, J L, Burdick, D S and Chu, K (1966) 'Computer Simulation Techniques'. Wiley, New York

Nemhauser, G L (1966) 'Introduction to Dynamic Programming'. Wiley, New York

Newell, G F (1971) 'Applications of Queueing Theory'. Chapman and Hall, London

Plane, D R and Kochenberger, G A (1972) 'Operations Research for Managerial Decisions'. Irwin-Dorsey, Georgetown, Ontario

Redfearn, D (1973) 'An application of queueing theory to the design and management of programmed learning'. In 'Aspects of Educational Technology VII' (Ed) R Budgett and J Leedham. Pitman, London

Thierauf, R J and Grosse, R A (1970) 'Decision Making through Operations Research'. Wiley, New York

Wagner, H M (1972) 'Principles of Operations Research'. Prentice-Hall International, London

APPENDIX: A MODEL EDUCATIONAL SYSTEM ANALYSIS CURRICULUM

Contemporary research and progress indicate that the mainstream of technological thought has been quantitative. Far from providing a restrictive scope, a good grounding in system analysis and operational research techniques should expand one's capacity of comprehension, regardless of one's special interests in selected aspects of educational technology. It can truly prepare one to be a generalist.

As an educational programme, the detail with which a curriculum may be specified varies from a terse, molar level (eg to develop competence in system analysis) to the extremely refined level of detailed behavioural objectives. In this model curriculum the following intended learning outcomes were established as the first level of resolution. In the Educational Systems Analysis course offered in the Graduate Programme in Educational Technology at Concordia University each of these is elaborated in considerable detail. (Time constraints permit only a cursory treatment of some.)

The student is expected to develop capability in:

1. Methods of system description and systems modelling using block flow diagrams and flow graph theory.
2. Scientific and technological research methodology.
3. Understanding, formulating and using probability theory.
4. Evaluating parameters of a theoretical model from available data by statistical inference.
5. Understanding, setting up and solving problems of rational decisions using the theory of games.
6. Understanding, formulating and using matrix methods to analyse system problems.
7. Understanding, formulating and using a Markovian Decision Model.
8. Setting up and solving the optimal assignment problem.
9. Setting up and solving linear programming problems.
10. Formulating and solving problems involving curvilinear or non-linear programming.
11. Setting up and solving dynamic programming problems.
12. Analysing, setting up and solving queueing (waiting line) problems.
13. Measurement and evaluation of educational systems.
14. Analysing and controlling costs of educational technology projects and proposals.
15. Establishing policies for decoupling systems through inventory control models.
16. Describing and using management planning models.
17. Educational systems management.
18. Computer programming.
19. Constructing, using and interpreting simulation models.
20. The student will begin to develop a cybernetic worldview in which static systems, dynamic systems, purposeful or goal-seeking systems, self-organizing and conscious systems evolve through an exceedingly complex series of mutually adaptive equilibrium responses.

Papers concerned with specific aspects of educational technology, related to the main theme

Television learning:
in search of a workable theory

M J COOMBS

ABSTRACT

Education technology is seen as impotent when confronted with problems of learning from television programmes in which information is presented as a continuous narrative with little reinforcement and few opportunities for overt response. This is a significant weakness when one considers that much of an adult's continuing education is via such programmes. The source of the weakness is perceived as the premature commitment of researchers to molecular theories of learning, in which the learner is seen as responding to a closely defined stimulus in a highly structured environment. This paper argues for the adoption of a more holistic theory which views both learning and recall as being mediated by the active construction and utilization of mental models of the stimulus. A method of identifying and measuring models is proposed.

INTRODUCTION

Educational technologists working with television producers in any kind of educational institution must at some time or other have faced the television credibility gap, if only at the level of the inattentive stare following a suggestion that some production technique might be subjected to a research investigation before being passed as educationally fit. However, if we take account of our diagnostic and therapeutic powers, an indication of their extent being given in a recent edition of the APLET Journal (Berry and Unwin, 1975), we cannot but be sympathetic with producers' suspicions. At best research confirms techniques already employed, whilst at worst the application of findings may actually interfere with a producer's style. The truth is that educational technology cannot cope with the complexity of a television programme, and in particular with conventional formats in which information is presented as a continuous narrative with little reinforcement and few opportunities for overt response. This weakness is very significant when one realizes that much of an adult's continuing education is via such television material.

132

TELEVISION RESEARCH: A MODEST FAILURE

Much of the television research that an educational technologist may draw upon falls broadly into two categories. These include studies of specific production variables and studies designed to find the optimum information loading across audio and visual channels.

Production variable experiments took some particular production device as the independent variable, and looked for learning effects in isolation from both the content of the message and the nature of the learner. The objective of such research was to develop general rules of production via the systematic testing of many different techniques, and eventually to formulate them into a television taxonomy. However, we may note that such research has often produced results that are either trivial or contentious when compared with the wealth of empirical knowledge to be found in standard television textbooks. Indeed, if we allow a sufficient, although not necessary, relationship between interest and learning, textbook principles may even be used as a guide to learning effectiveness. Let us take as an example the common research topic of the psychological effects of different lengths of shot.

An experiment by Williams (1964-65) examined the effect of variations in length of shot within a televised lecture on declared interest level. He concluded that if the relative tightness of shot is selected on the basis of the amount of interest inherent in the subject matter - that is close ups (CU) for the most interesting material, mid-shots (MS) for areas of middle interest and long shots (LS) for the least interesting material - an increase in interest will be achieved for medium interest subject matter but a loss of interest will be recorded for low rated sections. If the relative tightness of shot is in opposition to inherent interest, there will be an overall decrease in declared interest.

One may question the need to have conducted this experiment, as the results could have been predicted from the standard text 'The Techniques of Television Production', by Millerson (1961). With reference to the first finding, Millerson writes that in a situation where cutting corresponds to interest, a cut from an LS to an MS will tend to sharpen viewers' attention, whilst with a cut from a CU to an MS interest will increase because of the inclusion of new information that is close enough to the camera to be scanned in detail. A cut to an LS in a low rated portion will tend to decrease interest because of the loss of relevant detail. The effect of opposing cutting to interest needs no comment.

Cobin and McIntyre (1961) studied the relationship between length of shot and learning. Two live television programmes were made of a lecture using the same audio but with one and two cameras respectively. Results showed no significant difference in factual recall either between programmes or between material given in CU and LS. If we accept the principles of editing given by Bretz (1962) in his book 'Techniques of Television Production', we may suspect that vision would be largely redundant in a television lecture and so have little effect on the recall of factual information. Indeed, we may expect that a good producer would have taken pains to make the vision as unobtrusive

133

as possible.

An alternative approach to television research was to base experiments on information theory. In contrast to the foregoing, these studies sought to discover the unique effect of a particular information distribution between audio and visual channels on a specific learner or group of learners. The emphasis was therefore upon the dependent variable. However, in spite of this more precise orientation, findings still tended to be unimpressive.

The results of a large number of studies were reviewed by Severin (1967) and formulated into four propositions. These briefly predict that the greatest gain in learning will be from a multi-channel presentation giving complementary information, whereas redundant information on one channel will give the same level of learning as a single channel presentation, and irrelevant information will cause interference and reduce learning. We find again that similar advice is to be found in a production text. Millerson (1961) points out with regard to aural composition that sound should bear an informative relationship to vision, but that the two should be perceived as one unit. If this relationship is not achieved, either one channel will be redundant or interference will occur. We may also note that, in contrast to Severin's apparent assumption that interference is automatically undesirable, Millerson states that it may be used to effect in dramatic productions to suggest dissonance. Surely there are educational programmes in which we may wish to achieve a similar effect.

It appears, therefore, that educational technology has reached an impasse when concerned with analyzing learning from educational television. In this paper I wish to suggest possible reasons for this and to tentatively propose a way out.

AN INAPPROPRIATE PHILOSOPHY

It may be suggested that molecular psychological theories have been prematurely adopted as the sine qua non of educational technology. This is important because our psychological position strictly regulates our research behaviour by defining for us the research questions we may explore, the experimental designs and techniques we may employ and the solutions towards which we will aim. In television research all three factors appear to have conspired to produce trivial findings.

Molecular psychological theories take the philosophical position that man is essentially knowable as the sum of his parts, the path to understanding, and hence prediction, being from the lowest units upwards. This assumption has had three main deleterious effects. Firstly, with regard to permittable experimental hypotheses, television research has been satisfied to test the effects of single structural variables that have been subjectively selected by the researcher, rather than to first devise methods for objectively determining which variables are important (Baggaley, 1973). This has led to the absurd situation in which the manipulation of a single production device in a complex programme has been expected to reliably produce a significant increase in learning.

Secondly, experimenters have tended to look no further than the hypothesized effects of their experiments, and to regard as error all other outcomes regardless of their potential informativeness. In an attempt to reduce such error, researchers designed experiments in which the structure of learning materials was rigidly controlled and learning was measured via long MCQa with very high reliabilities. This latter factor alone would have had the effect of masking learning differences between conditions, without the added reduction of production variable effects due to the use of much simplified experimental programmes.

Thirdly, educational technologists have assumed that the learning outcomes of a programme could be explained in terms of a few powerful variable manipulations. In view of the fact that television conventions have developed via an attempt to extend the medium's range of expression, and that a learner's reaction to a programme is only as good as his interpretation of these conventions, this assumption fades as unrealistic.

Further to these problems, the information theory approach cannot readily be applied to television programmes in which information is presented as a continuous narrative. The concept of information in the parent mathematical theory is strictly quantitative, being a measure of the number of binary choices required to reduce uncertainty, where alternative choices are equiprobable. However, with a television programme there is no technique for assessing the total number of binary choices, hence experimental materials have been limited to simple prose passages combined with line drawings or easily recognizable pictures. Choices would also not be equiprobable, but would change in probability as the material was received and comprehended.

A 'MENTAL MODELS' APPROACH TO LEARNING

Given the difficulties of researching conventional education television using molecular designs, is there an alternative? If so, what form would it take and how could it be operationalized? Running parallel in psychology, and yet barely exploited by educational technology, is a more holistic philosophy. In contrast to the assumption of a passive organism underlying the work just discussed, this view conceives man as actively and consciously learning to control the events with which he is involved by seeking to predict them. This implies his developing perceptions of relationships between stimuli along with some notion of their individual reference to some specific task or problem.

A seminal experimental study applying the above philosophy, conducted by F C Bartlett (1932) and reported in his book 'Remembering: a Study in Experimental and Social Psychology', found that when subjects were required to reproduce perceptual and meaningful verbal material via various free recall techniques some features remained constant over time. These frequently consisted of a general outline of the learning material along with a few related details. The bulk of the detailed content, however, changed between reproductions.

In contrast to much earlier theorizing, Bartlett interpreted these findings as indicating that learning was not a process in which detailed analogues of

135

reality were imposed on the brain, but a process involving the gradual development of interpretive/mental models - schemata - of reality. Hence, recall could be seen as a constructive process employing these models, the subject first calling up the model relevant to a given task and then using it to infer detailed information. Detail, therefore, constituted hypothetical information, the accuracy of inference depending upon such factors as the specificity of the initial model and the time lapsed before recall. However, with visual material the reasons for recall and the subject's personal interests were also noted as relevant. In addition, these latter factors increased in importance as the learning material became more ambiguous, or remote from a subject's previous experience.

Applied generally to psychological processes, Bartlett's theory views perception and cognition as aiding a person's survival by permitting him to predict the covert properties of objects, or to establish their future actions, from limited sense data (Bruner, 1957a). Learning can, therefore, be seen as a process of establishing the nature of relationships between items of sense data: as learning to code sense data into appropriate mental models or model systems. Once a model has been formed, a coded stimulus should be sufficient for the inference of other characteristics.

However, in a complex environment a person may find situations in which it is not clear which model or model system should be employed. In this case, some system of selection would be required. Bruner (1957b) proposes a system in which models are assumed to have different degrees of accessibility, these being a reflection of the subjective probabilities of relationships between objects and events that exist within any given environment. It is further assumed that, as a model becomes more accessible, it will be activated by a weaker input and a wider range of input characteristics. There will also be a greater chance of alternative models being masked.

What might this approach tell us about learning from educational television? Most significantly it tells us that learning can take place in the absence of external reinforcement. However, as this will be entirely dependent upon a previously developed system of models, it will tend to be of a conservative nature. Moreover, it tells us that the specific information recallable from a programme will be dependent on the access order of the models in addition to their content. In other words, we may expect a dynamic relationship between background knowledge and a learner's objectives in viewing a programme. There may be occasions, therefore, when a learner is systematically misled in terms of the producer's objectives. A good example of this is given in Bates' (1975) address to the 1974 APLET Conference in which he mentioned that an Open University television insert to a programme on the perception of crowd behaviour led almost universally to a discussion on the morality of demonstrations. We may also expect students to be reluctant to accept new ideas in the face of an opposing model system and in the absence of information indicating the need for radical rethinking (Gregory, 1970).

A TENTATIVE MEASURE OF 'MENTAL MODELS'

Before the concept of mental models may be used in research, some means of recording and measuring them must be found. A possible solution may lie in a measure of cognitive complexity devised by Smith and Leach (1972).

It may be recalled that a mental model is conceived as having both content and some specific degree of availability. The concept of cognitive complexity was evolved by Bieri (1966), being defined as the tendency to construe social behaviour in a multi-dimensional way, such that a more cognitively complex person has a more versatile way of perceiving the behaviour of others than a less complex person. A more cognitively complex person is therefore likely to have a better predictive capability: to have available a wider range of models. Indeed, there is a close correspondence between Bieri's concept and the ideas outlined in the foregoing because his theorizing is founded on the writing of G A Kelly (1955), for whom a central idea is that man lives as a scientist, posing and testing hypotheses about the world in order to render it safely predictable. Moreover, the hypotheses - personal constructs - are conceptualized as bipolar, with a pole of affirmation and a negative pole. This would admit the possibility of describing a variety of relationships between models, as opposed to the simple inclusion/exclusion permitted between logical concepts.

The Smith and Leach measure employs a rated version of the repertory grid, which was developed by Kelly to provide a means of observing a subject's perceptions of relationships between sets of ideas, objects or names. Subjects are first presented with, or required to generate, a list of elements - ideas, objects or names - which are placed on the X-axis of a grid. In the case of Figure 1 the elements were given to subjects, each of them referring to a central idea in a medical video tape on epidural analgesia.

Using these as references, subjects are then asked to generate a list of ideas - termed constructs - for the Y-axis. Only the pole of affirmation is required. The subjects then rate the elements against the constructs for perceived relationship according to some given scale - in this case 0-10. A correlation matrix is then drawn up for the constructs, the units of which are the signed product-moment correlations of all possible rows of the grid, the magnitude of each correlation giving a measure of the similarity between the constructs to which it refers. A similar correlation matrix is drawn up for the elements, giving the signed product-moment correlations between all possible columns of the grid. Assuming constructs to be hierarchically organized (Kelly, 1955), the construct inter-correlations are now analyzed to give a hierarchical picture of the way constructs are grouped together.

The measure is now quantified by first impoverishing the subject's construct system by treating as a single construct all constructs that correlate above some critical level of significance - in this case the 10% level. The elements are then re-analyzed using the impoverished system. The difference between the groupings of elements in the first and second analysis is computed from a node count of the junction points between elements.

If the difference is large, the subject is deemed to be cognitively complex - to have a highly integrated, and hence powerful, system of constructs. If it is

Experimental reference: B6

Construct	#	Operation (10)	Cleanliness (9)	Spine (8)	Nervous system (7)	Circulation (6)	Drugs (5)	Nursing Staff (4)	Patient (3)	Epidural Space (2)	Entry (1)
Aseptic technique	1	10	10	4	0	9	0	5	0	0	8
Using Lignocaine 1.5%	2	10	0	10	10	5	10	0	10	10	8
Insert between Lumbar L4 and L5	3	10	0	10	8	3	7	0	6	10	10
Made sure nursing staff understand instructions	4	6	10	2	0	9	9	10	10	1	0
Attach 20ml syringe to thigh	5	2	6	0	0	0	0	0	3	6	0
Test fluid on hand of assistant for warmth	6	0	0	10	9	2	0	10	6	9	10
Do not bend or kink catheter	7	0	0	8	8	0	0	0	9	8	9
Make sure spine is flexed before inserting catheter	8	2	0	10	0	0	0	6	10	9	10
Inform patient of procedure	9	0	0	0	0	0	0	10	10	2	6
Catheter between Dura Mater and Vertebrae	10	5	9	10	10	0	0	0	0	10	10

Figure 1. Completed repertory grid for subject B6

138

Level of correlation

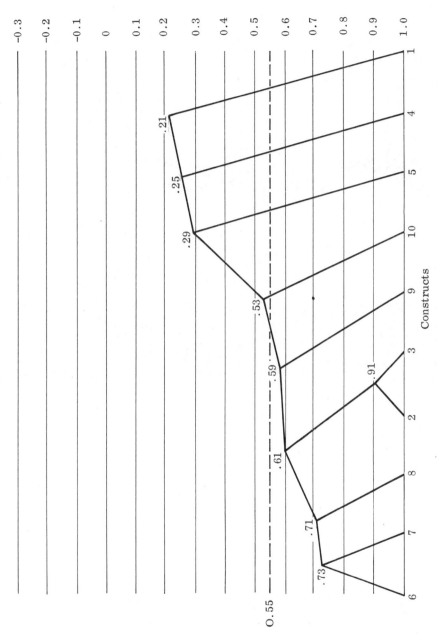

Figure 2. Hierarchical picture of groupings of elements from impoverished grid for subject B6

139

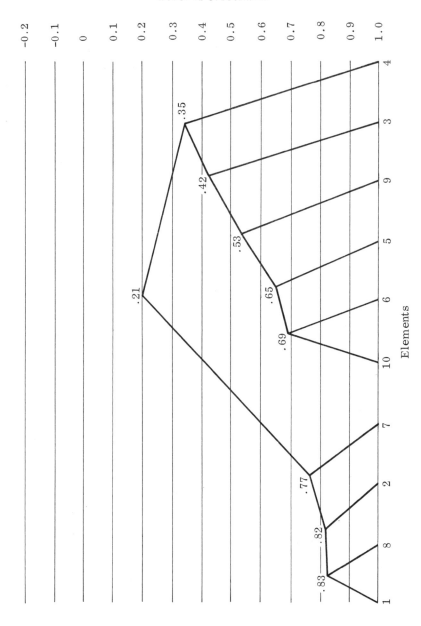

Figure 3. Hierarchical picture of groupings of elements from intact grid for subject B6

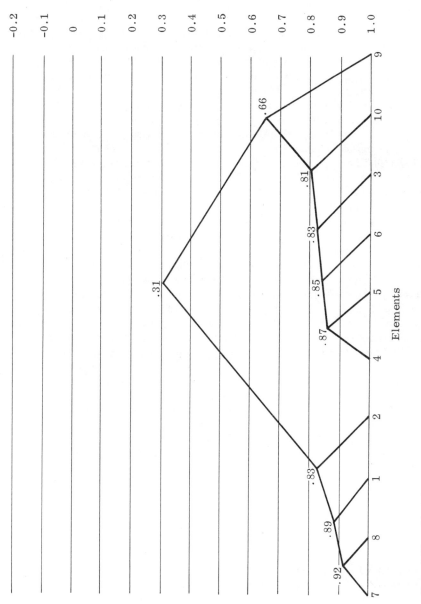

Level of correlation

Elements

Figure 4. Hierarchical picture of groupings of elements from impoverished grid for subject B6

141

small, he is deemed to be cognitively simple - his system lacks integration and so would have little predictive capacity.

CONCLUSIONS

To conclude we may ask two questions. Firstly, we may ask what advantages a mental models approach gives over the approach criticized at the beginning of this paper. Secondly, we may ask how far the repertory grid method goes to provide a measure of mental models and also to what specific experimental use could it be put.

The big advantage of the orientation proposed in this paper is that it admits to learning without overt feedback. However, the student would only be able to abstract information within the strict constraints of his present background knowledge and learning skills. He would, therefore, be unlikely to learn concepts that belong to an order not previously encountered. Presented with novel material, he would tend to adjust the message to fit his existing mental models. Likewise, learning that required new skills of analysis or synthesis would not be received. A number of interesting problems arise. We may first, of course, question the validity of our proposals, asking the meaning of different orders of concept and different types of learning skill. We may also question whether, from a production point of view, it would be possible to cue students either before or during a programme radically to alter their models to learn something very new. These are the subject of some of my current work at Liverpool and I will make no attempt to answer them at present but will simply put them forward as points for discussion.

Now to the grid itself. By putting few constraints on subjects, it promises to provide a relatively objective picture of cognitive structure. Assuming that construct clusters provide an adequate representation of mental models, the method could be used with a variety of conventional measures of recall to explore relationships between learning skills and learning outcomes. In particular, we could tackle the problems previously stated. However, it should be pointed out that the full meaning of the measure is as yet far from clear, some recent experiments showing little correlation between the constructs generated by students and their declared learning objectives. Nevertheless, although further validation is required, the grid as a measure of mental models combined with the theoretical background that has been outlined appear to offer an attractive path for studying learning from television. It remains to be discovered whether it will also be a profitable one.

ACKNOWLEDGEMENTS

The writer wishes to thank Dr J P Baggaley and Mr J O Thompson for their valuable comments during the development of the ideas discussed in this paper.

REFERENCES

Bartlett, F C (1932) 'Remembering: A Study in Experimental and Social Psychology'. Cambridge University Press, Cambridge

Baggaley, J P (1973) 'Developing an effective educational medium'. 'Journal of Programmed Learning and Educational Technology' Vol 10, pp 158-69

Bates, A W (1975) 'Obstacles to the effective use of communication media in a learning system'. In 'Aspects of Educational Technology' Vol VIII (ed) Baggaley, J P, Jamieson, G H and Marchant H. Pitman Press, Bath

Berry, C and Unwin, D (1975) 'PLET monitoring service: production and audience variables in film and television'. 'Journal of Programmed Learning and Educational Technology' Vol 12, pp 54-70

Bieri, J (1966) 'Cognitive complexity and personality development'. 'Experience, Structure and Adaptability' (ed) Harvey, O J. Springer, New York

Bretz, R (1962) 'Techniques of Television Production'. McGraw-Hill, New York

Bruner, J S (1957a) 'Going beyond the information given'. In 'Contemporary Approaches to Cognition' (ed) Bruner, J S et al. Harvard University Press, Cambridge, Massachusetts

Bruner J S (1957b) 'On perceptual readiness'. 'Psychological Review' Vol 64, pp 123-57

Cobin, M T and McIntyre, C J (1961) 'The Development and Application of a New Method to Test the Relative Effectiveness of Specific Visual Production Techniques for Instructional Television'. Illinois University, Urbana

Gregory, R L (1970) 'On how little information controls so much behaviour'. 'Ergonomics' Vol 13, pp 25-35

Kelly, G A (1955) 'Psychology of Personal Constructs' Vol 1. Norton, New York

Millerson, G (1961) 'The Techniques of Television Production'. Focal Press, London

Severin, W (1967) 'Another look at cue summation'. 'Audio-Visual Communication Review' Vol 15, pp 233-45

Smith, S and Leach, C (1972) 'A Hierarchical measure of cognitive complexity'. 'British Journal of Psychology' Vol 63, pp 561-68

Williams, R C (1964-65) 'On the value of varying television shots'. 'Journal of Broadcasting' Vol 9, pp 33-43

The mass media
with particular reference to television
as an instrument of continuous
education among Canadian Eskimos*

GARY O COLDEVIN

ABSTRACT

While a number of studies have demonstrated the influence of the mass media and particularly television as a primary source of non-formal education, few studies have examined the effects accompanying the injection of television into a previously isolated community. The present research analyses the impact of the CBC Frontier Television Service, a four-hour daily service in a remote Eskimo settlement, one year after its introduction. Four primary dependent variables are examined: (1) Information gain with respect to national issues; (2) Information gain and attitude posture towards international issues; (3) Social impact in terms of changes in social/psychological behaviour patterns; (4) Perceived information impact in terms of dominant information sources. Additional measures included the projected utility role of television within the context of community and educational requirements.

A survey was undertaken with 131 heads of households in the television community and compared with responses generated by 84 counterparts in a non-television settlement.

Data comparisons suggest that television has had limited impact on the development of cognitive acquisition of national issues but appears to have facilitated a conceptual framework for defining and proposing solutions to international problems. The more salient intercommunity differences were revealed in the social impact measures. Significant differences were detected in employment mobility aspirations for respondents' children, evaluation of life-style, perception of Eskimo differences from other people and desired travel destinations. In terms of information impact, radio was perceived as the dominant information source while television was viewed as providing only a minor support function. The influence of radio was primarily derived from news broadcasts in the native regional dialect. The major projected utility role for television as an educational resource was one of preserving traditional life-styles and values with programming in the regional language.

Suggestions are made as to the potential of the medium for both formal and non-formal educational broadcasting as well as implications of the study for developing nations currently initiating terrestrial and satellite television networks.

* This study was facilitated through a research contract with Communications Canada.

BACKGROUND

In 1958, legislation was passed by the Canadian Government to create the Canadian Broadcasting Corporation (CBC) Northern Service with provisals for the establishment of local radio stations in the larger Canadian Arctic communities. Originally, these major northern centres received weekly shipments of CBC network programmes for re-broadcast on a two-week delay basis. Additionally, the centres produced programmes of local interest such as community affairs, weather reports and regional information. The smaller Arctic communities continued to receive radio signals through the CBC shortwave service.

In 1967, television was introduced to the major Western Arctic centres through the CBC Frontier Coverage Package, a four-hour, 7.00 to 11.00 pm, two-week delay videotape service re-broadcast through a transmitter linked to a video playback machine. The programme content of the package was selected from regular CBC network broadcasts with the exception of 'direct' news and news specials. Within the Eastern Arctic, however, the Frontier Television Service was not introduced until 1972 and then into the predominantly Eskimo community of Frobisher Bay on lower Baffin Island. In contrast to the Western Arctic communities, the inception of television at Frobisher Bay heralded the introduction of a new medium into an area where native viewers had little understanding of the language or conventions of the medium. Those communities, which used English as the primary language of communication, viewed the Frontier Service as a natural supplement to daily information and entertainment. In Frobisher Bay, the television service provided sharp contrast to radio, much of which was broadcast in the regional Eskimo dialect. The community thus provided a uniquely valuable sampling area with which to examine the 'educational effects' of television on a virtually unexposed element of Canadian society.

PURPOSE

Two communities are examined in the present study: (1) Frobisher Bay for the present purposes is operationalized as the 'partial television' community (full-service television was introduced to the community immediately after the present sampling was completed) for direct comparison with (2) Fort Chimo, a 'non-television' community situated approximately 600 miles south of Frobisher Bay in northern Quebec. Fort Chimo was selected as the control community as it, like Frobisher Bay, is predominantly an Eskimo community but has only limited access to direct outside information through the CBC shortwave radio service. The primary, independent variable under study one year after the introduction of the medium is television (Frobisher Bay) vs non-television (Fort Chimo). Within this contect, the study examines four major dependent variables:

(a) information gain with respect to national issues;

(b) information gain and attitude posture towards international issues;

(c) social impact in terms of changes in social/psychological behaviour patterns;

(d) perceived information impact in terms of dominant information sources.

Additional measures undertaken in the television community included a projected utility role for television within the context of community information and educational resources.

The study was initially focused upon heads of households since they represented the hiatus between the traditional nomadic hunting and fishing culture and the present-day, relatively stationary community. Similarly, the predominant majority of this grouping have not been exposed to formal educational training. In terms of continuous education, the mass media may be characterized as the major supplier of non-formal education to this unique cultural grouping.

RATIONALE

While a number of studies have demonstrated the influence of the mass media and particularly television on socialization processes (eg Coldevin, 1972, 1974a), few studies have concentrated upon the injection of commercial television into communities previously isolated from the medium. The thrust from a relatively information-poor to information-rich environment and participation in the mainstream of information and entertainment which dominates much of the 'southern' leisure activities suggests a major impact on cultural solitude and its attendant social/psychological framework. Studies of this nature may prove to be of particularly high value to other countries currently initiating terrestrial and satellite network distribution systems (eg India and Brazil).

In relating the present study to those conducted in developing countries, the more general conclusion summarized by Rogers (1969) is that mass-media exposure is positively related to innovativeness, empathy and achievement motivation. Each of these relationships is only incidentally examined here. More parallel research has suggested that political knowledge is positively correlated with mass-media exposure (Chu, 1966; Deutschmann, 1963) as well as educational and occupational aspirations (Rogers, 1969). The majority of these latter studies were conducted with captive audiences in villages where teleclubs were formed for programme viewing (Coldevin, 1974b). In the present study respondents view programmes in individual home environments with no conscious attempts to incorporate pre- and post-viewing activities. The setting thus closely matches typical southern viewing environments. In essence the study may be viewed as one of the few remaining opportunities in North America to assess the educational effects of television in the form of mass information and entertainment on a previously unexposed population.

METHODOLOGY

Development of the Questionnaire

The final questionnaire assessing each of the major dependent variables was essentially composed of open-ended questions which allowed respondents to supply both attributes and decisions where required to the various dimensions. Since the questionnaire was the first of a developmental series, extensive information was also collected on demographic variables such as age, education, family size, employment patterns and language comprehension. Information gain with respect to national issues concentrated primarily on geographic unit identification and political structures. At the international level, information gain and attitude posture focused on the ability to define and provide solutions to major international problems. Social impact measures ranged from perception and evaluation of the Eskimo and southern life-styles to employment mobility aspirations for the respondent and his children. Source impact was probed through a four-point, Likert-type scale (No Useful Information - Much Useful Information) as to importance in responding to the various questions. Finally, each respondent was asked to project what he considered to be a primary utility role for television if the medium were to be employed as a community and educational resource.

Selected items of the final questionnaire were pre-tested with 40 heads of households in the control community. On the basis of pre-test responses, the final instrument was revised and considerably lengthened.

The Sample

Television Community. A sampling of 131 heads of households out of an approximate maximum total of 150* was undertaken during April, 1973. The date was deliberately chosen since it marked the hiatus between one year of exposure to the Frontier Coverage Package and the introduction of direct, full-service CBC television relayed via the ANIK I satellite. The initial survey was thus intended as both an evaluation of the Frontier Coverage Package and as baseline data toward assessing the developmental effects of full-service television.

The average age of the respondents was 41 to 50 years with 21% less than 30, 28% between 31 and 40, 30% between 41 and 50 and 21% over 51. Sex was divided into 87% male and 13% female. Although 7% of respondents did not have children, those with families averaged between four and five per household. In terms of occupational groupings, 38% of the sample were supported primarily through social welfare. Two per cent were supported through old-age pensions with 60% holding a job (often seasonal) in the community. The vast majority of these jobs were classified in the blue-collar category (Dominion Bureau of Statistics, 1961) with 8% holding white-collar and 2% professional positions. Seventy-seven per cent of the sample had no formal educational training with 18% having some primary grade exposure.

---

* No comprehensive data are available here. The figure is based upon an approximation of the principal interviewer at the time of sampling.

Five per cent had some high school training. None of the respondents had completed high school nor attended university. Seventy per cent of the sample indicated that they understood the Eskimo language only, with 30% understanding both Eskimo and English.

In terms of media accessibility, 95% of the sample reported having radio sets in their homes and 77% television sets. Those without radio or television receivers reported listening or viewing at neighbours' houses or public areas.

Favourite radio programmes were generally centred on Eskimo news (56%) followed in order by music (31%), myths and legends and Eskimo public affairs. Television preferences were centred on dramatic series (48%) with 'Cannon' being the overwhelming individual favourite. Variety and musical shows occupied the second-rank ordering, situation comedy third, with outdoor and wild-life and sports in fourth and fifth order of priority respectively.

Dominating the least-preferred television programme categories were public affairs and talk shows followed by 'non-formal education'. The former category is characterized by a great deal of talking, slow pacing and a dearth of physical action, any attribute of which may have contributed to the low rating. 'Sesame Street' occupied the foremost least-preferred individual programme category.

Non-Television Community. A sampling of 84 heads of households out of a maximum total of 109 units was undertaken directly following the television community sampling. Similar to the former community, all heads of households could not be included because of illness or seasonal absence on hunting or fishing expeditions. The average age of this sample was between 41 and 50 years with 11% less than 30, 26% between 31 and 40, 20% between 41 and 50 and 43% over 51. Sex was distributed into 77% male and 23% female. Although 8% of the sample reported having no children, the average family size was between four and five for those with children. Twenty-nine per cent of respondents were primarily supported by social welfare and 13% through old-age pensions. Of the 58% holding a job in the community, 94% were in blue-collar occupations (Dominion Bureau of Statistics, 1961), with 4% white-collar and 2% professional positions. Eighty-eight per cent had no formal education with 10% having had some primary grade exposure. One respondent had completed high school. None of the respondents had attended university. Sixty-five per cent indicated an understanding of Eskimo only, with 35% understanding Eskimo and English.

Radio signal accessibility is also high in this community with 87% of the sample reporting ownership of shortwave receivers. Those without personal sets reported daily listening either at neighbours' homes, work or public areas. Favourite radio programme responses in this community were overwhelmingly 'programmes in Eskimo' with no apparent distinction being made between the various categories.

In sum, the two samples closely parallel each other on a variety of demographic background dimensions and accordingly may be considered as highly satisfactory for comparison of the primary variables under consideration.

Questionnaire Administration and Content Analysis

Prior to administration, the questionnaire was screened for ambiguity and appropriate syntactical construction by experienced Eskimo translators. The translation from English to Eskimo syllabic script was undertaken by these same personnel. During the field administration, the questions were given in the regional dialect with responses being simultaneously translated into English for coding and content analysis. Two native interviewers trained in sampling techniques by the author participated in the on-site administration.

In developing the code book for content analysis, a sample of all responses given to each question was recorded and assigned to meaningful attribute categories (Backstrom and Hursh, 1963). With few exceptions, the code book developed for the television community was appropriate to responses generated by the control community. The matching of attribute categories provided further evidence of the mutual characteristics of the two samples and validity of direct comparisons of the primary dependent variables.

DATA ANALYSIS

Information Gain - National Issues

The influence of television on the development of cognitive acquisition of national issues appears limited (Table 1). Only one index out of six (identification of two main languages) was significantly higher for the television community. In total, the television community achieved 17% of maximum possible scores and the control community, 14%. In terms of information impact on national unit identification, television thus appears to be only marginally effective.

Table I. Information gain in terms of national unit identification

National Unit	Sample	Correctly Identified %	Incorrectly Identified %	Probability
Prime Minister	Television	37	63	
	Non-Television	33	67	NSD*
Number of Provinces	Television	9	91	
	Non-Television	6	94	NSD
Four Political Parties	Television	2	98	
	Non-Television	0	100	NSD
Leader of Opposition	Television	8	92	
	Non-Television	2	98	NSD
Capital City	Television	34	66	
	Non-Television	32	68	NSD
Two Main Languages	Television	36	64	
	Non-Television	15	85	.01

*No significant difference

Information Gain/Attitude Posture - International Issues

When respondents were asked to identify major international problems, significant differences were found between the two communities (Table II). While the percentage of no responses was slightly higher in the television community, a large portion of those in the control community felt unqualified to answer the question. In both communities, a number of respondents were inclined to identify as international, salient regional problems. Significant differences were also noted in the ability of the television sample to enumerate international problems.

Table II. Identification of contemporary world problems

Sample	No Response %	Feel Unqualified to answer %	Local Problems Enumerated %	International Problems Enumerated %
Television	40	11	14	35
Non-Television	36	30	12	22

$X^2 = 12.17$ df = 2   p $<$.01

While no significant differences were detected between the categories of world problems enumerated, war garnered the highest frequency for both samples. Interestingly, however, respondents in the television community were significantly more able to propose solutions to the problems enumerated (Table III).

Table III. Ability to propose solutions to international problems

Sample	No Response %	Not Applicable %	Solutions Proposed %
Television	15	65	20
Non-Television	19	78	3

$X^2 = 10.90$ df = 2   p $<$.01

These results appear to suggest in part that the conceptual framework for the general term 'international problems' may be more internalized within the television community as a result of exposure to a less abstract form of information reception.

Social Impact

Of all the measures included in the survey, the social impact comparisons produced the more striking intercommunity differences. While no significant differences were detected between the two samples in terms of individual

150

respondent's employment preferences, aspirations for gainful employment of sons (Table IV) and daughters (Table V) differed significantly. Respondents in the television community were also more inclined to forward opinions regarding occupational preferences for their respective offspring. The vertical mobility aspirations in the televison community are particularly striking for daughters.

Table IV. Perception of most interesting job for sons

Sample	% Not Applicable %	No Idea (Anything They Can or Want To Do) %	Lateral Mobility (No Change from Head of Household) %	Vertical Mobility (From Head of Household Position) %
Television	16	48	26	10
Non-Television	18	71	7	4

$$X^2 = 17.48 \quad df = 3 \quad p < .001$$

Table V. Perception of most interesting job for daughters

Sample	% Not Applicable %	No Idea (Anything They Can or Want To Do) %	Lateral Mobility in Relation to Mother %	Vertical Mobility in Relation to Mother %
Television	14	49	6	31
Non-Television	25	64	7	4

$$X^2 = 24.26 \quad df = 3 \quad p < .001$$

When asked the question, 'In what ways do you think the Eskimo people are different from other people?' significant differences were revealed in response patterns between the two samples. In the television community the primary differences were perceived as language and culture, while in the control community respondents felt that their ability to adapt to the northern environment was the primary distinction. It can be readily suggested here that television exposure as opposed to personal experience is the primary determinant of the two differing perceptions.

Expressions of life-style evaluation also produced significantly different postures. Respondents in the control community were more inclined to maintain their present life-style, while a corresponding greater percentage of respondents in the television community wished for change. The wish for change was primarily operationalized in the desire to 'return to traditional ways of life'.

Finally, travel aspirations produced significant differences in community orientations. While the predominant orientation in both communities was towards localized Arctic travel, a significant proportion of the television community respondents were more nationally oriented in desired travel destinations.

Information Impact

Source Ratings. Table VI indicates the rank-order comparisons of the most important sources according to scale-rating means. Respondents were asked

Table VI. Rank order comparison of most important sources according to scale rating means

Television Sample			Control Sample		
Source	Mean	Rank Order	Source	Mean	Rank Order
Radio	3.702	1	Radio	3.643	1
Church	3.122	2	Church	3.119	2
Family	2.695	3	Family	3.083	3
Store	2.595	4	Meetings	2.789	4
Neighbours	2.580	5	Teachers	2.750	5
Television	2.550	6	Neighbours	2.524	6
Press	2.542	7	Government Worker(s)	2.417	7
Government Worker(s)	2.374	8	Store	1.929	8
Meetings	2.366	9	Press	1.357	9
Teachers	2.282	10	Television	1.000	10

to rate each of the sources on a four-point rating scale as to their relative importance in answering the questions included in the three primary dependent variable categories analyzed previously. No attempt was made in this initial survey to separate media functions with regard to specific variables. The data reveal the perceived dominance of radio in both communities followed in respective order by church and family. The influence of television is ranked sixth in importance and is viewed as providing only minor support towards information levels and perspectives of the variables under study. Interestingly, the teacher was ranked in the lower position in the television community and in the fifth rank in the control community. The decreased social interaction as a result of television viewing may be a major factor in the apparent discrepancy. Similarly, the role of the press viewed as more prominent in the television sample was primarily due to the publication of a bi-lingual newspaper (Eskimo and English) in the community approximately two weeks prior to the survey. This type of print media is notably lacking in the control community.

Selection of Most and Least Important Source. The overwhelming dominance of radio as a primary information source was also noted in the responses generated for the one most useful source in answering the questions. Seventy-five per cent of the television community respondents mentioned radio, and 54% of the control community. Television was mentioned by only 2 respondents (1.5%) in the television community. The foremost least important source for the television sample was teachers, with newspapers garnering the greatest attention in the control sample. The extremes noted in the specification of the one most and least important source thus correlate exactly with the rank ordering of source ratings.

Projected Utility of Television Programming in Community

When the television respondents were asked to project what they considered to be a primary utility role for television within the context of community information and educational requirements, over 50% of the responses were centred on the 'preservation of traditional life-style and values'. Depiction of progress in the community and highlighting of major community problems ranked second and third respectively. An additional essential requirement suggested by 75% of the sample was that programming should be in the Eskimo language only. The remaining 25% opted for a mix of Eskimo and English. These results bring into sharp relief the potential application of educational television within the community. Building 'localness into production' through active native participation would appear as a minimal requisite towards effective communication.

CONCLUSIONS AND DISCUSSION

Prior to presenting general conclusions, it is useful to reiterate that the present study deals with a uniquely defined population with a paucity of directly related research with which to compare results. Equally important, the baseline data gathered may be influenced by a variety of independent variables other than those being primarily tested. Any firm conclusions concerning the effects of television in this perspective await the results of a developmental study presently in progress. With these reservations in mind, the following conclusions are cautiously advanced: ·
1. The influence of Frontier Television in terms of cognitive acquisition of national issues appears to be marginal with only one index out of six (identification of two main languages in Canada) being significantly higher in the television community as opposed to the control community.
2. At the international system level the yield was more striking. Significant differences were detected in the ability to define international problems as

well as to propose solutions to those enumerated. The conceptual framework for the general term 'international problems' appears to be more internalized within the television community, possibly resulting from exposure to a less abstract form of information reception.

3. The measures of social impact produced the more salient intercommunity differences. Television respondents held significantly higher employment mobility aspirations for sons and daughters, perceived language and culture to be more significant indicators of Eskimo differences from other people and held significantly more apparent dissatisfaction with their present life-style than their counterparts in the control community. Respondents in the television community were also more national-oriented in desired travel destinations.

4. No differences were noted between the two communities with respect to specification of major information sources. In both samples radio was rated as the foremost individual source, followed in respective order by the church and the family. Television occupied a tertiary role, being ranked in sixth place of importance in the comparison of scale-rating means. The influence of radio was particularly salient in the selection of the one most important source, being mentioned by 75% of the television sample and 54% of the control group. Television was rarely mentioned in this probe.

5. The preservation of traditional life-style and values was projected as the primary utility role for television within the context of community educational requirements. Associated with this specification was a perceived requirement for programmes to be broadcast in the native regional dialect. These measures left little doubt about the importance attached to affirming and reinforcing the traditional language and culture of the community.

On the whole, it cannot be concluded that television has greatly affected the community in terms of direct knowledge gain of both national and international issues and events. Even where significant differences were found, the comparative levels were low. Speculative reasons for this are numerous and perhaps best exemplified in the fundamental lack of understanding of the language of the broadcasting format coupled with the complexities of grasping the visual literacy demanded by the fast-paced, novel medium. The absence of a daily news programme (for those who do understand English) may also have been a major contributor to the low knowledge levels.

Significant differences found in the social impact indices, however, suggest a trend supporting the influence of television, an effect which in consideration of the knowledge levels, may be incidental. An analogous finding is suggested by Schramm (1961) when he notes, "...most of a child's learning from television is incidental. By this we mean the learning that takes place when a viewer goes to television for entertainment and stores up certain items of information without seeking them." In the present study, even though television is not perceived as an important source of information, the imperceptible influence of the medium may be operational. Thus, while radio is presently perceived as the dominant information source (even though it has not notably contributed to knowledge acquisition of international and national issues) primarily because of selected broadcasts in the Eskimo language, it is anticipated that this influence will decrease with the extension of full-service television and the gradual comprehension of both the language and conventions of the medium.

In summary, the initial results of this study suggest several implications for developing nations and regions. In the first instance, the 'incidental impact' of television as we have noted appears to have fostered a dichotomous position. On the one hand, the mobility aspirations for respondents' children suggest a vastly changing orientation from traditional stances. Unless property coordinated, however, as Schramm (1964) points out, the effect may be negative and one of 'raising the social temperature by raising aspirations when the existing conditions are not ready to satisfy them'. Conversely, the respondents' expressed valuing of, and adherence to, traditional ways of life imply a television mediated 'segregation from the past' effect and a reaction to irrelevant programming as reflected in the various dramatic series, variety and musical shows and, importantly, commercials. The wholesale exporting of a southern value system in this circumstance may be counterproductive and dissonance-producing. Rejection of the system may be the end-product of such an arrangement, rather than acculturation into the mainstream of national life.

Concurrently, however, the medium appears well intrenched in the community and viewing participation rates promise to increase rather than decrease. The feasibility of both formal and informal education broadcasting within this context appear significant. The fuller potential of the medium, however, may only be satisfied through sustained collaboration with, and the active participation of, the native target audience if a purposive educational application of television is to be relevant to both the deep-rooted culture and environment.

REFERENCES

Backstrom, C H and Hursh, C D (1963) 'Survey Research'. Northwestern University Press, Evanston

Chu, G (1966) 'When Television Comes to a Traditional Village'. Paper presented at the Pacific Chapter of the American Association for Public Opinion Research, San Francisco

Coldevin, G (1972) 'The impact of mass media upon the development of international orientations'. In 'Aspects of Educational Technology' Vol VI (ed) K. Austwick and N D C Harris. Pitman, London

Coldevin, G (1974a) 'The potential role of educational technology in the development of international perspectives'. 'British Journal of Educational Technology' Vol 5, No 67

Coldevin, G (1974b) 'Educational television research in India'. 'Public Telecommunications Review' Vol 2, No 1

Deutschmann, P J (1963) 'The mass media in an underdeveloped village'. 'Journalism Quarterly' Vol 40

Dominion Bureau of Statistics (1961) 'Occupational Classification Manual'. Queen's Printer, Ottawa

Rogers, E (1969) 'Modernization Among Peasants'. Holt, Rinehart and Winston, New York

Schramm, W et al (1961) 'Television in the Lives of Our Children' p 75.
Stanford University Press, Stanford, California

Schramm, W (1964) 'Mass Media and National Development'. Stanford
University Press, Stanford, California

Interactive instructional designs

DANNY G LANGDON

This paper describes seven specific instructional design formats and illustrates the components which comprise each. The majority of the designs were researched and developed by the author. Proper credit should be given for the conceptual framework of the Learner Controlled Instruction design to Robert F Mager, and Robert Meran for the Core Package. The remaining instructional designs were formulated by the author to meet specific student and teacher needs. The following designs are included:

(a) Learner Controlled Instruction
(b) Adjunct Study Guide
(c) Construct Lesson Plan
(d) Tri-Level Study Guide
(e) Audio/Workbook
(f) Core Package
(g) Interactive Text

I should like to emphasize that all of these designs were formulated with the student uppermost in mind, simply because it is the student who does the learning. Efficiency and effectiveness of student learning is always stressed. Each design is based on a minimum of three essential features:

(a) Learner goals and objectives
(b) Interaction
(c) Feedback

I am especially thankful to the American College of Life Underwriters, for it is an institution that truly believes in instructional technology and has provided the facilities, manpower, and financial resources for researching and developing many of these designs. Among others, the reader is referred to the following further instructional designs authored by other individuals:

Instructional Design	Principal Author
'Linear Programming'	B F Skinner
'Branch Programming'	Norman Crowder
'Individualized Learning Packages (ILP)'	Phillip Kapfer

'Personalized Systems of Instruction (PSI)'   Fred Keller
'Information Mapping'   Robert Horn
'Criterion Referenced Instruction'   Robert Mager

Before describing each instructional design, a definition is in order. An instructional design is, in simplest terms, a physical layout which prescribes the manner in which a student should proceed to learn, or a teacher to teach (or any given medium), or a combination of both. Instructional design is also a process by which we go about determining needs, writing, and validating; but this is more involved and would be impossible to cover in this brief paper. Thus, the author has chosen to deal only with the description of each instructional design format, how it is used by the student and/or teacher, and what outcomes can be expected from its use.

LEARNER CONTROLLED INSTRUCTION

Using the principle advocated first by Dr Robert F Mager, and in working in consultation with Dr Mager, I first designed a Learner Controlled Instruction (LCI) programme for the Bank of America, San Francisco, California, while employed by General Programmed Teaching Inc. This design is essentially composed of three major components: (1) behaviourally stated, learner objectives (see Illustration #1); (2) existing reference sources (books, media, persons, etc) keyed to the objectives; and (3) criterion test instruments (see Illustration #2). Students are given a procedural guide (see Illustration #3). * Essentially an on-the-job design, the course monitor is given a procedural guide as well. Students select and pursue the objectives as they wish, using whatever resources they desire. They initiate at what point they desire testing. All aspects of instruction are controlled by the students - hence the name, Learner Controlled Instruction.

The beauty of this design lies in its simplicity. It is so effective in promoting not only the learning of objectives, but also many other auxiliary outcomes, that it is somewhat hard for the individual who has never developed one or seen it used to believe such a design could produce such positive results.

An important aspect of this design, in addition to the variety of written and other media sources that might be made available as resource materials, is the availability of persons who have the expertise which the student is attempting to acquire. The student should have free access to such individuals, tempered only by real constraints on any interference it would cause these individuals in performing their own functions. As in the case of the Bank of America, this means access to tellers, equipment operators, managers, and so forth.

In simplest terms, the student selects which objectives he will work on and in what order. He uses the available resources (ie print, subject-matter experts) to the extent he desires, and then asks to be tested. The form of testing is related directly to the objectives, including written, oral

---

* All illustrations referred to are to be found together at the end of the paper.

presentation, task performance, simulations, or what have you. If the student enters with an existing knowledge or performance capability on any given objectives, he can be tested immediately. Entry-level knowledge, therefore, can be accounted for and thus an efficient programme exists.

Several outcomes can be anticipated from the use of the LCI design, including: higher levels of student confidence in his learning; instructional time reduced; resources being used on an as-needed basis; students being able to begin any time; development of a more positive attitude towards learning in that students do not compete with one another but rather with the external criteria of the objectives themselves; promotion of decision-making capabilities in that decisions must be exercised by the student throughout the use of the design.

Finally, although it might be thought that this design could have its widest application in industrial training needs, its application to the academic field should not be any less. It would require, as in industry, the freeing of administrative shackles and a reorientation to other means of 'grading' the student.

ADJUNCT STUDY GUIDE

Working on the idea that students using interactive (eg programmed instruction) texts receive confirming feedback (answers to questions) as isolated bits of information, the author has devised a direct means for students to tie these confirmations together. It is common for students to receive (or read) information, answer a question, receive confirmation, and to repeat this cycle on new information. By placing such confirmations within a summary (like a chapter summary to a book), the student is given the opportunity of not only receiving a confirmation but having these many confirmations tied together in the summary.

The Adjunct Study Guide is composed of three primary components:

(a) purpose and significance (Illustration #4)
(b) objectives and questions (Illustration #6)
(c) summary (Illustration #7)

Additional components can be added for specific learning needs - ie essay questions (#8), content outline (#5).

The unique feature of this design lies in the functions served by the Summary. The Summary consists of the answers to criterion questions (objectives), which have been connected by information that ties them together. This 'information' is not material we necessarily expect the students to be responsible for, but rather serves to tie the objectives together. The value of the Summary is both for obtaining confirming feedback and as a summary which ties objectives together. It serves a further added function for review purposes prior to some form of testing.

The order in which the student uses the Study Guide is as follows. For a given assignment (lesson unit) the student: (1) first reads the Purpose and Significance and Goals, so as to gain an overall appreciation of what the assignment entails and why it is of importance; (2) scans the Content Outline

159

to gain an overview of the assignment from a subject-matter standpoint; (3) completes each objective page, reading the suggested resource materials (or using any media specified), and answers the enabling and criterion questions provided; (4) checks the answer for each criterion question; (5) reads the summary from beginning to end after completing all the individual objectives. He may then answer any essay questions or similar components added to the Study Guide.

Uses made of the Adjunct Study Guide are primarily for independent study or as preparation for in-class instruction. It is especially effective in conjunction with the instructional design which follows.

CONSTRUCT LESSON PLAN

This design, the latest work of the author, was developed in response to a recognition that student-entry-level knowledge and preparatory study prior to instruction is generally not accounted for, and therefore not followed through within the classroom. Classroom instruction may be said to be inefficient in this respect. The author has devised two methods for accounting for student-entry-level knowledge, which have been labelled the Testing Pattern and the Screening Pattern. The author has devised a means for the teacher to then assemble a lesson plan based on this assessment of student-entry-level knowledge while in the classroom. Thus, the teacher constructs a Lesson Plan to meet the immediate learning needs of the students. A detailed discussion of this design may be found elsewhere under its title within these proceedings.

TRI-LEVEL STUDY GUIDE

Designed for independent study use, this design by the author recognizes varying entry-level knowledge by students. Thus, while not all varying degrees of entry-level knowledge could possibly be efficiently and effectively provided for, this design does attempt to account for entry-level knowledge at three specific levels:

(a) complete knowledge or mastery of an objective
(b) a general entry-level knowledge or one that needs only
   general reminders of content or skills previously learned, and
(c) no existing entry-level knowledge

Illustration #9 outlines the three entry-level stages this design is formulated to meet, and the parts of the design used by the students for each entry-level stage. These parts are illustrated by example in Illustration #10. A student with complete knowledge of the objective would simply read the objective and complete the criterion test item below it. A student entering with some knowledge, or needing only certain reminders, would read the objective, read the general information section, then complete the criterion test item. A student with no entering knowledge would read the objective, read the general information section, complete the instruction section, then answer the criterion test item. Additional criterion test items can be added so that a student trying all three avenues would not become attuned to the one criterion test item. Illustration #11 summarizes the three paths of entry level in this particular design. Additional levels could, of course, be added. In brief, levels are determined relative to the developmental testing programme that should be used in developing a given programme. It is within such testing that the levels are identified.

AUDIO/WORKBOOK

The author formulated this design in response to the emergence and widespread use of audio instruction in the cassette format. Of equal importance with the instructional format for this design is the developmental procedure which is used to produce the programme. Recognizing that traditionally we have produced written, audio, and visual programmes by first beginning with the written word, the author explored producing each 'media on its own terms'. The meaning of this is that rather than beginning the production of an audio programme, for instance, in the written word, we begin by making audio-recordings. The difference is a more free-flowing, natural mode of presentation.

As the title of this design suggests, the audio/workbook is a combination of audiotape (usually in cassette form) and response book (workbook). A response book is employed in order to require the listener to be more than a passive audience by requiring him to respond to activities and questions. The book can also contain relevant illustrations to the audio presentation. The latter is important when one considers that a student cannot read and look at an illustration (ie graph, chart, etc) at the same time, but he can listen and look at the illustration. Apart from illustrations that may be used, other essential features of the response book include:
1. A statement of the objectives for the audio programme, as shown in Illustration #13.
2. Space to respond to questions (enabling and criterion) as shown by Illustration #14. Note that questions may be printed or asked on the tape itself. Varying where the question is to be found is important to the extent that it keeps the listener attending to both the audio presentation and written materials.
3. Space to include the answer to questions, as in Illustration #15. Again, question answers may be printed or sometimes given on the audiotape itself. As with questions, attention considerations apply in determining where the answer will appear.

In terms of the audiotape itself, we generally begin with an overview of what the tape is concerned with and why it should be studied. An indication is then given to stop the tape and read the objectives for the unit under study. Illustration #12 provides an example. This is then followed by proceeding into a description of the first objective or set of objectives. After content presentation, the student is directed to stop the tape and answer a question or series of questions. He receives confirmation to his written answers in the response book or from the tape, as described previously.

As important as the physical design format itself, is the matter in which audio instruction is produced. Illustration #16 summarizes the approach recommended by the author. You are referred in particular to the three boxes to the left of box number 5. Rather than producing an audio programme by starting with a written script, it is recommended that once the objectives (and criterion questions and answers) are defined, the developer proceeds to produce in the audio medium itself. Since the programme is intended to be an audio programme, it is better to produce in the audio format initially. If there is a difference between the written word and the spoken word, then this procedure should be more sound. The author has also found it is quicker to produce the programme following this approach. The essential value lies in producing a programme that is much more natural and free-flowing. Care must be taken in editing transcriptions made of the audio recording to assure that the audio quality is not lost in editing and rewriting. As a further note, the implications for following a similar procedure in producing visual-based programmes should be obvious. That is, to what extent can we produce a visual programme by starting in the visual medium, testing to make the most out of it, and then adding audio or written media to support the visual? Further details on this approach may be found in the author's article entitled, 'Media Messages on their Own Terms'.

CORE PACKAGE

Basically used for skills-training programmes, this design is an attempt to tie several academic disciplines to facilitate the student's acquisition of a skill. Thus, in the study of electronics, for example, instructional components are provided for the related study of mathematics, science, or other such disciplines. The design used for each skill or discipline area is highly procedurally oriented; thus it may be used eventually as back-up on-the-job, job aid. This design was essentially formulated by Dr Robert F Meran for use by high school dropouts involved in government-sponsored skills-training programmes. The author personally worked with Dr Meran in developing and validating several packages of materials in this format.

Illustrations #17 to #22 exhibit the various design components. For example, a unit on learning to become a television cameraman begins with an overall description of the job responsibilities, as exemplified by Illustration #17. This is followed by a more detailed listing of the specific skills necessary to perform part of this job, as in Illustration #18, where the objectives are listed. Note that not only are the objectives listed, but the back-up components from certain academic areas, such as maths and science, are also listed.

For each job-skill objective, a Job Sheet is provided, as in Illustration #19. The student uses this to learn and practise a particular skill as defined by the objective. All necessary tools, material, reference sources, and the exact procedure he should follow are given. As mentioned earlier, while the job sheet is normally used for initial acquisition and practice of the skill, it may also serve as an on-the-job, job aid.

Illustration #20 shows a back-up component to a job sheet. As is often the case, before a skill can be acquired there is some necessary identification of component parts. This is the function of the Assignment Sheet as illustrated.

Illustrations #21 and #22 show how academic subjects are related to the acquisition of job skills. In this case the academic areas of maths and science have been used. Depending on the job skills, other academic areas may be employed, such as language arts, health, etc. Such areas are defined only as the specific job-skill objective itself requires it. The implication for teachers from various disciplinary areas working in concert with one another for the common benefit of their students should be obvious. Indeed, this is the real value of the Core Package.

INTERACTIVE TEXT

The Interactive Text draws on the principles and procedures of programmed instruction, although not in the sense of small-frame programming. The author draws a clear distinction between information and instruction, and in so doing makes a point that this design is for instruction. Essential components of the Interactive Text include Objectives (#24), which are treated in a descriptive manner rather than mere listing; Content (#25), which is directed specifically at the objectives, with necessary background and enabling questions and answers; and finally, criterion questioning and feedback (#26). Other necessary requirements are presented in terms of pre-testing (#23), and post-testing (#27).

SUMMATION

The foregoing descriptions can only, of course, serve as an introduction to each instructional design. The reader is referred to additional sources written by Langdon which are listed at the end of this paper. The purpose in presenting this thumbnail sketch of each design is to bring them to the foreground as possible designs to be replicated by the reader to meet his own student and teacher needs. It may well be that a combination of certain components among these designs can be restructured by the reader to meet learning requirements which any one of these designs does not specifically address itself to. As the author has found in his own application, it is usually a case of using two or more of these designs in combination to meet specific needs; for example a combination of the Adjunct Study Guide and follow up by use of the Construct Lesson Plan. The author would be only too happy to answer specific inquiries concerning any of these designs, particularly in terms of needs not filled by any of these or other design needs which the reader feels he has.

FURTHER READING

Additional information on these designs may be found in the following sources:
Langdon, Danny G 'Interactive Instructional Designs for Individualized
    Learning'. Educational Technology Publications, 140 Sylvan Avenue,
    Englewood Cliffs, New Jersey 07632

Langdon, Danny G (1970) 'Confirmation via (and a) summary'. 'NSPI Journal'
    September
Langdon, Danny G (1972) 'Media messages on their own terms'. 'Educational
    Technology ' June
Langdon, Danny G (1973) 'Instructional designs for a case study approach'.
    'Educational Technology ' October
Langdon, Danny G (1975) 'Construct lesson plan - improving instructional
    efficiency'. 'Educational Technology' April
Langdon, Danny G 'Constructing an Efficient and Effective Lesson Plan'
    (a book as yet unpublished)

ILLUSTRATIONS FOR INTERACTIVE INSTRUCTIONAL DESIGNS

The author wishes to thank Educational Technology Publications, Inc., Englewood, New Jersey for permission to reprint the following illustrations which appeared in a text of the author's, entitled, INTERACTIVE INSTRUCTIONAL DESIGNS FOR INDIVIDUALIZED LEARNING. All illustrations for each instructional design are presented in sequence as actually used by students or teachers.

ILLUSTRATION #1

III. STARTING PLANTS

      H.   Rooting Media and Equipment
           Goal: Upon completion of this unit, you will be able to properly
                   prepare rooting media, understand the need for proper
                   media to assure plant growth, and be familiar with the
                   tools and container requirements for growing plants prior
                   to planting in open ground.

Objectives	Proposed Completion Date	Criterion Test	Completion Date	Verification
1. List a minimum of five moisture-holding substances that can be used as rooting media for cuttings (MF-Chap. 9, SWGB-p. 81, SGC-pp. 16-17).		TW		
2. Describe two methods for sterilizing soil when soil is intended for use in a rooting mixture (MF-Chap. 9, F-"Better Gardens").		TO		
3. In terms of either ratios or percentage, list the component breakdown of at least two commonly used mixtures used as rooting media (MF-Chap. 9, Pamphlet-"Potting Plants").		TW		
4.				

Illustration #2

TW III-H-5

CRITERION TEST

Name .... Date ....

Certain types of chemicals can be used to treat wooden flats in order to prevent wood decay. Which of the following are correct chemicals to use?

........A. Copper Naphthenate
........B. Cuprinol
........C. Isopropyl Alcohol
........D. Petroleum
........E. Varnish

ILLUSTRATION #3

STUDENT GUIDE TO LCI

It will be necessary to provide students with a guide describing what LCI is and how it works. The outline of the more detailed contents of such a guide might be as follows:

I   What is Learner Controlled Instruction?

II   How LCI works

    A. General Description
    B. Components
        1. Objectives
        2. Criterion Tests

III   Responsibilities of the Evaluator

    A. Program Administration
    B. As a Resource Person
    C. As an Evaluator of Criterion Tests

IV   Responsibilities of the Student

    A. Objectives and Planning
    B. References and Resources
    C. Criterion Tests
        1. TW (with example)
        2. TO
        3. P
        4. FP

V   General Procedural Guide (checklist)

SYNTHESIS OF MONETARY AND FISCAL POLICY

PURPOSE

The two previous assignments covered the banking system, the mechanics of bank deposit expansion and contraction, and the tools of monetary policy. One purpose of this assignment is to examine precisely the impact of monetary policies on money, interest rates, investment, and output. The textbook refers to this as a synthesis of monetary analysis and income analysis.

Another purpose of this assignment is to identify the goals of fiscal policy and to examine the tools of such policy. As in the case of monetary policy, the material deals with the impact of fiscal policy on the level of income and employment.

SIGNIFICANCE

The Employment Act of 1946 committed the government of our country to promote favorable economic conditions. Monetary and fiscal policies are the major mechanisms used to attain those goals. The CLU candidate, as a responsible member of the community and as a member of a vital industry, is concerned with the profound impact of monetary and fiscal policy on the economic well-being of policyowners, the insurance industry, the community in general, and himself and his family.

The role of government in the economic and business life of the private sector is highly controversial. This assignment raises many important questions, but it also provides the analytical tools required for undertaking rational examination of them and for reaching mature, responsible judgments. Furthermore, it provides insight into the conditions of uncertainty under which governmental decision makers operate.

GOALS

1. To understand how an interaction of fiscal and monetary policy can be used to achieve a growing full-employment economy.

2. To understand why both the national budget and the national debt are measured in terms of their relationship to GNP.

TEXT REFERENCES

Samuelson - Chapters 18 and 19 (including Appendix to Chapter 19)

Summary Begins on Page 9.17

169

OUTLINE OF SUBJECT MATTER

1. Monetary and fiscal policy (S 334-345)

    a. Liquidity preference and marginal efficiency of investment
    b. Fiscal policy and income determination
    c. Interaction between fiscal and monetary policy

2. Fiscal policy (S 355-360)

    a. Goals of fiscal policy
    b. Automatic stabilizers
    c. Weapons of discretionary fiscal policy

3. The budget (S 360-363)

    a. Surplus and deficit financing
    b. The "new" economics
    c. Full-employment budget surplus or deficit

4. The public debt (S 364-371)

    a. Burdens
    b. External debt and internal debt
    c. Measuring the public debt

SYNTHESIS OF MONETARY AND FISCAL POLICY

MONETARY AND FISCAL POLICY

1 *Objective*   Given a liquidity-preference schedule, explain how monetary policy is used to effect a change in interest rates.

Reference   Samuelson pages 334-335 and Assignment 7 Objective 3

Notes

Question   Using the liquidity-preference schedule on pages 334-335 of Samuelson, expalin how monetary policy is used to effect a change in interest rates.

Answer   CHECK SUMMARY ITEM #1

SYNTHESIS OF MONETARY AND FISCAL POLICY

SUMMARY

Monetary and Fiscal Policy

The previous assignments have shown how changes in the level of national income could be achieved using either government tax and expenditure policies or government controls over the supply of money and credit. In the modern mixed economy, however, any attempt to achieve a desired change in national income requires the coordination of both fiscal and monetary policies. This assignment will show how these stabilization policies work and interact to achieve such a change.

Assume that the desired economic goal is to increase GNP. Such an expansion could be initiated using either monetary policy or fiscal policy. First, let's consider how monetary action to increase the supply of money could be used to initiate a chain of responses resulting in an increase in GNP.

#1 The equilibrium rate of interest is determined by both the supply of money and the demand for money. The supply of money is controlled by monetary policy. The demand for money is determined by the various motives for holding money. One factor which influences the demand for money is the interest rate, with demand varying inversely with the level of interest. As interest rates decline, the demand for holding money increases. This relationship between interest rates and the total demand for money is graphically illustrated by the blue line in Figure 18-1 (a) on page 335 of Samuelson. Samuelson refers to this blue line as the "liquidity-preference schedule." Since the interest rate is determined by the intersection of the demand for money and the supply of money, the liquidity-preference schedule actually shows the relationship between the demand for money, the supply of money, and the interest rates. It illustrates why an increase in the supply of money leads to a reduction in the interest rate. In Samuelson's graph, the increase in the supply of money from A to B means that the new supply of money intersects the liquidity-preference line (demand for money) at point B, which is at a lower interest rate than the previous intersection at point A.

#2 An increase in the supply of money can also provide an increase in the availability of credit. As the level of interest rates declines, investment projects which had been delayed because of prevailing interest rates now become more profitable to undertake. Other projects are also undertaken. The marginal-efficiency-of-investment schedule illustrates the induced increase in investment that results as interest rates decline. The decrease in interest rates from A to B shown in Figure 18-1 (b) on page 335 of Samuelson results in an increase in investment from A' to B'.

ILLUSTRATION #8

ILLUSTRATIVE ESSAY QUESTION

Explain how each of the so-called "built-in (or automatic) stabilizers" may operate to minimize fluctuations in our national income.

Answer   SEE PAGES 9.25 AND 9.26

ILLUSTRATION #9

LEVEL	ENTRY LEVEL KNOWLEDGE
1	Complete knowledge of objective
2	High but not complete knowledge of objective, or needs only reminders of content
3	Low or no existing knowledge of objective

LEVEL	PARTS OF DESIGN USED
1	Objective. Criterion Test Item
2	Objective. General Information. Criterion Test Item
3	Objective. General Information Instruction. Criterion Test Item

ILLUSTRATION #10

STUDY GUIDE

OBJECTIVE: Given the lengths of two sides of a right triangle, calculate the length of the third side so as to demonstrate the Pythagorean Theorem.

Criterion Test:

If side a is 6 in. and side b is 8 in. in the triangle at the right, what is the length of side c? (check p. 14 for answer)

(Depending on students, the following discrimination-type question might be a suitable substitute for the above:
Which of the following equations and/or problems correctly express the relationship between a, b, and c in the given triangle (of the illustration above)?

.....a. $a^2 + b^2 = c^2$

.....b. $b^2 + c^2 = a^2$

.....c. $b = \sqrt{c^2 - a^2}$

.....d. side c equals 10 in.

.....e. $6 + 8$ equals $\sqrt{14}$

.....f. $c = 14$

GENERAL INFORMATION

The Pythagorean Theorem is one of the most useful theorems in mathematics. It states an important relationship between the lengths of the legs and the length of the hypotenuse of a right triangle. The theorem states that in any right triangle the square of the hypotenuse is equal to the sum of the squares of the legs.

INSTRUCTION

Read pages 265-266 of JDD, then answer the following: (Answers—p. 14)

1. State the Pythagorean Theorem.
2. The Pythagorean Theorem applies to:
   .....a. all triangles   .....c. right triangles
   .....b. equilateral triangles   .....d. isosceles triangles
3. If the hypotenuse of a right triangle is expressed as c and the sides as a and b, how would the equation be expressed for the Pythagorean Theorem?
4. Calculate problems 1-5 on page 269 of JDD.
5. Calculate the Criterion Test Item above. (check page 14 for answers)

ILLUSTRATION #11

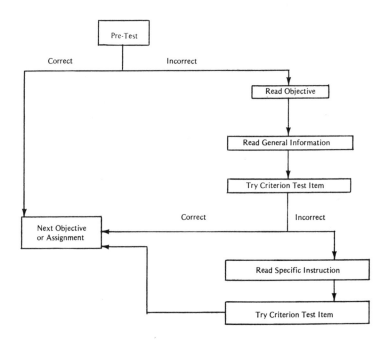

ILLUSTRATION 12

Course 3
Assignment 13

SCRIPT

NARRATOR: This is the beginning of the review of assignment 6, entitled *"Premiums, Experience Rating, and Reserves."* This assignment is basically concerned with the cost of group life insurance. The first aspect dealt with is that of premiums. This is followed by a discussion of the net cost of group insurance, due to experience rating, and then by a discussion of acquired reserves. At the tone, stop the tape and turn to page 139 in your response booklet. (PAUSE.) Read the objectives on assignment 6, then restart the tape.

(TONE)

Rates for group life insurance must meet two objectives. First of all, they must be adequate. Secondly, they must be equitable. An *adequate rate* is one that provides, in the aggregate, enough premium income to meet the total expected losses, establish proper reserves, and pay for administrative expenses. An *equitable* rate means that a rate charged to a policyholder must reflect the value of the risk assumed for that particular policyholder plus his fair proportion of the expenses required. In other words, a particular policyholder that presents a risk which is higher than average should pay a premium that is higher than average. Now turn to page 140 in your response booklet and write your answer to question 1. (PAUSE.) You are to: "Describe the objectives of rate making as they apply to group life insurance."

(TONE)

ILLUSTRATION 13

Course 3
Assignment 13

When you have completed the Review of *Assignment 13*, you will:

1. State how an injured worker recovered damages from his employer under common law, and list the three common law defenses that the employer could use to defeat the worker's claim for damages.

2. Explain the fundamental principle of workmen's compensation in terms of employer liability and legal interpretation.

3. List the five fundamental objectives of workmen's compensation.

4. List the five major requirements that an injured worker must fulfill to collect workmen's compensation benefits.

5. Describe the four major types of workmen's compensation benefits that are available to injured workers.

6. Given a list of possible statements regarding the effectiveness of workmen's compensation, identify any correct statements.

Turn on the tape.

177

Illustration #14

Course 3

Assignment 13

Question 5

Describe the major types of workmen's compensation benefits that are available to injured workers.

Check your answer on page 149.

Course 3

Assignment 13

Question 3

(When you hear the tone, write your answer below.)

The Answer Is Given on the Tape.
Turn on the Tape.

ILLUSTRATION #15

ANSWER TO QUESTION 5

Four major types of benefits are available:

1. The costs of hospital care, physician care, surgical and medical services are normally paid in full in most jurisdictions.

2. Disability income benefits are paid for stated periods depending on the degree of disability. Disability can be temporary total, permanent total, temporary partial, and permanent partial. The amount paid for disability benefits depends on the degree of disability.

3. Death benefits to the dependent survivors may be paid. These benefits include cash payments for stated periods and a funeral allowance.

4. Rehabilitation services are often provided to the injured worker.

Turn on the tape.

ILLUSTRATION #16

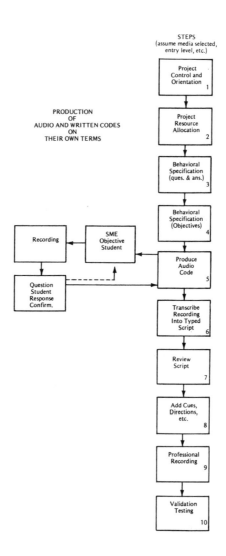

STEPS
(assume media selected, entry level, etc.)

Project Control and Orientation — 1

PRODUCTION
OF
AUDIO AND WRITTEN CODES
ON
THEIR OWN TERMS

Project Resource Allocation — 2

Behavioral Specification (ques. & ans.) — 3

Behavioral Specification (Objectives) — 4

Recording

SME Objective Student

Produce Audio Code — 5

Question Student Response Confirm.

Transcribe Recording Into Typed Script — 6

Review Script — 7

Add Cues, Directions, etc. — 8

Professional Recording — 9

Validation Testing — 10

ILLUSTRATION #17

PURPOSE AND SIGNIFICANCE

TELEVISION CAMERAMAN

Within the total system of television operations, the TV Camera-man plays a unique and special role. He is, in effect, the eyes of the audience. His camera is not simply a device to capture images before it, but rather his camera must be thought of as an extension of his own field of vision that will then become the field of vision for the audience that will immediately or ultimately view a live or taped program.

Under the direction of a Program Director, the TV Cameraman will use a video camera to photograph scenes for taping and broadcasting. This necessitates a great deal of knowledge and artistry on the part of the cameraman. He must know how to operate different types of video cameras and perform correct camera procedures, such as panning, tilting, dollying, and shot selection. Furthermore, his function in the total effort of television operations necessitates discussing dramatic and presentational effects, mood, and photographic composition of scenes with the Program Director. Knowledge related to basic physics principles, such as levers, is important because he must alter angles or distance of shots for effects.

As you progress through your course of study, it is important that you keep in mind the following goals:

1. Gain the necessary skills to effectively operate the video camera.
2. Appreciate the artistic necessity to produce a pleasing shot commensurate with the effect and mood desired.
3. Understand and cooperate within the total operation of television programming, including especially your role with other personnel.

See also: Dictionary of Occupational Titles, listing 143.062.

ILLUSTRATION #18

PERFORMANCE OBJECTIVE CHECKLIST

NAME	DATE ENTERED..........	DATE COMPLETED..........

TELEVISION CAMERA OPERATION

When you have completed this course, you will: COMPLETION
                                                                   DATE

1. Identify five major types of television cameras based on their use in the small studio, classroom, industrial training program, or large commercial studio.   ....

2. Describe the principles of photo-electricity, persistence of vision, and scanning as they relate to video camera operations. Sc. Sheet #1. Math Sh. #1.   ....

3. Describe four differences between a vidicon camera and an image orthicon camera. Assign. Sheet #1.   ....

4. Identify five different types of camera mounts. Assign. Sheet #2, 3, 4, 5. Sc. Sheet #2.   ....

5. Identify parts of a panning head and operate with smooth function. Assign. Sheet #6. Math Sh. #2.   ....

6. Identify and operate the major camera adjusting mechanisms of focusing control, panning tension control, lens turret control, tilting tension control, panning handle (guide arm), and handle angle adjustment. Sc. Sheet #3, Math Sheet #3, Assign. Sheet #7.   ....

7. Demonstrate proper focusing procedure on a static object. Assign. Sheet #8. Sc. Sheet #4.   ....

8. Operate the diaphragm opening (f-stop) of a video camera to demonstrate how the lens affects the depth of field. Assign. Sheet #13. Sc. Sheet #5, Math Sheet #4.   ....

9. Demonstrate proper focusing on subject moving toward and away from camera. Assign. Sh. #8. Sc. Sheet #6.   ....

10. Demonstrate simultaneous dollying and focusing. Assign. Sheet #9.   ....

(continued, next page)

ILLUSTRATION #19

JOB SHEET 8

NAME .... APPROVED ....

1. OBJECTIVE:
   To be able to operate the diaphragm opening (f-stop) of a video camera to demonstrate how the lens affects the depth of field.

2. TOOLS AND MATERIALS NEEDED:
   A.   Television studio camera
   B.   50mm. vidicon lens

3. GENERAL INSTRUCTIONS AND INFORMATION:
   For a specific lens, a large diaphragm opening (small f-stop number) will decrease the depth of field; a small diaphragm opening (high f-stop) will increase the depth of field.

4. REFERENCES:
   Assignment Sheet #13
   Television Production Handbook, Zettl, p. 29, 30
   Math Sheet #4
   Science Problem #5

5. PROCEDURES:
   A.   Set up camera for studio production.
   B.   Set 50mm. lens at f/1.9.
   C.   Place three objects in front of camera; one 6 feet away, one 15 feet away, and the third 20 feet away.
   D.   Note how many of the three objects are in focus.
   E.   Focus on center object.
   F.   Change f-stop to f/8 setting.
   G.   Note number of objects still in focus and compare to results of f/1.9.
   H.   Repeat procedures for f/22 setting.

6. QUESTIONS:
   Listed below are possible answers to the questions. Choose the correct answers and *WRITE* or *PRINT* them in the spaces provided.
   increase   decrease
   A.   If a 50mm. lens diaphragm setting is changed from f/1.9 to f/8, the depth of field will_____ .
   B.   If a 50mm. lens diaphragm setting is changed from f/22 to f/8, the depth of field will_____ .
   C.   If the diaphragm opening of a lens is increased, the depth of field will_____ .
   D.   See Instructor. Demonstrate objective.

ANSWERS:	
A.	Decrease
B.	Increase
C.	Decrease

Illustration #20

ASSIGNMENT SHEET 13

NAME .... APPROVED ....

I. OBJECTIVE:
To be able to identify parts of a lens.

II. GENERAL INSTRUCTIONS AND INFORMATION:
The function of a lens is mainly to produce a small, clear image of the viewed scene on the television picture tube. The lens you use determines how close or how far away an object will appear (assuming a fixed distance from camera to object). Some lenses make an object seem far away, although the camera is comparatively close to it; other lenses show the object or action at close range, although the camera may be located at some distance from it.

III. REFERENCE:
Television Production Handbook, Zettl. Job Sheet #8.

IV. QUESTION:
Identify the following parts:

..... f-stop adjustment ring   ..... mounting threads
..... f-stops   ..... lens grip
..... distance (in feet)   ..... focus adjustment ring
..... optics   ..... mount

ANSWERS	
1	8
4	7
2	6
5	3

184

Illustration #21

NAME .... APPROVED ....

I. OBJECTIVE:
   To be able to calculate problems using the Inverse Square Law as it applies to determining Relative Aperture Ratios (a factor used in calculating depth of field).

II. MATERIALS NEEDED:
   A. Pen and Paper.

III. GENERAL INSTRUCTIONS AND INFORMATION:
   Depth of Field is that area in which all things appear to be in focus. It is measured from the point nearest the camera which is acceptably sharp to the point farthest from the camera which is acceptably sharp. In the accurate calculation of Depth of Field, several mathematical concepts are brought to bear, including among others the "Inverse Square Law." This law, in turn, involves knowledge of basic concepts related to how numbers are squared and how ratios are expressed.

IV. REFERENCES:
   JDD, Chapter 7
   HFB, Chapter 4
   RM, Chapter 2

V. PROCEDURE (INSTRUCTION):
   A. Review the meaning of ratios (JDD, pp. 229-230).
   B. Review the procedure for squaring a number (RM, p. 48).
   C. State the mathematical relationship expressed in the Inverse Square Law (HFB, Chapter 4, p. 41).
   D. State the formula for calculating relative aperture ratio (f/number).
   E. State the relationship between the Inverse Square Law and the relative aperture ratio formula.
   F. State the effect on f/number when the diameter (D) of a lens decreases; increases. (HFB, p. 42).

VI. QUESTIONS:
   A. As the diameter of the lens opening (increases/decreases) _____, the f/number will be increased.
   B. If the focal length of a given lens is 8 in. and the diameter of the maximum effective aperture is 2 in., the relative aperture would be?_____
   C. If the focal length of a given lens is 4 in. and the diameter of the maximum effective aperture is 1 in., the relative aperture would be?_____
   D. If the focal length of a given lens is 2 in. and the diameter of the maximum effective aperture is 4 in., the relative aperture would be?_____

FOR ANSWERS, SEE
NEXT PAGE

ILLUSTRATION #22

NAME .... APPROVED ....

I.   OBJECTIVE:
     Describe the position and characteristics of the images formed by a
     convex lens for different positions of an object; cite an application
     appropriate for each.

II. MATERIALS NEEDED:
     A.   Convex lens (of known focal length)   C.   Meter stick
     B.   Light box with wire screen   D.   Cardboard screen

III. GENERAL INSTRUCTIONS AND INFORMATION:
     You are going to perform an experiment to demonstrate the relationship
     between the position of an object relative to the focal length of a convex
     lens and the size of the object as it is projected on the opposite side of
     the lens on a screen. The importance lies in the practical application to
     which such relationship is necessary for the lens in a TV camera. You are
     to set up the experiment as described in TC, page 199, and position the
     object (the light source) as specified in the left hand column of the table
     below. Record your observations in the remaining three columns. The
     references listed below will provide you sufficient background to set up
     and record your observations.

IV. REFERENCES:
     Taffel, Visual Physics, pp. 199-205
     UNESCO, p. 180
     TC Workbook, pp. 199-200

V.   PROCEDURE:
     After reading the references listed above, position the object as
     described in the left hand column of the following table. Record your
     observations.

Position of Object	Position of Image	Description of Image	Applications
1. Infinitely far from lens			
2. At a distance from lens greater than twice the focal length (2F)			
3. At twice the focal length (2F)			
4. Between one and two focal lengths (F and 2F) from lens			
5. At the principal focus (F)			
6. Between the principal focus (F) and the lens			

FOR ANSWERS, SEE
NEXT PAGE

ILLUSTRATION #23

CHAPTER I PRE-TEST

You should be able to work each of the following problems on your computer. If you are unable to work any given problems, or you do a problem incorrectly, check the page reference given with the correct answer and proceed directly to that part of Section I dealing with the problem in question. Page numbers are given next to the answers to tell you where in the program to go for detailed instruction. Work all problems before checking answers.

1. Using your computer, divide 420 by 35.   Answer..........

2. Using your computer, multiply 85 times 36.5.   Answer..........

3. At what speed would you be flying to have covered a distance of 200 miles in two hours and thirty minutes?   Answer..........

4. What would be the fuel consumption rate for an aircraft that in 1:30 used twenty gallons of fuel?   Answer..........

5. What would be the True Airspeed of an aircraft showing an Indicated Airspeed of 140 mph, at a Pressure Altitude of 18,000 feet and a temperature of -20°C?   Answer..........

6. What would be the True Altitude of an aircraft showing an Indicated Altitude of 24,200 feet, at a Pressure Altitude of 22,000 feet and a temperature of -10°C?   Answer..........

ANSWERS	IF MISSED, PROCEED TO PAGE:
1. 12	p. 4
2. 3102.5 (approx. 3100)	p. 6
3. 80 mph	p. 8
4. 13.3 GPH	p. 12
5. 185.9 mph	p. 16
6. 26.000 feet	p. 20

ILLUSTRATION #24

CHAPTER I

INTRODUCTION AND OBJECTIVES

This text has been divided into three chapters for the purpose (1) of providing a logical breakdown of related problems; (2) to provide a block of calculations to be learned in one sitting; (3) to learn problems in the same order in which you will most likely use them during training.

It is suggested that you learn all the problems within a chapter in one sitting, then take a break before going to the next chapter.

Chapter I introduces you to the basic layout of an E6-B Flight Computer and to the very essential computations for both preflight planning and inflight calculations. You begin with a basic introduction by identifying the five basic parts of a flight computer. This is followed by direct application of these parts of a flight computer in the calculation of two preflight planning problems. The first type of problem involves giving you two of the three values for Time, Distance, and Speed, and you are to calculate the third, unknown value. The second problem involves giving you two of the three values for Fuel Consumption, Gallons Used, and Time, and you are to calculate the value of the third, unknown value. You will again note that both of these are preflight-type calculations, although there are occasions when they are also made during flight.

Finally, two basic inflight calculations will be learned—True Airspeed and True Altitude. To calculate the True Airspeed, you will be given the values of Pressure Altitude, Temperature, and Indicated Airspeed to then calculate the True Airspeed. True Altitude calculations involve some of the same given values as in calculating T.A.S. You will be given Pressure Altitude, Temperature, and Indicated Altitude to calculate the True Altitude.

Now turn to the next page to begin Chapter I.

Illustration #25

FUEL CONSUMPTION

Objective— Given any two of three values for Fuel Consumption, Gallons Used, or Time, calculate the value of the third (e.g., given gallons used and time, find fuel consumption).

This type of problem is a proportion, represented by the formula:

$$\text{Gallons per hour (fuel consumption)} = \frac{\text{Gallons Used}}{\text{Time}}$$

There is no need to memorize this formula as it can easily be remembered by knowing the expression Gallons Per Hour (GPH) and what it means:

Gallons   is an expression of (fuel) gallons used

Per   is an expression the same as the sign — in a fraction

Hour   is an expression of time

$$\frac{\text{Gallons Used}}{\text{Time}}$$

Gallons Per Hour is an expression of two values, which are .... and ....

Answer
Gallons Used
and Time

Fuel consumption problems are worked exactly the same as Time-Distance-Speed problems. Both are proportion-type problems. Since fuel consumption problems involve an expression of time in hours, you will again have to remember to use 60 on the movable scale as your index under GPH in the proportion. The proportion, from the formula, looks as follows:

$$\frac{\text{GPH}}{60} = \frac{\text{Gallons Used}}{\text{Time}}$$

Which two values in the proportion above would appear on the movable scale when the problem is set up on the computer? .... and ....

Answer
60 & Time

Look at Figure 7. (Not shown in this illustration.) Suppose that thus far in your flight you have used 40 gallons of fuel and have been flying for a period of 3:30. What would your fuel consumption be? As a proportion, the problem would look like this:

$$\frac{\text{GPH}}{60} = \frac{40}{3:30}$$

Here you simply move the time, 3:30 on the inner (movable) scale, under the gallons used, 40 on the stationary scale, and then find the answer to GPH by reading it on the stationary scale above the 60 on the movable scale. What is the GPH? ....

Answer
11.4 GPH

189

Illustration #26

It should be obvious in fuel consumption problems that you could be given the fuel consumption (GPH) and some other value, such as Time, and be asked to find the gallons used. Given a fuel consumption of 15.8 GPM over a flying time of 1:50, how many gallons of fuel would have been used? Work as a proportion and write your answer here:............

Answer
20 Gallons

Here are some additional problems to practice on:

	Fuel Consumption	Time	Gallons Used
(1)	12.65 GPH	1:30	....
(2)	....	2:40	34.2 gallons
(3)	11.1 GPH	2:20	....

ANSWERS

(1) 19 gal.   (2) 12.8 GPH   (3) 25.9 gal.

ILLUSTRATION #27

CHAPTER I POST-TEST

You should be able to work each of the following problems on your computer. If you are unable to work any given problem, or you do a problem incorrectly, go back and review that part of Chapter I dealing with the problem in question. Page numbers are given next to the answers to tell you where in the program to go for review, or you may wish to use one of the other references listed. Work all problems before checking answers.

1. Using your computer, divide 420 by 35.　　　　　Answer..........

2. Using your computer, multiply 85 times 36.5.　　　Answer..........

3. At what speed would you be flying to have covered a distance of 200 miles in two hours and thirty minutes?　　　　　　　　　　　　　Answer..........

4. What would be the fuel consumption rate for an aircraft that in 1:30 used twenty gallons of fuel?　Answer..........

5. What would be the True Airspeed of an aircraft showing an Indicated Airspeed of 140 mph, at a Pressure Altitude of 18,000 feet and a temperature of -20°C?　　　　　　　　　　　Answer..........

6. What would be the True Altitude of an aircraft showing an Indicated Altitude of 24,200 feet, at a Pressure Altitude of 22,000 feet and a temperature of -10°C?　　　　　　　　　　　　Answer..........

ANSWERS	IF MISSED REVIEW PAGE	OR READ
1.　12	p. 4	MR p. 10
2.　3102.5 (approx. 3100)	p. 6	MR p. 12
3.　80 mph	p. 8	MR pp. 4-5
4.　13.3 GPH	p. 12	HFR p. 48
5.　185.9 Mph	p. 16	HFR pp. 49-50
6.　26,000 feet	p. 20	MR pp. 13-15

A teaching laboratory for continuing education

S O'CONNELL, S J PENTON, S M KAY

If continuing education is defined as the educational process which carries on where formal education finishes, then tertiary education above all has a responsibility to make some provision for this. People who leave tertiary education should be adequately prepared to fulfil whatever need for further learning arises, not just graded and stamped as apparently finished products. This grading and stamping of graduates is invariably related to the subject content of science degree courses, whereas preparation for on-going education involves other considerations less specific to particular subjects, for example, developing the abilities given in Table I.

Table I. Examples of non-subject abilities

Ability to:	learn	plan ahead
	work independently	critically analyse
	work in groups	communicate
	identify problems	adapt to unfamiliar situations
	solve problems	keep an open mind
	make decisions	

Learning related to subject content is readily examinable whereas learning related to these other considerations is not. Also what is not examined tends not to be taught, and is therefore not learnt. These facts may account for the lack of attention which such non-subject considerations receive in science degree courses. There seems to be a general agreement amongst university teachers as to the desirability of a graduate possessing these abilities, but when asked how a particular course teaches them, the answer so often starts with 'Well ...' and finishes with 'it all comes out in the wash at the end', or words to that effect. These problems stem from the modular method of teaching science; each course is made up of separate course units (typically sets of twenty or so lectures on particular topics) given by different lecturers. The lecturers can take steps to ensure that their subject content is related to that of other course units but can rarely consider non-subject content in this way, simply because it is taught implicitly whereas the subject content is taught explicitly. Even if the former were to be taught explicitly, there would still be problems where students have a choice of course units. Should each unit include all the desired non-subject considerations? If so, it is unlikely to cover many of them adequately. Or should each unit cover only those considerations appropriate to the topic, in which case how can each student achieve adequate coverage when his choice is made on the basis of subject matter only?

Accepting the existing situation of the modular structure of science degree courses, it seems therefore that there is little chance of including non-subject considerations in a planned and systematic way within these subject based courses. However, there is a possibility of doing this in the context of a laboratory based course, provided that the course is broad enough.

There are four reasons why this is so:

1. Laboratory work can be less constrained by syllabus

The present climate of opinion is less inclined to insist that laboratory work should consist of a definitive set of bench experiments related to specific lecture courses. This means that it is possible to use suitable subject matter as a means rather than as an end in itself. For example, in an exercise designed to develop a student's decision-making abilities, material of the appropriate type is vital but the actual subject matter chosen is not critical. Thus the subject matter is the means, but decision-making is the end.

2. Laboratory work is less constrained by assessment

The proportion of a student's total assessment allocated to laboratory work is relatively low. Typically 40% of a student's time-tabled hours are spent in a laboratory but the marks given for this amount to 15-20% of the final assessment. If a student is to develop the ability to learn independently it is important that he should be motivated from within rather than by the pressure of an assessment procedure specific only to his present situation. It is also important that a student is self-monitoring and does not tend to rely on external assessment as a measure of his progress. Some assessment is inevitable but at least it can be given a low profile.

3. A laboratory course can provide continuity

MacKenzie, Eraut and Jones (1970) have emphasized the need for a progressive destructuring of a student's learning experience if he is to develop independence in learning. This takes time - too rapid a change can be confusing. A laboratory course is one (often the only one) of the few courses which potentially extend over three years. Instead of the usual situation in which laboratory work comprises unrelated termly or yearly sections, it is possible to consider the sequence as a whole and to plan the three years together. Such continuity can then provide an opportunity for progressive destructuring.

4. Laboratory work can be integrated

By combining laboratory work over three years into a single course, it becomes practical to design the course to give adequate coverage of all the

193

non-subject considerations in Table I.

In addition, the laboratory has a number of practical advantages over other situations. It has a large degree of flexibility: people and equipment can be mobile or static, situations can be set up for study over prolonged periods, both individual and group activities can be accommodated.

Also, special facilities exist in laboratories - not only is there apparatus of various kinds, but there are support staff concerned with the running of the laboratories. The technical staff, for example, can assist in the use of teaching aids, and they have skills going beyond the maintenance and setting-up of equipment which enable them to take an active part in teaching basic skills.

As a consequence of the above, a wide variety of activities is possible in addition to those traditionally associated with practical work. Examples of these are not only discussions, seminars, paper exercises, example classes, role-play and lectures, but also coffee and chat. Since the laboratory has such a high potential, it is a waste of a valuable learning resource to restrict its use to the provision of traditional bench experiments.

DETAILS OF AN INTEGRATED THREE-YEAR LABORATORY COURSE

A laboratory course incorporating the ideas outlined above has been planned by the authors as a collaboration within the Nuffield sponsored Higher Education Learning Project (HELP). The course is in experimental physics and is currently being run in the Physics Department of Royal Holloway College. It is integrated over the three years of an undergraduate's degree course, and is specifically designed to cover those non-subject abilities to which we have already referred (Table I).

We have begged, borrowed and stolen valuable material and ideas from a number of institutions within the HELP organization and others. To all of these we are grateful.

Implementation

The destructuring of activities is carried out in a progressive fashion by beginning with highly structured activities, such as learning basic skills, and finishing up with a project which is a completely unstructured activity. As previously discussed, this destructuring must be done progressively. It is no use expecting students to make a discontinuous jump from relatively structured experiments in their second year to a completely unstructured activity when they come to tackle a project in their third year. Similarly, the size of any task must be increased progressively. Students cannot be expected to make a good job of writing a full report unless they have had practice in writing shorter pieces.

The overall plan (extending over three years) is outlined in Table II. Year 1 begins with orientation. Students arriving at university have conceptions of laboratory work which are necessarily limited by what they have so far experienced in their education. They must therefore be given the chance in the first few weeks to find their feet and to settle down in their new environment.

Table II. Overall plan

Year 1	Year 2	Year 3
orientation	higher skills	real or true
attitudes	higher abilities	experiment (project)
basic skills [1]	specialized knowledge	
abilities [2]	specialized apparatus	
application of [1] & [2]		

This involves getting to know each other and the staff involved in the course.
It also involves their gaining confidence in this new environment, and students
differ greatly in this respect, depending upon their previous experience. For
example, some are really scared of even the simplest apparatus, whilst
others confidently refer to quite sophisticated equipment.

The formation of attitudes is just as important. Since these will depend to a
large extent on early impressions of the course, it is essential that the scene
is correctly set right at the beginning. In the first few weeks, activities are
therefore introduced which are designed to arouse interest in the course,
which allow students to appreciate the open nature of the laboratory situation,
and which also allow a large amount of staff/student interaction. Students are
helped to gain confidence, through exercises designed to cover basic skills
and experimental 'know-how'; for example, skill in handling some commonly
used instruments.

In parallel with the acquisition of such skills, there are activities which
cater for the non-subject abilities. In each case, an activity is chosen which
seems most appropriate for the particular ability. This need not be a practical
exercise, for the course includes many different types of activity. It is
important whilst students are building up their abilities that they are not
confused by having to cope with a large number of aims simultaneously. The
specific aims of each activity are therefore limited and clearly spelt out. For
example, it would be unwise to assume that students somehow acquire skill in
written communication merely by tacking on a written account to the end of
another activity. So, for a first go, this is better achieved with a simple,
single aim exercise in which students are asked to describe a specific event
(say, a short sequence from a film loop).

Finally, at the end of the first year all the skills and abilities which have
been acquired are brought together in a somewhat structured project-type
activity.

In Year 2, skills and abilities formulated in Year 1 are developed to a
higher level. This is largely an on-going process of development, with the
introduction of higher level skills such as developing critical attitudes or
adapting to unfamiliar situations. Also, the second year is the time for the
introduction of specialized techniques and knowledge - what one might call
'real' physics, for example, vacuum work, advanced techniques of
spectroscopy, microwaves, nuclear work. Students thus get the chance to
handle specialized equipment.

Throughout the second year, the activities become progressively more open, so that the activities of Year 2 lead naturally to the third year work, which for the student is an experiment in the true sense. In this the student has overall responsibility for his own work. Although he may be guided by a supervisor, he carries out the project independently, working within the constraints of time, space, facilities and money. The work need not be restricted to individuals - it might be carried out as a group project.

Types of activity included in the course

The types of activity included in the course so far fall into five main categories. These may be carried out singly, in pairs, or in groups, whichever is appropriate.

1. Practical work of various types, including:

  (a) Packages covering basic skills, eg learning how to use a cathode ray oscilloscope.
  (b) Problem-solving experiments, eg 'Determine the factors which influence the sinking time of a model boat'. The end point of such an experiment is given, but students decide how to go about solving the problem in their own way.
  (c) Investigations, eg 'Investigate the fracture of glass'. For such investigations a short article may be given to the students which describes a few simple experiments, so that the starting point of the exercise is fixed (ie the scene is set), but the approach to the investigation and the end point are left open.
  (d) Projects of various kinds, both group and individual.

  The examples given here are obviously from physics, but these types of work could be applied to other subjects.

2. Paper exercises including: analysis of data, computation, writing reports, library work (including compiling bibliographies and the use of abstracting journals).

3. Discussion plays a large part in the activities. This is important from the point of view of encouraging interaction between staff and students, and between students themselves. Hence discussion goes on informally; on a one-to-one basis, eg during criticism and comment sessions; in small groups, eg during project planning, or as exercises in design studies and critique of methods.

4. More formally, group seminars are included to encourage oral communication.

5. The final category includes informal activities, such as coffee and a chat. We believe that having coffee available in the laboratory is important from the point of view of encouraging interaction and getting the atmosphere right.

At present, Year 1 is nearing completion of its first run, and Year 2 is in the planning stage. Third year projects exist in the system already.

REFERENCE

MacKenzie, Eraut and Jones (1970) 'Teaching and Learning'. UNESCO

APPENDIX

Example of exercises related to specific aims

1. Critical thinking - a problem in space

Students are given a student generated solution to the problem of monitoring the mass of an astronaut in a space capsule, in which the astronaut is suspended between two springs and set into oscillation. The students are asked to criticize the method.

2. Open-mindedness - Mpemba's experiment

At this point in the talk, printed sheets describing Mpemba's experiment were circulated and members of the conference were invited to take part in the exercise as students in a laboratory situation.

The printed sheets are in fact an edited version of an article which appeared in 'Physics Education', May 1969, in which an African boy gives an account of his accidental discovery that hot water freezes more quickly than cold water, and describes the reactions of various people to his findings. These reactions ranged from frank disbelief to cautious acceptance.

Students are asked to write down their own reactions which are collected and discussed as a group.

Unconventional aspects of educational technology in an adult education programme

L F EVANS

As part of the development of the City University it was decided to inaugurate a programme of adult education in September 1971. In its 'previous existence' as Northampton Polytechnic there had been some courses of a non-academic, non-vocational nature, but these had ceased after the Polytechnic became a College of Advanced Technology.

The programme was based on the interests of a number of members of academic staff who were concerned to develop the university's links with the locality and the large working population surrounding it in the City. The subjects offered in the programme reflected both the personal extra-mural interests of some contributors, and the more 'popular' aspects of the academic interests of others. Topics included in the first programme were: 'Some mathematical puzzles', 'Seeing your way', 'Some engineering disasters', 'Pure and impure food' and 'Wine and vine in Europe'.

The last-mentioned was a course of my own devising, based on a series of lectures previously given in an undergraduate liberal studies programme, and it is with certain experiences within that course that this paper is concerned.

The purpose of the course was to survey the development of viticulture in Europe, to familiarize students with wines from the major producing regions and to enable them to taste, distinguish and recall a representative series of specimens.

To this end the students were first given samples of three wines with markedly different characteristics, and were then given the following printed instructions:

1. Take a small (2-3 ml) sample.
2. Examine against a white background for colour and clarity.
3. Swirl wine in the glass with a circular motion and examine for alcohol content.
4. Swirl again, insert nose in mouth of glass, inhale and adjudge aroma and bouquet.
5. Take a small quantity (0.2 - 0.5 ml) into mouth and taste - note sweetness/dryness.
5. Take second small sample into mouth, 'aerate', note 'flavour'.

Each of these actions was demonstrated to the students, their purpose explained, and the sequence then carried out. Students made their own notes of their reactions, and were reminded of the need to be able to recall the wine's characteristics at a later date.

The process was repeated with a further three wines, the total number sampled being chosen to illustrate all the basic attributes to be identified.

> Colour: Red; Rose; White;
>
> Alcohol: 8⁰ – 18⁰;
>
> Still – Sparkling
>
> Dry – Sweet

with a wide range of aroma, bouquet and flavour.

During the course a total of 48 wines were tasted, the techniques described above being practised and refined as the students developed their abilities.

At the end of the course a 50-question multiple-choice test was used to estimate the assimilation of information presented, and five of the wines which had been tasted during the course were given as a test of the students' ability to 'identify and recall'.

In the class of 54 students, 46 scored 80% or above in the multiple-choice test. Only two, both incidentally female, correctly identified all five samples, 34 students failing to identify more than two.

It was clear from this experience that the ability to learn and recall information presented in written and oral form was clearly well developed but, no doubt due to the general influences of our culture, which does little to encourage the critical analysis and retention of smell and taste stimuli, the ability to 'learn and recall' with the nose, tongue and mouth was sadly lacking.

In preparing for the next course, which involved 58 students of essentially similar characteristics - age, sex, cultural background - as the first, considerable thought was given to the solution of the problem of improving performance in the 'taste and recall' area.

Tests were made in collaboration with a small group of students from the first course to devise a means of codifying some of the more subjective aspects of the 'tasting' procedure. The method by which alcohol content was estimated was first considered, and a more detailed explanation, including the use of the illustration in Figure 1, enabled the trial group to distinguish between wines with 2⁰ difference in alcohol content, with better than 80% certainty.

8 – 10%alcohol   16 – 18% alcohol

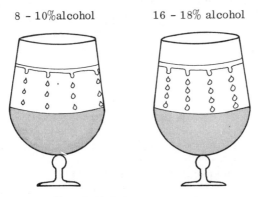

Figure 1. Alcohol content comparison

199

After a discussion of the varying reference concepts used by each of the students to identify and recall smells and flavours, a simple ternary diagram was developed, as illustrated in Figure 2, to quantify, albeit in a very crude manner, the impression received on 'sniffing' and 'sipping'. Wines were tasted and located as a point within the triangle dependent upon the taster's estimate of the ratio of each of the three attributes.

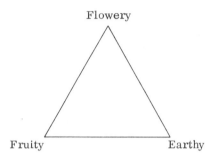

Figure 2. 'Tasting Triangle'

The area covered by the scatter of the 'points' of each individual, for a group of five (three male, two female) was never greater than 10% of the area of the triangle

It was therefore decided to introduce these adjuncts into the next course programme.

The same printed instructions (1 - 6) were issued. A more extensive explanation was given, orally, of 3., illustrated with the diagram referred to above and photographic slides showing wines of 8°, 12°, 14° and 18° in identical glasses, immediately after 'swirling'.

The diagram shown in Figure 2 was duplicated and distributed at 4., and each wine tasted marked by the taster as a point on the diagram. These marks were transferred to a transparency enabling the entire class to relate their own subjective impressions to those of their fellows.

In all the first series of six wines tasted the scatter of points was never greater than 12% of the area of the triangle, and it seemed that a feasible method of identification for recall had been devised.

Later in the course, however, as more esoteric wines, Turkish Buszbac and English Rieslaner, for example, were sampled, there was a marked increase of scatter, sometimes covering 60% of the triangle. It would seem that to some extent 'de gustibus non est disputandum' is still apposite.

The use of the method continued throughout the course, however, and at the conclusion the same multiple-choice test was given, and five wines tasted during the course were again used in the 'taste and recall' test.

In this class of 57 students, 48 scored 80% or above in the multiple-choice test. 16 correctly identified all five wines, 21 correctly identified four wines and only four failed to identify more than two.

It is perhaps rare that the basic concepts of a systematic approach to learning are used in what tends to be a somewhat esoteric field where phrases such as 'a naive little wine with an intriguing aftertaste' are bandied about, and legendary feats of identification of rare wines often fail to stand up to objective examination.

Since the application of an essentially 'Ed Tech' approach produced such convincing proof of efficacy, it seemed appropriate that some practical demonstration should be included in the presentation. Accordingly, the audience at the presentation were given the instructions enumerated above, and a series of characteristic samples.

By the second sample a measure of accord had been reached on the location of that sample, of the same order as that obtained with the second class described above.

It is, of course, open to doubt as to whether this is an indication of the efficacy of the system, the persuasiveness of the presenter, or the naivety of the wine.

It did, however, add an olfactory and gustatory dimension to what was primarily an audio-visual conference.

New uses of the telephone in adult education

BEN TUROK, JOHN S DANIEL

SUMMARY

Telephone conferences (the linking of a number of telephones simultaneously) can remove some of the obstacles to the wider provision of adult education. Recent telephone teaching activities in the Open University are described and their future development is discussed in terms of systems in use at the Université du Québec and the University of Wisconsin. It is suggested that the psychological barriers to a wider use of teleconferencing have been exaggerated and that the most successful telephone teaching techniques correspond closely to the best adult education practice in ordinary classrooms.

INTRODUCTION

The drive towards continuing education has raised two related problems which arise from the fact that most of those seeking continuing education are working adults. The first problem is to prepare courses that are flexible enough to be taken part-time by large numbers of people and the second problem is to provide these courses at a reasonable cost. Let us examine briefly the methods which can be used in the provision of continuing education.

Correspondence tuition was historically the first technique employed to make adult education available on a large scale. It remains a highly flexible way of providing courses, for it allows the student to work at his own pace at any location. There is also an element of two-way exchange between tutor and student although, since these exchanges take place by post, they are not instantaneous. Some correspondence tutors succeed remarkably well at introducing the human touch into these contacts with students but this requires considerable skill.

Another arm in the arsenal of educators is broadcasting, both television and radio. Here the personality of the tutor or lecturer is allowed considerable scope and the student comes to know him as a particular person. But broadcasting is a one-way process and the student is sometimes left frustrated with unanswered questions. Broadcasting may also be insufficiently rigorous from an academic point of view since programmes are short and the demands of presentation sometimes predominate over academic content. Both correspondence and broadcasting however have the supreme virtue of wide distribution in both numbers and space.

The traditional classroom tutorial group is another major means for adult education support and this method is in general use in most countries. But face-to-face provision is expensive and the economies of scale sought by advocates of continuing education are hard to achieve, particularly on more specialized courses where the density of student population is low. Even if the state is willing to make substantial investments in buildings and teaching staff, classroom tutorials can impose quite considerable strain on students in terms of travel costs, time and effort.

The development of continuing education is likely to proceed more rapidly if these constraints are taken into account, which means placing a high priority on taking education to the student. Given this premiss it is natural to investigate the instructional possibilities of the telephone since this is a medium of communication which already reaches into the homes of a large proportion of adult students in developed countries.

ONE-TO-ONE TELEPHONE CALLS

Nearly all correspondence colleges make considerable use of the telephone on a one-to-one student-to-tutor basis. In some cases the student must pay the call charges involved but in others the college itself provides this facility as a part of its service. A notable example is the De Vry Institute, a US correspondence college offering home study courses in electronics. This institute receives some 2,000 calls daily on the toll-free WATS (Wide Area Telephone Service) line telephone consultation service which is available to its 140,000 students.

Although the telephone is obviously playing an important role in such courses two criticisms can be made. Firstly, the use of a tutor in a series of one-to-one exchanges is not very cost-effective if many students have similar problems, and secondly such tutor/student conversations do not allow for the student/student interactions which have been shown to be a highly effective element in any instructional strategy designed for adults.

Both these criticisms can be countered if the use of the telephone is extended to groups involving both students and instructors/tutors.

TELEPHONE CONFERENCING: LINKING HOME-BASED STUDENTS

Most telephone companies have available, although they do not advertise it energetically, a conference facility which, if booked 24 hours in advance, can link up to eight phones. An example of the use of such a facility for educational purposes is an ongoing project run by the London region of Britain's Open University. The University's teaching system is based on correspondence units backed up by television and radio broadcasts and supported by a face-to-face tutorial programme. Tutorials are available for most of the 50,000 students at 260 study centres dotted around the country. These tutorials are conducted by some 5,000 part-time staff who are recruited from other universities and educational institutions. However, a considerable number of students are unable to attend the tutorials either because the study centres are too far away or because they are housebound by virtue of disablement or for other reasons. The problem of student attendance is made worse by the fact that the university is expanding its course provision proportionally faster than student intake so that higher level courses may have a comparatively smaller number of students. It is this 'scatter' problem, together with the needs of the housebound, which has drawn attention to the possibilities of teaching by telephone.

In the first type of application seven students are linked up with a tutor on their home telephones so that each can hear the others simultaneously in a conference-type situation. This project, as well as the other Open University application discussed below, was assessed by Holloway and Hammond (1975) from the Communication Studies Group of London's University College on the basis of interviews with students and tutors. While the numbers involved were small, the results were sufficiently convincing to encourage the extension of the scheme. Of 13 participants in the conference call system the following reasons were given for taking part: four had psychological problems which made leaving home or meeting new people at study centres difficult, two needed extra academic support on top of the normal tutorial provision, two were shift-workers who could not attend study centres in the evening, three were volunteer participants, one was unable to travel to the study centre and one was physically handicapped. It is likely that in the larger regions like Scotland or South West England, attendance would be affected even more by travel problems than is the case in London.

Holloway and Hammond found that satisfaction with the method was high and that most participants wished to continue with it. On the other hand several problems surfaced. Most obtrusive was the uncertain quality of the telephone line which varies a great deal. The reason for this seems to be the rather primitive equipment used by the Post Office in setting up the calls, which will have to be modernized if the technique is to become widely used. However, the motivation of the students was so high that they were prepared to tolerate line problems in most cases.

Participants drew attention to the impersonal character, in the initial calls, of the disembodied voice, particularly as the students had not previously met the tutor. Other commentators on telephone conferencing have urged the interspersal (Daniel, Fortier and Simard, 1974) of these meetings with face-to-face meetings so that voices could be tied to faces, but this is not always possible in the Open University. Students and tutors also complained of the fatigue and discomfort of holding the telephone handset for an hour at a time although some have turned to the use of a headset, rather like the conventional telephonists' equipment, which is available for hire from the Post Office.

The absence of graphics was also raised and this is obviously a major deficiency in telephone work. The lack was made up to some extent by reference to the diagrams in the bound course units provided by the University, by precirculated sheets or by ingenious descriptive techniques by the tutor in the case of graphs. The University is currently working on a device which will transmit graphics from a pad to television screens and if this can be produced at low cost it may be that future Open University students will be able to be taught at home by the combination of telephone and television screen

204

in a two-way system (Pinches, 1975).

Among the merits mentioned by the students were the obvious ones of savings in time and fares for travel, the greater degree of concentration required on the telephone than in a classroom since there are no distractions, and the greater degree of discipline the medium imposes on participants. Since they cannot see each other, a high degree of restraint and courtesy is required so that no one dominates the proceedings. The convenor, who is usually a tutor, conducts the meeting with a firm hand, asking each person to comment in turn once the formal presentation is over. In the same way each question may be referred 'around the table' if warranted. The session is therefore rather more structured than the conventional tutorial and this is particularly advantageous for slower students who are normally left behind. Furthermore, since time is limited, there seem to be fewer purely anecdotal interventions. Personal problems are saved for an individual call later on. A surprising number of participants found the method more conducive to active participation since the shy students were shielded by their anonymity. Students also found the method less formal, more lively and less aggressive than conventional tutorials, though it was also less entertaining and more tiring.

An experienced teletutor has commented that a social unit emerges after a few calls especially if this is encouraged by allowing some free time at the end of each call for casual chat. There can be no doubt about the way the isolation of the home learner is overcome. Tutors find the absence of visual cues a considerable handicap. They are unable to resort to many of the techniques normally used in the face-to-face situation and this means that their presentation has to be clearer and more structured than usual. The tutor has to concentrate to hear every comment clearly and to conduct the meeting firmly without dominating it. Students are often willing to be bolder in their criticism of content. All in all, tutors are required to prepare more for a teletutorial, although this burden on them is probably a boon to the students. On the other hand the tutor is also spared the bother of travel and in many cases conducts the tutorial from the comfort of his study at home.

LINKING STUDY CENTRES TO DISTANT TUTORS

The second application of telephone teaching in the Open University has been to link students who are met at one of the University's study centres to a tutor or resource person at a distance. A striking example is the connection of a study centre on the Isle of Man to tutors in Liverpool, 80 miles across the sea. In such a case the tutor may still be at home using an ordinary handset, but the student group obviously requires some sort of loudspeaking equipment.

The loudspeaking telephones available from the British Post Office (models LST 1 and LST 4) were designed for office use rather than for instruction. However, this equipment does allow a group to listen and speak to a distant person. Feedback howl is prevented by a voice switch in the set, which means that the line is opened for speech automatically without any need to press buttons.

The Open University has found that by adding an extension speaker and microphone and deploying the students carefully in a room with fairly soft acoustics, a tutorial can be held satisfactorily. However, technical problems, having mainly to do with 'clipping' caused by the voice switch, have been more troublesome than in the case of the conferences linking home-based students. Holloway and Hammond (1975) suggest that the loudspeaking equipment be used for tele-lectures rather than discussions, but this conclusion is probably premature, particularly as those involved with the Wisconsin system discussed below tend to the opposite view.

TELECONFERENCING: LINKING REGIONAL OFFICES AND STUDY CENTRES

The next stage in the Open University project will combine the key aspects of both applications, ie conferencing and loudspeaking telephony. This development will have implications not only for instruction but for the administration of the University since teleconferences could easily replace some meetings of regional representatives. In fact the proposed network, in which the central campus will be linked to the regional offices, which will in turn be connected to their study centres, combines features of two North American systems, those of the Université du Québec and the University of Wisconsin. A brief discussion of each of these systems will help to clarify the issues involved.

Telephone conferencing at the Université du Québec

Apart from its recently created Télé-université the Université du Québec is essentially a multi-campus conventional (as opposed to distant study) university. However, the different campuses and centres are located in seven cities spread over a territory 800 miles long, and right from the University's creation in 1968 ways were sought of using telecommunications to reduce the travelling which university committee meetings would otherwise entail. After early experiments using the telephone company conference facility to link 'speakerphones' in the various campuses the university acquired its own system which has been in operation since late 1972. Since this system has been described elsewhere (Daniel, Fortier and Simard, 1974; Daniel, 1975) only a brief account will be given here.

The key element in the system is the conference bridging console which forms part of the main switchboard in the University's head office in Quebec City. This equipment can bridge up to seven parties and the purpose of having it on the university premises, rather than at the telephone exchange, is twofold. Firstly, it allows conferences to be set up at short notice by a telephonist familiar with the university but secondly, and more importantly, it permits use of the telephone lines to the various campuses which the university rents permanently.

Although this equipment can be used to link any seven telephones, experience has shown that best results are obtained using a conference telephone set. At present the University rents some twelve Western Electric portable 50A sets which can be plugged in at any of over 50 offices and meeting rooms in the university. This means that most people involved in committees which meet by teleconference can join in without having to go far from their own office.

Statistics show that over 150 different people on more than 25 committees have used the system in the last two years. At present, over 15 teleconferences are held each month and a detailed study of system use has been carried out by Barrette et al (1975). Due to the growth in teleconferencing in the university a new, electronic conference bridge is shortly to be installed. This will allow up to 15 lines to be bridged simultaneously and, more importantly, will allow several smaller teleconferences to be held at once.

Although there has been some teaching by telephone at the Université du Québec, the majority of teleconferences have been for administrative purposes and at the current rate of system use each meeting held in this way saves the university some $300 without counting the time lost in travelling to face-to-face meetings.

The Université du Québec system thus provides a model for that part of the Open University system which would link the 13 regional offices to the central campus at Milton Keynes and be used chiefly for meetings of university committees. However, the second part of the Open University system, linking the study centres to the regional offices, finds a better model in the University of Wisconsin Educational Telephone Network.

Teaching by Telephone in Wisconsin

The use of the telephone in the University of Wisconsin is a remarkable application of educational technology by any standards. This Educational Telephone Network (ETN) as well as the successful techniques of telephone teaching in adult education, has been described in a key paper by Parker and Baird (1975). A four-wire dedicated telephone network links more than 200 specific sites (courtrooms, libraries, hospitals, etc) in 120 different towns in the State of Wisconsin. The system is in use from early morning until late at night and in 1974-75 the courses offered over the system attracted more than 25,000 students. The facility is also used by government departments to disseminate, for example, emergency agricultural information to officials around the state.

The excellent technical quality of this system obviously depends on the care taken over all components of the system and on constant attention to the quality of the telephone lines. However, the feature which more than any other seems to represent a technical breakthrough is the Darome Edu-Com conference set installed in each of the sites. This set includes two loudspeakers and four microphones which can be arranged as desired in each room. The microphones include a bar which must be depressed in order to activate the voice switch and the Wisconsin experience proves that this is a perfectly satisfactory arrangement. This is an important point since 'hands free' voice switching is often held up as an ideal. In fact, it seems clear that even the best voice switch cannot be used alone in a big system, for this means that every dropped book or squeaky chair at every site is heard throughout the network.

Nor does the 'press to activate' system work, as might be supposed, simply because the students are listening passively to a tele-lecture. In fact, as we hinted earlier, Parker and Baird (1975) indicate that most courses taught over the Wisconsin ETN resemble lectures a lot less than most courses given on campus. However, it is important to realize that, unlike the Open University applications in which the telephone provides special tutorial back-up for sophisticated multi-media courses based on correspondence and broadcasting, the telephone is the main instructional vehicle for the University of Wisconsin courses which use the ETN.

It is no accident that the first major educational telephone network should appear at the University of Wisconsin, for this institution has a tradition of extending the boundaries of the campus to the boundaries of the state which reaches back to the turn of the century. In other words, the University could draw on its long experience of extension work to identify the best way of conducting telephone courses and the ingredients which it is useful to add to the non-visual voice link.

Besides the obvious need to furnish students with the key visual elements of each course (diagrams, figures, etc), Parker and Baird (1975) insist on the importance of sending out documents which help to personalize the course. These might include a welcome letter explaining the ETN system, a photo and biographical sketch of the instructor and any guest speakers, and a class list indicating not only the names of students, but also their addresses, phone numbers and professional activities.

These authors also give an inventory of the techniques which have been found effective for the telephone sessions themselves. The striking thing about these techniques is that they correspond very closely to the best practice of adult education as outlined by authors such as Knowles (1970). Emphasis is placed on obtaining the active participation of students in the course not only by ensuring group and sub-group discussions but by including group projects and student reports which lead to peer teaching. Parker and Baird describe some 20 techniques which can be used to achieve these objectives and leave the clear impression that the very absence of visual feedback makes ETN instructors adapt to the special requirements of adult education more completely than they would in a classroom.

CONCLUSION

In the literature on both the administrative and instructional uses of teleconferences much space is given to recondite discussions of the psychological problems engendered by this type of communication. In the opinion of the present authors these problems have been vastly exaggerated. Indeed many of the so-called psychological problems boil down to the simpler questions of unfamiliarity and technical quality. If a teleconferencing system is clearly useful and free of technical problems, people rapidly gain familiarity with the particular characteristics of the medium and little talk is heard about psychological hang-ups. Of course, the fact that psychological problems are at root technical problems is not necessarily a great help, since behind the technical difficulties often lie political questions related to the organization of telecommunications in a particular country. It is evident that the technical quality of a teleconference will be a direct reflection of the quality of the telephone network in the country concerned. However, where this quality is adequate the only remaining problem is the equipment specific to teleconferences, ie the bridging equipment and the conference set. Excellent equipment now exists - the only difficulty is that there is something less than a free market in telecommunications hardware. Fortunately the present energy crisis has given considerable impetus to the greater use of telecommunications. Telephone companies are aware of an upsurge of interest in teleconferencing in business and industry and educational institutions will be able to take advantage of the technical and attitudinal changes which this interest produces.

Although invented over 100 years ago the telephone remains the basic instrument of the new communications technology. During its first century the telephone was neglected as an educational tool but the signs are that its second century will see a rapid expansion of its use in adult education.

REFERENCES

Barrette, R, Kilfoil, J C, Morin, C and Dumas, P (1975) 'La Télégestion à l'Université du Québec: bilan et perspectives'. Rapport de recherche, Vice-présidence aux Communications, Université du Québec

Daniel, J S (1975) 'The Use of Teleconferences in the Administration of a Geographically Dispersed Organization'. Proceedings Open University Seminar on Telephone Conferencing, London, July 1975

Daniel, J S, Fortier, J and Simard, P (1974) 'The Use of Audioconferences in University Teaching and Administration'. Proceedings International Conference on Frontiers in Education, IEE London, pp 70-73

Holloway, S and Hammond, S (1975) 'Tutoring by Telephone: A Case Study in the Open University'. Ref P/75025/HL Communications Studies Group, University College, London

Knowles, M S (1970) 'The Modern Practice of Adult Education: Andragogy versus Pedagogy'. Association Press, New York

Parker, L A and Baird, M A (1975) 'Humanizing Telephone Based Instructional Programs'. Proceedings International Conference on Frontiers in Education, ASEE/IEEE, Atlanta

Pinches, C (1975) 'Some Technical Aspects of Teaching by Telephone'. Teaching at a Distance Vol 3, pp 39-43, Open University Press

Scale effect, and its relevance for resource-based learning

JOHN COWAN

ABSTRACT

The writer claims that a significant change of scale is almost inevitably accompanied by radical changes in the features, problems and characteristics of any given situation. Parallels are briefly drawn between scale effects in the natural and applied sciences, and the growth of resource-based learning. The sheer unpredictability of the problems which can arise in the process of development is instanced through a range of examples related to various parameters which are characteristic of the size of a resource centre and the scope of the facilities which it offers.

INTRODUCTION

The famous progress of Hannibal's army through the Alps was frustratingly hampered by a simple restriction: elephants can't jump! Some of the Carthaginian cavalry may perhaps have wondered why the mighty elephant, with a similar skeleton and muscle structure to the horse, could not at least attempt to emulate the smaller and more nimble animal, when required to do so. The historian Livy did not tell us if they discovered the explanation of the elephant's incapacity - but at least we know now that the reason is to be found in what engineers call 'scale effect'.

Scale effect is manifested in the form of unexpected and unpredicted phenomena, which occur when the important features, problems and characteristics of any given situation are radically changed by a significant change of scale. Scale effect may be a reason for these changes, or it may simply be an excuse; but it is certainly a generally accepted fact that, when size is increased, new and hitherto unexpected problems become critical. In the present paper the writer hopes to consider the influence of such scale effect in the growth of resource-based learning.

THE RELEVANCE OF SCALE EFFECTS IN A RESOURCE CENTRE

It might be as well to begin by giving a simple example of the way in which a growth problem in a resource centre can be solved, apparently to everyone's satisfaction, only to be succeeded by an unpredictable second-generation problem, of a rather different nature. This is really what is meant in the present context of scale effect.

For example, even the obvious problem of storage of materials can have many completely different ramifications, depending on the scale of operations. In the beginning, once there is somewhere to store all the materials methodically (and that can be a big problem in itself), the next hurdle comes when the volume of materials reaches the level at which some process of selectivity must be introduced, so that formal arrangements are made to prune the supply and review the stock for deadwood. Once that problem has been solved (apparently for all time), the resources will continue to accumulate until they can only be stored in such a way that some are more readily available to users than others. At this point the cataloguing and retrieval system (which had previously proved quite adequate), must be drastically revised to provide the searcher with much more guidance regarding the relative usefulness of various likely sounding items. It is also about this time that the physical problem of accommodating a number of searchers and retrievers within the storage and cataloguing area demands a new arrangement of cupboards, shelves and open space, so that more than one person may search or retrieve at the same time. And the sequence presumably does not stop there; it is merely truncated because the writer has reached the limit of his own experience!

The reader is asked to note the diversity of the problems which have been mentioned. Storage space, selection of materials, cataloguing and retrieval, multiple utilization - these were each new difficulties following succeeding growth steps. It appears that problems are multiplied, rather than magnified, by growth.

THE SCALE OF RESOURCE-BASED LEARNING

If a development in resource-based learning is to be examined, then the size or scale might be measured in terms of any one of a number of relatively simple, but interrelated, variables.

These include:
(a) Student numbers, measured by the total size of the undergraduate population served by the centre.
(b) Utilization of facilities, indicated by the proportion of the available time taken up for study purposes.
(c) Range of material, as reflected by the scope of the subject matter covered by the material located in the resource centre.
(d) Staff numbers, measured by the size of the staff group involved in the preparation and use of resource materials.
(e) Extent of autonomy, indicated by the availability to students of alternative study paths, study rates and assessment procedures.

The writer proposes to trace the influence of scale effect due to each parameter taken separately, before going on to consider briefly the implications of scale effect in respect of future planning and development.

Factor 1: Growth of Student Numbers

As the student population increases, the problems which are highlighted change frequently, with all the unpredictability of a discotheque lighting system.

1. With a very small group, the relatively high preparation time per student capita inevitably prompts the lecturer to ask 'Is it really profitable? Could I not make better use of my time by devoting it to personal contact, for instance?' The problem at this point is a simple question of expediency.

2. With slightly increased numbers, the lecturer encounters the need to set up some kind of operational system; he may also begin to find some slight loss of the staff/student 'team feeling' which assists in any innovation.

3. After further growth, the risk of a feeling of impersonality in the system has to be consciously combated. At the same time, security, the prevention of pilfering and the control of facilities, all demand attention. Prediction of the likely fluctuations in demand, and adjustment of the same for maximum running efficiency, also raise new difficulties.

4. When the student numbers are large (by departmental standards), 'one-at-a-time' facilities (such as those offered for cataloguing and issue) are inadequate: multiple-use facilities are the obvious answer, but they often call for a complete rethinking of methods, while the interruptions caused to such systems during updating, maintenance, etc are now likely to be serious.

   The writer has no experience of large numbers by university standards, and can therefore offer no further comment under this heading.

   The problems which have been mentioned here do not need to be summarized: it will again have been evident that entirely different aspects of organization, administration and economic viability will demand attention at the various stages in the growth pattern.

Factor 2: Increased Utilization of Available Facilities

1. A <u>low</u> level of utilization (2-6 hours/week) makes it difficult to justify the cost of equipment, and to maintain complete control of it.

2. <u>Moderate</u> use (6-10 hours/week) requires the management and timetabling to follow non-conventional forms, which must first be developed, and then justified to one's colleagues! Back-up staff are now necessary, but cannot be kept employed full-time.

3. <u>Fairly adequate</u> utilization (10-15 hours/week) highlights the need to set up some scheme to resolve timetabling problems both amicably and constructively.

4. <u>Average</u> utilization (15-20 hours/week) creates situations in which peak demands (at changeover and popular times) become a nuisance within the resource centres, due to queues, etc. Supervision and management of the supporting staff is now an appreciable responsibility.

5. <u>High</u> demand (20-25 hours/week) almost inevitably leads to loss of freedom in booking, or to the purchase of further under-utilized equipment. Fast access immediate storage is virtually essential by now, which implies a 2-tier system of storage.

6. A <u>very high</u> demand (25-30 hours/week) can only be met by flawless

organization of extensive numbers of back-up staff.

Notice how the emphasis, which centred originally on relationships with people outside the centre, switched to timetabling and organizational aspects within the centre and finally led to human problems for both the staff and the users of the centre.

Factor 3: Scope and Volume of Material

1. If only part of a course is resource-based, the staff member concerned will tend to concentrate his energy on that one line of development or, conversely, he may diversify his interests elsewhere, to the detriment of purposeful growth in the resource centre. The problem at this stage is one of conflicting demands or interests for the lecturer.
2. When only one course, with linear programming, is offered, the need for documentation of the materials reaches the stage that it cannot be left to the lecturer's memory - and a 'system' must be devised. At the same time students must be taught by someone to use the new method of learning, or else it must be arranged that they have sufficient time to discover this for themselves.
3. If more than one course is based on a resource centre, then differences in course structures begin to present study problems for the individual student. They also lead to timetable clashes with courses outside the centre, and create additional work for support staff, who must be kept informed of many of the details of the courses - and their consequences.
4. An average centre, with several courses and several learning routes available, will have to consider very seriously the desirability (or necessity) of arranging for storage of some of the materials in satellite areas.

(Higher volumes of widely ranging material are beyond the writer's experience).

Again the examples quoted indicate the diversity of the problems which can arise. It is difficult to see any strong family resemblance between them.

Factor 4: Numbers of Staff Members Actively Involved

1. A solitary lecturer, unless he is a superman, will be continually limited in his efforts because he is not accomplished in all the necessary skills.
2. Two or three staff members, working as a group, must learn how to subdivide their duties, and yet maintain overall continuity of teaching philosophies. How to brief colleagues to run materials they have not produced is an associated problem. And the feeling of not having absolute control of your own materials (particularly where good young men are concerned), is difficult to combat in team working.
3. As staff numbers rise to half a dozen, thought must be given to the training of the new recruits, and to the (understandable) reaction from many staff who are unwilling to tackle supposedly menial tasks. At this point, contact with students is becoming less frequent for any one particular lecturer, since more members of staff are involved. For that reason, the centre will perhaps appear more impersonal.

(The writer has no experience of the workings of larger teams.)

Factor 5: Autonomy offered to Student

1. Rigid control creates, as a natural reaction, a desire from the user for more freedom, and even a demand for alternative study routes.
2. The introduction of some flexibility permits the student to explore all the options (in case he misses anything), although this additional activity on his part may well be neither necessary nor desirable.
3. When wide flexibility is available, advice and direction on the use of materials must be available. The difficulty is to offer this advice in a non-authoritarian manner, and to give the student some feedback on his study rates.

DISCUSSION

This paper had its early beginnings in the belief that we make our most significant advances when facing serious problems. Structural engineers learnt more about torsional instability from the aftermath of the failure of the Tacoma Narrows Bridge than would ever have been discovered in a trouble-free development period. A similar spin-off has followed the recent failure-plagued phase in the development of box-girder bridges, from Milford Haven to Melbourne. So the writer idly wondered if the problems he has encountered (frequently) in educational innovation had proved equally instructive.

A first review made it clear that, although the details were likely to be of little interest to others, there had been a curious but significant lack of continuity in all of these experiences: one difficulty had not given forewarning of the next problem.

In the beginning the writer had faced problems which demanded creativity or inventiveness in their solution. Of course, this demand arose because he had never taught in the new manner, nor had he prepared materials in the (for him) unusual form which the method demanded. In the fullness of time, the traumatic initiation passed its peak, and a completely new problem emerged: how to get his activities organized methodically, in order to reach an optimum production rate, consistent with a reasonable standard of materials and content. After that had been arranged, the situation changed once more; the innovation became almost an established part of the teaching scene, and the manpower devoted in his department to resource-based learning was augmented. Suddenly management, delegation and communication became the new problem areas, until a reasonable working scheme could be developed - at which point the greatest problem of all arose. How does one maintain and encourage one's own enthusiasm to move forward constantly? Despite apparent success, there is surely always a need for further innovation and development.

Although few of us are sufficiently blessed with second sight to predict accurately and comprehensively, it is easy to be wise in retrospect, and to point out that most, if not all, of these points could have been foreseen. But each succeeding problem represented the emergence of a new dominant factor, rather than the growth of a previously familiar difficulty. The new factor could not really have been predicted as a direct result, or an extrapolation of earlier experience.

CONCLUSION

Insects have the rigid parts of their body frame on the <u>outside</u> of their limbs. But if a man-sized insect were created, its armour-plated limbs would have to be so heavy that the insect would be less mobile than a 2-year-old in a suit of medieval armour. For the <u>relative</u> values of bone strength, bone stiffness and bone weight alter appreciably with size, which explains why we humans must have our bones inside our limbs - and also why the worst fears of science fiction could never be realized by the emergence of a race of super-insects.

This further digression into bio-engineering has brought us back full circle to our starting point. The problems of the large mammal, like its skeleton, are quite unlike those of its small neighbours. Insects can all jump: but elephants can't.

In the same way the problems of the large resource centre are quite different from those of the smaller-scale activity. The common thread in all that has been said is the opinion that problems arising after growth are seldom extrapolations of difficulties encountered in smaller scale situations.

Papers concerned with other aspects of educational technology

The formative evaluation of tape/slide guides to library instruction

P J HILLS, MRS L LINCOLN, L P TURNER

1. INTRODUCTION

This paper is concerned with a description of the development and refinement through application, of a procedure for the formative evaluation of tape/slide guides to library instruction. It examines the context in which the formative evaluation is taking place and outlines the rationale for and design of a formative evaluation procedure. It is hoped that the issues emerging will also be of relevance to those involved in the broader applications of evaluation in teaching and learning.

2. THE CONTEXT IN WHICH THE EVALUATION IS TAKING PLACE

2.1 It is essential that an evaluation procedure be designed to meet the needs and constraints imposed by the context in which it is taking place, if it is to provide <u>useful</u> information to the client* upon which decision alternatives may be judged. If evaluation is defined as "... the process of delineating, obtaining and providing useful information for judging decision alternatives ..." (Stufflebeam, 1971) then before evaluation can be said to have taken place the usefulness of the information must be established.

The formative evaluation procedure to be described has been developed and is being refined in the context in which it is intended to be used to ensure that the emerging procedure will be sensitive to the provision of useful information in that context. To understand the rationale behind the development of this evaluation procedure, it is necessary to describe the context in which the procedure is being carried out.

2.2 The SCONUL cooperative scheme

In 1970 the Standing Conference of National and University Libraries (SCONUL) set up a steering committee to coordinate the cooperative venture of the production of tape/slide guides to the use of the library and its resources, being undertaken by a number of libraries in

---

* That person or group for whom the evaluation is being conducted.

institutions of higher education in Britain.

Each tape/slide guide is produced by a working party of (usually) three librarians from different institutions, with, in some cases, help from an audio-visual unit.

Each guide relates to a particular aspect of library instruction of common interest to the members of the working party.

The tape/slide guides in the scheme are designed to instruct various types of library users in using the library and its resources effectively. The aspects of instruction covered fall into three main groups:

(a) The techniques of using bibliographic resources such as 'Chemical Abstracts'.
(b) The structure of the literature and methods of bibliographic control of a particular subject such as Biology.
(c) The systematic retrieval of information from the libraries' resources.

The guides are intended to be transferable to users of libraries other than the producing library, and the content matter is therefore as far as possible not institutionally specific.

The process of design and production of a tape/slide guide in this cooperative scheme begins with a librarian submitting a topic for which he perceives there to be a need for instruction to the Steering Committee. The committee consider the topic for inclusion in the scheme and ensure that it is not being covered by another tape/slide guide. The working party is formed and the production process begins.

The cooperative scheme only accommodates tape/slide guides and should a librarian decide his treatment of the aspect of instruction is more suited to an alternative medium, then the proposed production would not be included in the scheme.

In a first round of the operation of the cooperative scheme, 10 tape/slide guides were produced and approximately 60 copies of each have been sold to date (Spring, 1975).

The librarian/producers involved in the scheme tend not to be permanently concerned with teaching or instruction, and often have little previous experience in producing tape/slide materials.

3. THE NEED FOR EVALUATION IN THIS CONTEXT

The completion of the first round of tape/slide guides provided the basis for discussion on production experiences and problems between those who were involved.

A booklet entitled 'Tape/slide Presentations: Recommended Procedures' was published by SCONUL in 1973 giving guidelines for future producers in the scheme based on the experiences gained in the first round of productions.

During discussion of these experiences by the Steering Committee of the scheme the issue of evaluation emerged. In the first round the members of the working parties contributed their subjective comments about the guides, and in some cases qualitative and attitudinal questionnaires were distributed with the guides.

On discussion it was felt by the Steering Committee that this was not enough, in that little account was being taken of the effects of the guides on the intended audiences.

It was suggested that it would be useful for a producer to be able to assess the effectiveness of his particular guide in advance of its distribution to other institutions. Thus, if the guide proved inadequate then modifications could be made to it before releasing it for sale.

Towards this end an initial procedure for evaluation was designed by members of the project team and was submitted to the Steering Committee. It was accepted in principle and a description of the methodology of the procedure was included in the SCONUL booklet mentioned above.

This evaluation procedure is essentially formative, in that its main aim is to provide the feedback of information to the producer of the tape/slide guide which enables him to make decisions about change to improve the effectiveness of the guide in the instructional situation while the production is still in the developmental stages.

4. BACKGROUND TO THE TAPE/SLIDE EVALUATION PROJECT

The project began on 1st January, 1973 with the main aim of developing and refining this formative evaluation procedure by investigating its implementation in the context of a second round of production of tape/slide guides in the SCONUL scheme. This round of productions is nearing completion (Spring, 1975).

One of the outcomes of the work of the project will be an instructional package designed to teach librarian/producers how to carry out a formative evaluation procedure as an integral part of the process of producing a tape/slide guide.

If the librarian/producer is to conduct the production/evaluation procedure independently of the project team it must not be so sophisticated that it becomes unmanageable. The prime criterion for the success of the procedure is that it shall provide the producer with useful information to aid him in making decisions about changes to his guide without either involving him in a large investment of time or requiring him to have the expertise of a social scientist.

5. THE RATIONALE AND DEVELOPMENT OF THE FORMATIVE EVALUATION PROCEDURE

The formative evaluation procedure has been designed with the intention of satisfying the following criterion:

To provide a producer of a tape/slide guide with a process of delineating, obtaining and providing useful information for judging decision alternatives. This process should:

(a) be valid;

(b) be suited to the constraints of time and expertise on the part of the producer;

(c) be flexible, ie adaptable to the specific producer and tape/slide requirements.

These issues will be discussed in Section 7.

The formative evaluation procedure is being used by 11 producers in the second round of the SCONUL scheme. The project team have adopted the role of helpers and administrators with regard to the implementation of the procedure while examining the procedure against the stated criterion.

6. THE FORMATIVE EVALUATION PROCEDURE

The procedure essentially provides information:

(a) from the librarians (working party) on:
    (i) the worth of the aims and objectives
    (ii) the design of the tape/slide to achieve its objectives.

(b) from the audience (library users) on:
    (i) the audience's ability to achieve the objectives of the guide
    (ii) the areas of the guide with which the audience have problems and the nature of these
    (iii) the attitudes of the audience to the guide.

The processes by which these types of information are retrieved are the following:

(a) A working party of three librarians is formed to design the guide. Meetings of the working party with a member of the project team present define the target population for the guide and write the aims and objectives.

(b) When these are finalized an initial script for the guide is written, the working-party members comment on this from a subject and teaching point of view, ie is the content factually correct, is the teaching approach such that the objectives will be achieved, is there a harmony between visual and spoken material, will additional printed material be required to go with the presentation, is the script in spoken rather than written English. and so on.

    In some cases the primary producer of the guide has consulted both academic staff and students from relevant departments to get comments on the script, aims and objectives.

    When the script has been finalized the physical production of the guide is undertaken.

    The means by which this information is obtained by the producer is largely through interaction between the members of the working party and in some cases outside agencies such as audio-visual experts, academic staff and students.

    The procedure aims to ensure that such issues as who is to be taught, what is the teaching intention, and how the teaching material is to be organized, are resolved and made explicit by the working party; this ensures that the outcomes of decisions relating to these issues are more readily open to debate.

When the guide exists as a physical entity it is then possible to obtain the information from the student audience in the following way:

(c) The preliminary version of the tape/slide is shown to a small sample of approximately 6 representatives of the target population. These individuals are then interviewed, using a non-structured approach, on their reactions to the guide. The purpose of this process is to identify evaluation issues that are specific to this guide and that may not have been anticipated by the working party and the evaluator.

Any issues that do emerge are then examined with a larger sample of approximately 30 representatives of the target population during the trial stage of the guide.

(d) The trial evaluation material is designed. This consists of:

    (i) The construction of pre- and post-knowledge tests to measure gains in achievement of the objectives which can be attributed to the guide. The results of these tests provide information on the achievement of the objectives.

    The working party decide upon an acceptable level of achievement, say 70% of the sample audience achieve 70% of the objectives after viewing the guide, and if this level is not reached during trials this is considered evidence that the guide requires modification to improve its performance in the instructional situation.

    (ii) The construction of a diagnostic questionnaire to elicit information on specific areas of the guide which pose problems to the learners. This questionnaire contains items of four different types:

    (1) Standard questions appropriate to determining the quality of any tape/slide guide, concerned with matters such as pace, clarity of voice, academic level and so on.

    (2) Questions specific to the guide on trial based on the issues identified in stage (d) above.

    (3) Standard questions designed to indicate the particular areas of the guide with which the learners have encountered problems. In order to help the learner indicate precisely these areas he is issued with a set of contact prints of the slides and a typed copy of the commentary. The nature of these problems is identified by interviewing the learners after they have completed this section of the questionnaire.

    (4) Standard questions related to the learners' attitudes to the guide concerned with matters such as relevance to the learners' needs, boredom, whether they thought tape/slide a good way to learn the information presented.

(e) The trials are then organized and administered. This involves selecting a sample of approximately 30 library users which represents the target population of the guide. If the guide is designed primarily for the self-instructional situation, then the guide is shown individually in the trials session.

The trials involve:
  (i) the administration of the pre-test
 (ii) the audience watching the guide
(iii) the administration of the post-test and the diagnostic and attitude test
(iv) the audience is then interviewed using the responses from the diagnostic and attitude test as a focus.

The final interview retrieves in detail, information on the nature of problems the students have had with the guide and also attempts to identify any unspecified outcomes on attitudes not addressed in the previous test material.

(f) The results from the trials are analysed and on the basis of the outcome of this analysis the producer decides on changes that need to be made. If the guide is modified the producer is advised to carry out a re-trial. Information from a re-trial may be used summatively and be published with the guide.

7. PROGRESS IN THE IMPLEMENTATION AND REFINEMENT OF THE PRODUCTION/EVALUATION PROCEDURE

Eleven of the producers in the second round of the SCONUL scheme are collaborating with the project team on the implementation of the procedure and in Spring, 1975 they are at varying stages of progress, those most advanced being at the stage of trials with the learners.

Some of the issues emerging from their use of the procedure will be discussed below, against the criteria for the evaluation procedure mentioned in section 5.

(a) Validity

The procedure requires that the working party formulate the aims and objectives for the tape/slide guide and these form the criteria against which the performance of the guide in the instructional situation is measured.

The assumption made here is that the aims and objectives for the guide are worthwhile in the sense of repaying the time and effort expended by the learner to achieve them. Eraut (1972) raises this issue and develops the argument that the issues of the worth of the programme objectives must not be avoided in formative evaluation.

Lincoln in a working document (see References) discusses the implications of this assumption in the context of library instruction where the knowledge and skills to be learnt are not an end in themselves but a means to an end, that end being the efficient retrieval of information.

In the context of library instruction it is proposed that the worth of objectives for the SCONUL tape/slide guides lies in their relevance to the information requirements of the type of library users for whom the guide is designed; for example "if a student may never use a given index, it

223

serves little purpose to teach him and then to take pride upon evaluation that he has indeed mastered its intricacies" (Vogel, 1972).

In order to help the librarian/producer to ensure that this assumption is justified, the project team has developed a procedure which guides the librarian through a process of consulting other sources of information on which to base decisions about the worth of objectives.

These sources include: studies of the users' needs in the library; discussion with academic staff in the relevant departments who dictate, via the course requirements, the kind of use the students make of the resources of the library, discussion with graduates on their perspectives of library instruction.

This procedure is designed to provide the librarian with more information about the kind of instruction needed on which he can make more reasoned decisions about what to teach than if he relied on his own intuition and experience as a librarian.

Issues relating to the internal validity of the formative evaluation procedure can only be resolved at the end of the present programme of use of the procedure by the producers when all data has been collected and analysed.

However, some possible sources of invalidity have emerged, these being: (i) sample design; (ii) test construction; (iii) institutional variables; (iv) real and experimental settings for the trials of a tape/slide.

We are attempting to reduce possible invalidity in these areas whilst still satisfying the criterion of usability. This involves a compromise between a vigorous scientific approach and one of expediency.

(b) Usability

In making decisions with regard to the general validity of the formative evaluation procedure, it is necessary that the quest for validity does not result in a process of formative evaluation which becomes too cumbersome and time-consuming for the librarian/producer to use. The investment in evaluation resources must not outweigh its usefulness in providing the required kind of information.

(c) Flexibility

The procedure, whilst defining a general approach to formative evaluation, has to adapt to a producer's specific and unique evaluation needs within a group of users of the procedure. These aspects of differing needs are being examined and an assessment of changes to the procedure required to account for such needs is being made. The experience gained in the implementation is providing information on the validity, usability and flexibility of the procedure which will result in the following outcomes:

   (i) A report on the investigation and examination of the formative
       evaluation procedure in the context of the second round of the
       SCONUL cooperative scheme will be published at the end of 1975.
   (ii) A teaching package will be published at the end of 1975 which will
       make available instructional guidelines and sample test material
       to enable those who are not solely evaluators to carry out a
       formative evaluation during the production of their tape/slide
       guides.

224

REFERENCES

Eraut, M (1972) 'Strategies for the evaluation of curriculum materials'. In 'Aspects of Educational Technology VI'

Lincoln, L 'A procedure for deciding what are worthwhile aims and objectives in a course of library instruction'. OSTI/TSEP/D5, available from project team

Stufflebeam, D L et al (1971)'Educational Evaluation and Decision Making'. F E Peacock, Itasca, Illinois

Vogel, J T (1972) 'Critical overview of the evaluation of library instruction'. In Drexel Library Quarterly, Vol 8 No 3, July

This report covers one aspect of the work of the Tape/Slide Evaluation Project, funded by the British Library Research and Development Department, a joint project in the Institute for Educational Technology and the Library at the University of Surrey.

Some aspects of 'modelling' in the microteaching context

S GILMORE

Although the term 'model' and its cognates is used in teacher training, it should not be assumed to have only one meaning. It is necessary to distinguish, at least, two distinct meanings of the term: firstly in a general sense, when it refers to paradigms of teacher training which describe or predict a set of outcomes as, for example, in the <u>instructional process</u>, or the <u>teacher-pupil</u> interaction paradigms; secondly in a more particular sense, when it refers to the act of 'modelling' when an individual demonstrates a particular behaviour pattern as in, say, <u>inquiry strategies to be used in the classroom</u>, which the trainee learns through imitation.

A consideration of the interrelationship and interdependence of the general and particular uses of the term provides us with a guide to approaches in the training of teachers. In the past, the trainee adopted what has been described by Stolurow (1965) as the 'model the master teacher' approach.

As Stones and Morris (1972) explain, the training of a teacher is: "...viewed as a process of initiation in which the master teacher's teaching skills, performance, personality and attitudes are acquired by the student through observation, imitation and practice." Historically, this training procedure was based on the apprenticeship system which had roots far back beyond the rise of industrial societies in the nineteenth century. This basic pattern of skill acquisition can still be observed in primitive or non-industrial societies where skills are transmitted to the young and inexperienced by a process of direct imitative interaction with the adult members of the community. While attempts have been made to modify the 'apprenticeship concept' in teacher training by the introduction of theoretical courses as a background to practical teaching, it is generally agreed that these courses have failed to blend theory and practice in teacher training. It was the recognition of this failure which provided some of the impetus for inquiries into teacher education and training carried out by the DES in England and Wales (1972) and the GTC in Scotland (1972). It is arguable whether the recommendations in these reports face up to the major criticism of the 'model the master teacher' approach in that in this approach the trainee is not given or is allowed to acquire any explicit teaching of teaching.

On the contrary, these official reports appeared to be more concerned with the organizational and structural aspects of teacher training rather than with an appraisal of the underlying principles of teacher training. However, a more fruitful inquiry had been undertaken in the USA in the early 1960s. As a result of much rigorous thinking an alternative approach to teacher training began to be formulated. In contrast to the former 'model the master teacher' approach, trainees were required to 'master the teaching model'. The underlying assumption of this new approach does not rest on the notion that the trainee teacher is able to grasp the complexities of the ongoing process of teaching simply by observation and imitation - the characteristics of the older approach - but rather by means of systematic observation and analysis of teacher behaviours - the characteristics of the newer approach - the trainee is enabled to 'master teaching models'. Central to the mastery of these models is the trainee's acquisition and practice of a repertoire of previously defined technical skills. These technical skills have been defined by Gage (1968) as: "...specific instructional techniques and procedures that a teacher may use in the classroom. They represent an analysis of the teaching process into relatively discrete components that can be used in different combinations in the continuous flow of the performance".

Such analytical procedures permit the trainee to understand and control his teaching behaviours in a way that has proven to be altogether impossible by observing experienced teachers over hours, days and weeks, even if these periods of observation are punctuated by highly-structured 'demonstration' lessons given by gifted teachers or teacher trainers. In the acquisition and practice of teaching skills, the trainee is expected to focus attention upon teaching behaviours within a highly circumscribed situation. It is postulated that microteaching provides such a circumscribed situation wherein the trainee can practise these technical skills in a scaled-down teaching exercise. Scaled-down in terms of time - 5-15 minutes; in class-size - not more than five pupils; and in task - the trainee practises one technical skill in a single microlesson.

Microteaching's technical-skills approach is used to give trainees a clear idea of the skill to be learned. Instruction in a particular skill is usually given in a number of ways, but a preferred mode is by means of videotape. The particular skill is usually demonstrated by a 'model' on the videotape and is shown to the trainee before he practises the skill in a microteaching situation.

It is worth remembering that in the original microteaching programme developed at Stanford University, modelling and/or feedback by VTR was not envisaged. It was a happy chance that a prototype model of the original portable VTR became available at the same time. This association of microteaching with VTR was a crucial one in developing the new approach to teacher training. Not only was the VTR a feedback device but also it provided the medium whereby the technical skill could be 'modelled' to the trainee before he undertook his microlesson.

It was hoped that the student would imitate the behaviours exemplified by the 'model'. It is useful at this point to make a distinction between two main types of models used in microteaching: perceptual and symbolic. A perceptual model refers to videotaped teaching episodes which, usually, exaggerate a specific teaching skill. On the other hand, a symbolic model is a verbal description of the skill to be practised by the trainee in the microteaching session. Our immediate concern, however, is with the perceptual model provided by the VTR. Two basic patterns for the use of videotaped models have been developed: prior-practice and self-contained. Allen and Ryan (1969) distinguish these patterns by stating that: "In the prior-practice pattern, an instructional model is shown to the trainee teachers in which a skill is demonstrated before the student practises the skill. In the self-contained pattern, the videotaped model is employed with different students who are given no indication of the skill being modelled. It is employed primarily as a research instrument to discover which patterns of exposing the model tape provide the most powerful training treatment. It can also be used as part of the process to identify teaching skills."

The use of prior-practice videotaped models to facilitate the acquisition of teaching skills is still at a very early stage of development.

The rationale for the use of models in microteaching derives from earlier studies of imitative behaviour conducted by social psychologists. In a review of literature on the subject, Bandura and Walters (1963) concluded that behavioural modification was possible almost entirely through imitation and that modelling cues proved more effective than operant procedures, ie by reinforcement. At the same time an important investigation, as far as microteaching was concerned, carried out by Bandura and Ross and Ross (1963), found that filmed models were as effective as live models in affecting behavioural change. While the available empirical evidence seemed to provide some justification for the introduction of modelling procedures in the microteaching context, the complexities involved in the use of such producedures would have to be more fully understood before their validity could be established as a means of enabling the trainee teacher to acquire specific technical skills. Young (1969), in a review of research of the modification of teacher behaviour using audio videotaped models, focuses attention on a number of related questions. It is probably useful to consider these questions as falling broadly into two groups: firstly, the types of model used to modify teaching behaviour; and secondly, the conditions under which the modelling takes place.

The types of model used bring into focus such questions as the relative effectiveness of (1) perceptual and symbolic models; (2) modelling a specific teaching behaviour in the context of a lesson and out of content; (3) an audio (only) model of teacher behaviour followed by the trainee verbalizing the desired behaviour; and (4) positive models (ie displaying the unwanted behaviour). As an indication of the kind of research undertaken to provide a tentative answer to one of these questions, the use of positive or negative models, brief reference is made to three studies.

Allen and others (1967) studied the effect of teachers viewing a model displaying positive examples of the desired behaviour and having them view a model displaying both the desired and unwanted behaviour. Their findings suggest that when teachers attempt to transfer the positive instances into new lessons they do so more effectively after viewing the positive rather than being exposed to negative models.

Koran (1968) on the other hand, compared the effectiveness of positive and/or negative models of trainee behaviours but found no significant differences between the relative effectiveness of the models.

Gilmore (1975) in his initial findings reported that those trainees who were exposed to positive models used more prescribed questioning behaviours than those trainees who were exposed to negative models. No statistically significant differences, however, were found between those trainees who received no modelling compared with the trainees who received positive or negative modelling treatments.

Because of the relative paucity of research findings in this area it is difficult to draw any firm conclusions on whether the use of videotaped models is a determining variable in the trainee's acquisition of teaching skills in microteaching. While most microteaching programmes are organized so as to include modelling in the instructional sequence two contrasting developments in microteaching may throw further light on the degree of strength of the model as a constructed teaching-learning episode in influencing teaching behaviours.

In 1968, at the University of Malawi, a microteaching programme was devised without the use of videotaped models. Instead, demonstration lessons were used which took the form of a simulated teaching situation during which a trainee teacher practised a specific teaching skill to a microclass composed of fellow students who assumed the role of pupils. In this situation the focus of attention lies not only on the trainee teacher and his microlesson but also on the controlled and structured observation of the lesson by fellow students who then take part in a discussion and analysis of the lesson.

As Lawless (1971) describes the procedure: "every effort is made to ensure that the lesson plan is a clear list of behaviours or activities for both teacher and pupils and not just a list of topics to be taught". It is claimed that replacing modelling by simulation and observation, students were able to relate both curricular and theoretical elements to the teaching situation in the classroom. To the best of my knowledge, no empirical evidence, as yet, has been presented to support this claim.

A striking contrast to a pattern of microteaching which does avail itself of filmed and videotape recordings is the self-instructional minicourses developed at the Far West Laboratory in California. The minicourse is a self-contained package of materials designed for trainee teachers to use special teaching skills. In the first of three main steps in the course, the trainee is required to: (1) read the teacher handbook about a limited number of specific teaching skills; (2) view a videotape or film in which each of the skills is described and illustrated; and (3) view another videotape or film which shows a teacher using the skills in the context of a lesson. This extended modelling phase combines symbolic modelling, perceptual modelling which serves the dual function of providing a clear performance model and discrimination training among the skills, and direct instructional sequences on the skills to the practised, before the trainee plans his microlesson. For Borg and others (1971) the technical skills approach in microteaching is justified on the grounds that it is much easier for the teacher to incorporate a behaviourally defined, technical skill into his classroom behaviour than a vaguely stated exhortation such as 'be non-directive', 'establish rapport with the student', or 'individualize instruction'. Clearly, the modelling procedures used in the minicourses could be a useful aid to the trainee in acquiring specific teaching skills to be later included in the actual classroom behaviour of the trainee. The effectiveness of this form of microteaching has been substantiated by field testing of, for example, Minicourse 1 (Effective Questioning) by Borg (1969) in the USA and replicated in a pilot study by Perrott (1974) in a British adaptation of Minicourse 1. It is doubtful if one could use these tests solely as a basis to make firm generalizable conclusions on the relative effectiveness of minicourses. This is, of course, to be expected in an area of continuing investigation. Later results may strengthen the earlier claims.

These contrasting developments in microteaching lead one to consider the second of the two sets of theoretical and practical issues mentioned earlier, namely, the conditions under which the trainee views the model. These issues centre on the question of how far, and in what degree, ought the trainee to be cued and his attention focused during either the 'modelling' or 'planning' period prior to his teaching of a microlesson. Young (1969), referring to his own research, stated that: "...the addition of auditory and/or visual cues to a videotape model provided a 'contingent' focus for the viewer and, in essence, provided the reinforcement and discrimination training previously provided by the supervisor sitting with the teacher. This protocol proved to be significantly more effective than viewing a model with a 'non-contingent' focus,(eg written directions and explanation of what to look for in the model). The latter protocol produced no behaviour changes." But as Griffiths (1972) argues, this raises the question of the troublesome aspect of the prescriptive nature of the introduction of technical skills in microteaching programmes. As he points out: "the use of model tapes, and operational definition of specific skills, do seem somewhat off-key in this context of considerable ignorance."

If we accept Professor Peters' dictum that all learning is ultimately self-learning, and if we wish to develop in our trainee teachers self-learning habits and skills, problem-solving and decision-making abilities, individuality, and capabilities of continuous self-renewal and self-understanding, we are required to formulate and develop a technology of teacher training which will enable the trainee more actively to shape and control his own teaching behaviours.

Perhaps the assumptions of the stimulus continuity and mediational theory developed by Bandura and its effect on 'modelling' practices in microteaching ought to be re-examined. Briefly stated, this theory is based on the assumption that when a trainee views a perceptual model the sensory images which the trainee forms become structured and his perception responses are strenthened through contiguity. In addition, it is postulated that the trainee, when presented with symbolic modelling, ie verbal instructions, acquires verbal representations of the model's behaviour which become associated with the perceptual images. It is suggested, therefore, that if the learner verbalizes the model's behaviour he will acquire it more readily. This

230

problem of learning through models with its vaguely mechanistic overtones is open to the criticism that our knowledge of the trainee's processes of information-selection carried out by the trainee when viewing is so little known: a point made by MacLeod (1973) in the related context of the trainee's self-viewing of his own performance on videotape.

An alternative paradigm to Bandura's theory is offered by Richmond (1975) under the title of a generative theory of education derived from Chomsky's theory of language acquisition. We cannot avoid the fact that there appears to be no explanation for the ways in which the subtleties and complexities of grammatical rule learning are acquired by the child in the absence of anything resembling formal instruction other than by a recourse to the recognition of innate principles operating in language learning.

From this position Richmond indicates how a theory of learning may be built which is at variance with the current assumptions upon which modelling in microteaching rests. As he indicates: "the mother-child relationship which makes possible the 'miraculous birth of language' must be the paradigm for any humane learning theory. As an example of that 'minimum of priming' which enables the educative process to become self-directing, it cannot be bettered: by comparison, a paternalistic theory which purports to shape behaviour as if it were composed of bits and pieces of a jig-saw which needed to be put together by someone - parent, teacher, any except the learner himself - is made to appear not so much procrustean but absurd. How else to explain the fact that the most difficult feat of human learning, articulate speech, is performed during the first two years of life?"

The implications for the use of videotaped models in microteaching is clear. Neither the Stanford model of microteaching nor the so-called self-instructional minicourses allow the trainee sufficient freedom to be more responsible for his own learning of desirable teaching behaviours. Obviously some cueing and focusing, especially in the initial stages, is necessary but microteaching in the future has to develop new contexts for learning where the trainee is given credit to develop his inborn capacity for decision-making and problem-solving. This does not mean a return to unguided trial-and-error learning which was a characteristic of the 'model the master teacher' approach nor does it imply that the only alternative is for the trainee to 'master the teaching model' with its corollary that the analysis of teaching into special skills reduces the complexities of teaching and gives direct practical guidance to the trainee about the behaviour desired and provides reliable criteria by which mastery of the skills can be assessed. The contrast between the two approaches is not as distinctive, particularly in the area of modelling, as one might first suspect; the role of the trainee is essentially a passive one. In the older approach, the trainee 'observes' the master teacher; in the newer approach the trainee 'views' the model. In a generative approach the task of the trainee is to 'teach the model teaching' with the model in this metaphorical sense regarded as an embodiment of the latent capabilities for teaching skills possessed by the trainee revealed in the mirror image of himself on videotape. In this dialogue with himself, provided by means of videotaped recording, the trainee assumes the role of a participant-observer in the study and acquisition of his own self-directed teaching behaviours.

If we were to evolve such a form of teacher training we would, in fact, be responding to the plea so eloquently and wisely made by Sir James Pitman yesterday that the learner ought to be more involved in educational technology than has been the case in the past.

REFERENCES

Allen, D W and others (1967) 'A comparison of different modelling procedures in acquisition of a teaching skill'. Paper presented at AERA Conference, New York

Allen, D W and Ryan, K (1969) 'Microteaching'. Addison-Wesley, London

Bandura, A, Ross, D and Ross, S A (1963) 'Imitation of film-mediated aggressive models'. In 'Journal of Abnormal Social Psychology' Vol 66, pp 3-11

Borg, W R (1969) 'The minicourse as a vehicle for changing teaching behaviour: the research evidence'. Paper presented at annual meeting of AERA, Los Angeles

Borg, W R (1971) 'The minicourse - a milestone on the road to better teaching'. In 'British Journal of Educational Technology' Vol 2, pp 14-23

Department of Education and Science (1972) 'Teacher Education and Training'. (James Report). HMSO, London

Gage, N L (1968) 'An analytical approach to research and instructional methods'. In 'Phi Delta Kappa' Vol 49, pp 601-6

General Teaching Council of Scotland (1972) 'Report on the Training of Graduates for Secondary Education'. HMSO, Edinburgh

Gilmore, S (1975) 'The use of videotaped "models" in teacher training'. Paper presented at NECCTA Conference, Edinburgh

Griffiths, R (1972) 'Some troublesome aspects of microteaching'. Paper presented at NECCTA Conference, Leeds

Koran, J J (1968) 'The relative effectiveness of imitative versus problem solving in the acquisition of a complex teaching skill'. Unpublished doctoral dissertation, Stanford University

Lawless, C J (1971) 'Microteaching without hardware developments at the University of Malawi'. In 'Teacher Education' Vol 12, pp 53-63

MacLeod, G R (1973) 'A study of student self-viewing during microteaching'. Paper presented at BPS Education Section Conference, London

Perrott, E (1974) 'A study of self-instructional microteaching systems'. In 'Educational Development International' Vol 2, pp 19-25

Richmond, W K (1975) 'Education and Schooling'. Methuen, London

Stolurow, L M (1965) 'Model the master teacher or master the teaching model'. In 'Learning and the Educational Process' pp 223-247 (ed) Krumboltz, J D. Rand McNally, Chicago

Stones, E and Morris, S (1972) 'Teaching Practice: Problems and Perspectives'. Methuen, London

Young, D B (1969) 'Modification of teacher behaviour using audio videotaped models in a microteaching sequence'. In 'Educational Leadership' Vol 26, pp 394-403

The typography of college prospectuses: a critique and a case history

PETER BURNHILL, JAMES HARTLEY,
SUSAN FRASER, MARGRETTE YOUNG

ABSTRACT

This paper is divided into three parts. Part 1 surveys the typographic design features of fifty-one college and university prospectuses; Part 2 describes the re-design of one of these prospectuses; and Part 3 describes an experimental comparison between the original and the revised document. The results of this study indicate superiority in terms of cost-effectiveness for the revised prospectus.

PART 1. A SURVEY OF COLLEGE PROSPECTUSES

"Writing, whether typographically or electronically, is not an inborn talent, but a way of thinking, a rational attitude and a mental discipline. Only when thought is constructed orderly and rationally, can a corresponding orderly, rational structure be given to its transcription - its layout and design." (Baudin, 1967).

How orderly and rational is the typographical structure of our work-a-day documents? And if it is not, who is to blame for our typographical Tower of Babel?

As part of our work on Typography, Communication and Learning (sponsored by the Social Science Research Council) we have become involved in evaluating the re-design of a prospectus for a College of Further Education. As a part of this project we assessed the typographic design features of over 50 prospectuses sent to the University of Keele during the academic year 1973-74. In the first part of this paper we summarize what we found.

Table I lists in summary form the main typographical attributes of these documents. Some of the terms used may need explanation. 'ISO Standard formats' refers to the recommendations of the International Organization for Standardization for the dimensioning of printed paper sizes, recommendations which are now accepted by the national bodies of most of the world's technologically advanced countries.

Of the 51 prospectuses, 36 used inconsistent word spacing; that is, what is sometimes misleadingly called 'justified' text. But 15 used consistent word spacing - or 'unjustified' text. Research evidence suggests that unjustified text (the more economical method) causes no difficulty for normal readers,

Table I. Typographical analysis of 51 college/university prospectuses

Typographical attributes	ISO Standard Formats			Non-standard Formats	
	Vertical A5	Horizontal A5b	$\frac{2}{3}$A4b	Vertical	Horizontal
Columns per page:					
One	28	–	–	15	1
Two	2	2	–	2	–
Three	–	–	1	–	–
Word spacing:					
Consistent	9	1	1	4	–
Inconsistent	21	1	–	13	1
Word breaks at line ends:					
Not present	9	1	1	4	–
Present	21	1	–	13	1
Line spacing:					
Systematic	1	–	–	2	–
Unsystematic	29	2	1	15	1
Type size/interline space relationship:					
Satisfactory	9	2	–	4	–
Unsatisfactory	21	–	1	13	1
Number of type sizes used:					
One	–	–	–	1	1
Two	11	2	1	13	–
Three or more	19	–	–	3	–
Paragraph coding method used:					
Indentation	2	–	–	–	1
Line space	21	1	1	10	–
Indentation + line space	7	1	–	7	–
Position of headings:					
Left ranging	27	2	1	11	1
Centred + left ranging	3	1	–	6	–
Position of page numbers:					
Top, centre	1	–	–	–	–
Top, left and right	1	–	–	–	–
Bottom, centre	10	–	–	6	–
Bottom, left and right	10	1	1	7	1
Bottom, left and left	7	1	–	2	–
Not used	1	–	–	2	–
Total cases	30	2	1	17	1

and, in fact, that it may be helpful for less able ones (Hartley and Mills, 1973).

In 36 of the 51 prospectuses words were occasionally divided at line-ends as a consequence of the use of 'justified' composition.

Of the 51 prospectuses, 48 used irregular and unsystematic line spacing in order to produce text areas of a fixed depth. Only 3 prospectuses used line space systematically for the purpose of grouping parts functionally. Thirty-six of the prospectuses were set with too little interline space; that is, the difference between word space and interlinear space was insufficient to stress the horizontal, as sense and research (Tinker, 1963) suggests. At the same time, space was wasted by having wide margins which, in some cases, accounted for as much as 50% of the total area of the page.

The remaining design features summarized in Table I are self-explanatory.

This survey seems to indicate that, in prospectus design at least, transcription from thought to type is not as orderly or rational as it should be.

PART 2. RE-DESIGNING A PROSPECTUS

The designer's brief

The function of the prospectus was that of a working document of some 200 pages giving detailed information for use both within the college and externally. The re-designed version would continue to serve these ends, and, except for updating, would follow the original in content and sequence. The designer saw in the design situation the need to maintain and, if possible, to improve performance standards at a time when rapidly rising prices called for a strict watch to be kept on the cost of printing the prospectus.

Design analysis

An analysis of the typography of the previous year's prospectus showed that heavy demands had been made on hand-setting in what was basically a machine system of typesetting. The root cause of the need to revert to hand-work - the more costly method of typesetting - was the traditional convention that 'text' should be seen as a rectangle of a fixed width and depth surrounded by wide margins. This tradition requires the internal spacing of the information to be adjusted inconsistently in order to produce a rectangle of consistent dimensions. From the point of view of economy in production on the one hand, and of concern for the syntactic demands of the information on the other, it seemed necessary to draw up a specification for control of the layout, and to do so in a way which would make maximum use of the keyboard for both the assembly of characters and for the overall spatial organization of the page.

In the original prospectus, the absence of a consistent spatial system for the functional grouping of parts had led to the use of two type styles and five type sizes in an attempt to define heading levels and other features of the text. These variations made further demands on hand-work. Furthermore, the absence of a detailed typographical specification, the possibility of which had been precluded by compliance with tradition, had contributed to a high charge being made for author's corrections.

The specification of the revised version of the prospectus

The construction by keyboarding of the typography of the re-designed version was controlled by a line-numbered reference grid. The grid was planned to work in conjunction with a written specification and with a system of copy mark-up based on that recommended by British Standard 1219:1958, 'Proof Correction and Copy Preparation' (currently being revised). A consequence of this procedure was that the overall page arrangement could be seen and checked against the specification at first proof stage. Page turnover problems could also be resolved at this point. The specification also had contractual implications.

The construction and dimensioning of the reference grid stemmed from a close analysis of the syntactic demands of the copy in terms of horizontal and vertical grouping. That is to say, the reference grid was related to the intrinsic structure of the information, and was not imposed upon it by a concern for renaissance systems of geometrical proportioning.

In brief, the main points of difference between the typography of the original and the re-designed versions of the prospectus (illustrated in Figures 1 and 2) were:

1. Page size
    Original: 144mm x 215mm
    Revised: 148mm x 210mm (A5)
2. Production method
    Original: Letterpress. Character assembly system - Monotype
    Revised: Lithography. Character assembly system - IBM (a choice determined by estimates submitted as a result of tendering, not the designer's preference).
3. Information area
    Original: Occupied 55% of total page area.
    Revised: Occupied total page area, less allowance for binding margin and trim at head, foot and fore-edge.
4. Lines of text, maximum possible per page
    Original: 62
    Revised: 49
5. Number of pages
    Original: 208
    Revised: 232 (about one-third of increase due to additional information)
6. Internal spacing, horizontal axis
    Original: Word space varied from line to line to produce lines of equal length. Words broken and hyphenated to avoid excessively large word spaces in the line.
    Revised: Word space standardized throughout. No word breaks permitted.
7. Internal spacing, vertical axis
    Original: Varied from page to page. Hand set.
    Revised: One, two or four units of line-feed (10-pt). Choice of interval

determined by structural analysis. Specified at mark-up
stage. Machine set.
8. Type sizes and variants
   Original: Two styles, including roman, bold and italic. Five sizes.
   Revised: One style. Two sizes. Roman and bold, no italic.
9. Basic text type size
   Original: 8-pt, set solid (ie line-feed, 8-pt).
   Revised: 8-pt, 2-pt interline space (ie line-feed 10-pt).
10. Page numbers
   Original: Foot of page, centred.
   Revised: Head of page, left and right.
11. Colour coding
   Original: Coloured pages used to code the nine departmental sections.
             Eg Green - Business Studies; Yellow - Design, etc.
             In addition, white paper was used for preliminary pages.
   Revised: White paper throughout. Running heads set over departmental
            pages to replace function of colours.
12. Tables
   Original: Use of horizontal, hand-set rules and 'ditto' marks.
   Revised: No rules. Column heading set in bold face. All entries spelt
            out. 'Subject' heading moved to last column to minimize
            need to carry entries over to a second line. Ranging axes
            specified on master reference grid.
13. Contents pages, main and departmental
   Original: Page numbers ranged extreme right of type area.
   Revised: Page numbers positioned left of entries with fixed space
            between.
14. Cost
   Original: £1470, excluding charges for author's corrections (These
             amounted to several hundreds of pounds). Quantity 8000
             copies.
   Revised: £1180. No charge for author's corrections, these being
            set off against errors made by printer with respect to the
            specification. Quantity 7500 copies.
(The prospectuses were both designed in the college, so there were no extra
design charges).

PART 3. EXPERIMENTAL COMPARISONS

Having satisfied ourselves that the revised prospectus was less costly to
produce, we next turned to the question of whether or not the revised
prospectus was easier or more difficult to use than the original.

Method

The most appropriate measures of effectiveness, or of ease of use, appeared
to us to be (i) the time taken to retrieve information from the prospectuses,
and (ii) the number of errors made in retrieval. A work-book was constructed

Part-time Vocational Courses

City and Guilds Creative Studies Courses

The undermentioned courses have been designed mainly for those mature students who wish to follow a course for vocational and personal reasons. The Courses are made up of two parts: Part 1, involving 2 years' study and Part 2, involving one years' study. External examinations for both Parts involve written papers and Coursework assessment.

Fashion CGLI 780
Part 1, 1st and 2nd Years

The aim is to develop an awareness of fashion as a whole in addition to a high standard of Craftsmanship using modern methods of making up.

Day Course

Course Symbol: **DF1**　　　　　　　　　　　*Course Tutor:* Miss M. Jeavons

Class Number	Subject	Day	Time	Room
71004	Practical	Tues.	$9\frac{1}{2}$—$12\frac{1}{4}$	Ov16
71014	Common Core/Millinery	,,	$1\frac{1}{2}$—4	Ov16
71024	Theory and Textiles	Thurs.	$9\frac{1}{2}$—$12\frac{1}{4}$	Ov20
71034	Design and Pattern Cutting	,,	$1\frac{1}{2}$—4	Ov20

Evening Course

Course Symbol: **EF1**　　　　　　　　　　　*Course Tutor:* Mrs. H. E. C. Keeling

71064	Practical	Mon.	$6\frac{1}{2}$—$9\frac{1}{2}$	Ov20
71074	Common Core/Theory	Tues.	7—9	Ov20

Embroidery CGLI 782
Part 1, 1st and 2nd Years

Students will be trained to develop a creative approach to the Craft, design being an integral part of the study. A knowledge of traditional techniques will form a background to contemporary developments.

Day Course

Course Symbol: **DE1**　　　　　　　　　　　*Course Tutor:* Mrs. M. P. Archer

71104	Design and Experimental Work	Tues.	$9\frac{1}{2}$—$12\frac{1}{4}$	Ov17
71114	Conmon Core/Practical	,,	$1\frac{1}{2}$—4	Ov17
71124	Drawing	Thurs.	$9\frac{1}{2}$—$12\frac{1}{4}$	Ov17
71134	Practical	,,	$1\frac{1}{2}$—4	Ov17

Evening Course

Course Symbol: **EE1**　　　　　　　　　　　*Course Tutor:* Mrs. D. Wilson

71164	Common Core/Theory	Tues.	7—9	Ov17
71174	Practical	Thurs.	$6\frac{1}{2}$—$9\frac{1}{2}$	Ov17

Soft Furnishing and Upholstery CGLI 783
Part 1, 1st and 2nd Years

The Course will develop the appreciation of colour, tone, texture, pattern and the influence of light in the choice of furnishings for the home. A high standard of craftsmanship will be required from students throughout the Course.

Course Tutors: Miss M. Jeavons

Course Symbol: **DSF1**　　　　　　　　　　　Mrs. H. E. C. Keeling

71204	Practical	Tues.	$9\frac{1}{2}$—$12\frac{1}{4}$	Ov20
71214	Common Core/Theory	,,	$1\frac{1}{2}$—4	Ov20

153

Figure 1. A page from the original prospectus

Part-time Vocational Courses

■ **City and Guilds Creative Studies Courses**

The undermentioned courses have been designed mainly for those mature students who wish to follow a course for vocational and personal reasons. The Courses are made up of two parts: Part 1, involving 2 years' study and Part 2, involving one year's study. External examinations for both Parts involve written papers and Coursework assessment.

Fashion CGLI 780

Part 1
1st & 2nd years

The aim is to develop an awareness of fashion as a whole in addition to a high standard of Craftsmanship using modern methods of making up.

Part 2
3rd year
Day Course

A more advanced study of the items in the Fashion Part 1 syllabus.

Course Symbol: DF1   Course tutor: Miss M Jeavons

class	day	time	room	subject
71004	Tues	9¼–12¼	Ov15	Practical
71014	Tues	1½–4	Ov15	Common Core/Millinery
71024	Thurs	9¼–12¼	Ov20	Design and Pattern Cutting
71034	Thurs	1½–4	Ov20	Theory and Textiles

Evening Course

Course Symbol: EF1   Course Tutor: Mrs HEC Keeling

class	day	time	room	subject
71064	Mon	6½–9½	Ov20	Practical
71074	Tues	7–9	Ov20	Common Core/Theory

Embroidery CGLI 782

Part 1
1st & 2nd years

Students will be trained to develop a creative approach to the Craft, design being an integral part of the study. A knowledge of traditional techniques will form a background to contemporary developments.

Part 2
3rd year

The subject is studied in greater depth with emphasis laid upon advanced techniques and historic research.

Day Course

Course Symbol: DE1   Course tutor: Mrs MP Archer

class	day	time	room	subject
71104	Tues	9¼–12¼	Ov17	Design and Experimental Work
71114	Tues	1½–4	Ov17	Common Core/Practical
71124	Thurs	9¼–12¼	Ov17	Drawing
71134	Thurs	1½–4	Ov17	Practical

Figure 2. A revision of the same page

- somewhat like a programmed text - which required the reader to complete a series of search tasks, using either the old or the new prospectus. The search tasks were designed to cover a range of retrieval problems which might be differentially affected by the different typographic aspects of the two prospectuses.

Task One involved retrieval from the General Information section which occupied several pages at the beginning of the prospectus. The work-book required readers to find and write down the answers to questions such as 'What are the opening hours for the library during the vacation?' 'What is the fee for a student under 18 years of age doing a full-time vocational course?', and so on. There were ten questions on this section. This task demanded retrieval from complex materials (calendars, tables and prose) and required searching backwards and forwards.

Task Two required the readers to find a particular page in the prospectus (the Contents pages for separate randomly listed departments) and to write down the last item listed on it. The aim of this task was to see if there was any difference in the time taken using the two prospectuses to locate separate departmental sections. There were six departments to be located.

Task Three required the readers to write down the page numbers of particular items listed on various Contents pages. The aim of this task was to see whether or not there was any difference in time taken to locate page numbers due to the revised layout of the Contents page. Twenty-eight page numbers were to be recorded.

Task Four involved readers in retrieval of material from 'continuous text'. Two main methods were used here. Questions were asked about the information (as in Task One), and sentences taken from the information pages were presented in the work-book with words omitted. The reader's job was to write in the missing words. There were fifteen questions, and twenty missing words to complete. Again, as in all the tasks, the aim of this task was to see how typographic differences in the prospectuses might affect retrieval speed.

Task Five was concerned with retrieval from the tables, and was divided into four parts which tested different aspects of the tabular layouts.

> In part one readers were given course symbols and subject titles, and they had to write down appropriate class numbers.
> In part two readers were given course symbols and class numbers, and they had to write down appropriate subject titles.
> In part three readers were given course symbols and class numbers, and they had to write down appropriate days.
> In part four readers were given course symbols and class numbers, and they had to write down appropriate room numbers.

Thus the aim of Task Five was to examine how the layout of the tables in the original and the revised prospectuses affected the retrieval of different kinds of information from the tables.

Task Six required the reader to locate courses offered by the college which were difficult to retrieve because of the lack of an index in both prospectuses. The reader had to find four entries, each of which demanded considerable searching. The aim of this task was to compare the relative effectiveness in the two prospectuses of the text headings and typographic coding for locating elusive material.

The general procedure utilized was for readers to work in pairs. While one member of the pair completed tasks in the work-book, his/her partner recorded the time taken for each of the tasks. After a break, these roles and the prospectuses were changed and the procedure was repeated.

Thus each reader worked with one prospectus only. This arrangement was decided upon because a pilot study with university students had revealed possible asymmetrical transfer effects from the first to the second prospectus if readers used both prospectuses. It was found that using the original prospectus first appeared to help use of the revised one when it was studied second, but that using the revised prospectus first did not have such an effect. Poulton (1966) has indicated the difficulty of interpreting asymmetrical effects from balanced experimental designs.

Subjects

The readers employed in this study comprised potential and actual college students: the former were 15- and 16-year-old schoolchildren, the latter students attending Stafford College of Further Education. Both groups were classified in terms of high or low academic ability according to the particular courses they were taking. The composition of the readers was as follows:

Potential Students	Male	Female	Total
High ability	18	17	35
Low ability	16	13	29
Actual Students			
High ability	10	7	17
Low ability	23	8	31
Totals	67	45	112

The work-book used with the less able students was shorter (it contained only Tasks Two, Three and Five, and had less items in Task Five) and it had more explicit instructions.

Results

Time taken. The results obtained were examined using the Mann Whitney U test (Siegel, 1956). Comparisons within each prospectus group for main effects (more able versus less able, potential versus actual students, and males versus females) were non-significant. The detailed results on the different tasks provided so few significant differences that it did not seem worthwhile to present these analyses here. What we have done, therefore, is to present in Table II the results in terms of the high- and low-ability students for each prospectus group, showing the median time taken, ie the mid-score of the total range of scores, and the range of times recorded on

241

Table II. Medians and ranges of times recorded for each task on the original and the revised prospectus for able and less able students. (NB not all students completed all of the tasks in the time available to them.)

Able Students		Task 1	Task 2	Task 3	Task 4	Task 5:1	Task 5:2	Task 5:3	Task 5:4	Task 6
original prospectus	median	6min 24sec	3min 8sec	4min 0sec	8min 6sec	2min 8sec	2min 4sec	2min 21sec	1min 58sec	2min 47sec
	range	2.53-15.05	1.14-8.45	2.35-6.20	4.45-12.01	1.21-3.36	1.01-2.26	1.28-3.43	1.16-2.55	1.35-5.48
	N	25	22	23	17	16	16	13	12	11
revised prospectus	median	6min 11sec	3min 4sec	4min 1sec	8min 53sec	2min 26sec	2min 8sec	2min 25sec	2min 6sec	2min 58sec
	range	3.40-15.25	1.58-9.30	3.06-6.29	5.01-14.05	1.48-4.09	1.35-3.17	1.50-3.37	1.34-3.01	0.45-6.00
	N	27	21	26	16	15	15	15	14	12
Less Able Students										
original prospectus	median	*	3min 8sec	4min 49sec	*	1min 39 sec	1min 39 sec	1min 34 sec	1min 16 sec	
	range		1.40-5.45	2.39-7.49		0.41-2.44	0.52-2.24	0.51-2.54	0.45-2.40	
	N		29	31		31	29	27	26	
revised prospectus	median	*	3m 15sec	4min 35sec	*	1min 44sec	1min 58sec	1min 31sec	1min 13sec	*
	range		1.36-5.36	3.00-6.12		1.04-2.48	1.02-4.49	0.55-2.31	0.45-2.38	
	N		28	29		29	25	19	22	

* Less able students did not do this task

each task. (The differences shown in the Table between the able and the less able students on Task Five reflect the fact that the less able students were required to find fewer items).

A comparison of the results in terms of the original versus the revised prospectus shows that <u>none</u> of the differences between the times recorded for the two prospectuses on any task was significant, either overall, or within any particular group. Indeed, in view of the wide time ranges reported for each task, the differences shown in Table II can be regarded as negligible.

<u>Errors</u>. Errors made by readers were of two types: (i) misinterpreting the instructions in the work-book, and (ii) misreading the prospectus. The data from the one or two subjects who misinterpreted the instructions were discarded. Very few readers made any mistakes in retrieving information from the prospectus - only one or two errors were recorded within each task for the whole sample - and they occurred equally in retrieval from the original or the revised prospectus.

Thus the data from the error analyses, and from the times recorded for readers to retrieve different aspects of information from the prospectuses, indicate that the revised prospectus could be regarded as effective as, but no better than, the original in terms of use. And, as has been noted, this effectiveness was achieved at a much reduced cost.

Some additional data

In addition to the study described above, two more investigations were carried out by some of the writers' undergraduate students which used university students as readers. These studies examined in more detail (i) retrieval from 'continuous text' using the method of scanning (Poulton, 1967) and (ii) retrieval from the tables. The results of both of these investigations paralleled the results we have reported here: no significant differences were found in retrieval times from the two prospectuses.

One interesting finding which did emerge, however, (but which was not quite significant at the accepted level of $p < .05$), was that women students scanned the revised prospectus faster than they scanned the original. (This difference did not emerge with the men.) It appeared that the women students scanned more systematically than did the men, but it is not clear why they should obtain better results with one prospectus than another because of this. The findings are of interest because (i) they tie in with other research which suggests that females are better at scanning than are males (Hartley and Burnhill, 1971; Hartley et al, 1975) and (ii) they suggest, <u>contrary</u> to the research literature, that typographical variants not detected by less able readers may be detected by more able ones.

The attitudes of users

The people who most used the college prospectus continually appeared not to be the students of the college (some of them denied ever having seen it) but the administrative staff. We thought it would be of interest, therefore, to ask the college secretaries who were concerned with admissions and enquiries about their attitudes to the revised prospectus. In the event we were able to interview eight such secretaries shortly after the introduction of the revised prospectus. It is fair to record that six of these secretaries were, at that time, extremely hostile towards it. It appeared, however, from our interviews, that the main reason for this hostility lay in the fact that the revised prospectuses had arrived for the secretaries on the first day of the new academic year; consequently they had had to use a new prospectus whose layout was different from the one they were accustomed to, at a time when they were exceedingly pressed in terms of enquiries. As one secretary put it, 'The first thing that struck me was that I couldn't find anything!' The loss of colour coding was the change that affected them most. Some secretaries had cut the edges of the text to make departmental section entries clearer, and indeed one secretary had torn the book apart and separately grouped each departmental section in a large ringed folder, but, as she did this for the original one too, this was not such a radical innovation as we thought. It illustrates, however, that there are problems of using prospectuses with which this report has not been concerned.

In our discussion with these secretaries it appeared that the initially aroused hostility had partly abated, but that it was still present. When pressed to make detailed points of criticism of the revised prospectus with reference to the original, a variety of criticisms were elicited. However, what one secretary appeared to like another one disliked!

PART 4. CONCLUDING COMMENTS

This paper has shown that most college and university prospectuses use a traditional approach to a design problem that needs fundamental rethinking. Our study has shown that it is possible to rationalize typographic conventions, to save money and to produce a prospectus which, to all intents and purposes, is no more difficult to use. However, it is important to observe, in reaching these conclusions, that our method of collecting data was somewhat rough and ready: differences in time taken for retrieval may have been swamped by the time taken to write the answers down. Furthermore, of course, working against the clock and being timed by a friend may in itself by highly motivating. Klare (personal communication) has argued that high motivation sustained over a period of time is likely to render insignificant any small effects due to typographic variables.

It is important to note in conclusion that our re-design of the prospectus, of course, produced only one re-designed version. In the act of designing, a typographer will examine mentally the typographical image of a range of possible solutions, each one having the status of a hypothesis to be tested and, if necessary, rejected on logical, economic and/or technical grounds. (Furthermore, the process is holistic, not a one-step-by-one-step procedure.) In principle therefore we could have systematically varied a number of parameters (eg the amount of space between main, secondary and tertiary headings) and thus provided several re-designed prospectuses. The research we have carried out, however, suggests that it would be extremely difficult to assess in a practical situation the effectiveness of such changes relative to each other. There may be a case, therefore, for examining in a laboratory situation variations produced in this way. In particular we would be interested in comparing the typographic codings between different entries of differing kinds to see if in fact the number used by printers are really needed (or even seen by non-typographers). In brief, we are interested in how far space and a minimum number of typographic variables can be combined to indicate structure compared with more traditional methods which use multiples of typesizes and typefaces. The research reported in this paper has indicated that a more rational approach to print design can produce cost-benefits, but there is still a need, one feels, for more precise investigation in this area of enquiry.

ACKNOWLEDGEMENTS

We are grateful to the Social Science Research Council who financed our research, and to all those people who generously assisted us with our studies. We are indebted to pupils and staff at the Regis School, Wolverhampton, and to students, secretarial staff, and Miss R Brody of the Liberal Studies Department at Stafford College of Further Education. We are particularly indebted to Mr Edmund Brown who was responsible for the typographical design of the new version of the prospectus.

REFERENCES

Baudin, F (1967) 'Typography: evolution and revolution'. 'Journal of Typographic Research' Vol 1, No 4, pp 373-86

Burnhill, P and Hartley, J (1975) 'Psychology and textbook design: a research critique'. In 'Aspects of Educational Technology VIII'. (Eds) J Baggaley et al. Pitman, London

Hartley, J and Burnhill, P (1971) 'Experiments with unjustified text'. 'Visible Language' Vol 5, No 3, pp 265-77

Hartley, J, Fraser, S and Burnhill, P (1975) 'Some observations on the reliability of measures used in reading and typographic research'. 'Journal of Reading Behavior' (in press)

Hartley, J and Mills, R L (1973) 'Unjustified experiments in typographical research and instructional design'. 'British Journal of Educational Technology' Vol 2, No 4, pp 120-31

Poulton, E C (1966) 'Unwanted asymmetrical transfer effects with balanced experimental designs'. 'Psychological Bulletin' Vol 66, pp 1 - 8

Poulton, E C (1967) 'Skimming (scanning) news items printed in 8 point and 9 point letters'. 'Ergonomics' Vol 10, No 6, pp 713-16

Siegel, S (1956) 'Non-parametric Statistics for the Behavioral Sciences'. McGraw-Hill, New York

Tinker, M A (1963) 'The Legibility of Print'. Iowa State University Press, Ames, Iowa

Audio video composition:
a pilot experiment

SALAH EL-ARABY, JUDITH GOULD

Composition writing poses a continuing challenge to learners of English as a second language because it is a test of integrative language skills. Educators have been searching for effective devices to help learners through the gradual transition from controlled, guided composition to authentic free expression. This paper discusses the procedures, results and implications of a pilot experiment designed to estimate the relative effects of self-teaching video and audio aids in controlled composition writing.

PURPOSE

During the last five years videotape programmes seem to be gaining ground as an invaluable means to help learners view, criticize and evaluate their performance. It has been used, according to Brown, Lewis and Harcleroad (Brown, et al, 1973) as an aid in teaching demonstrations and recording performance for analysis and microteaching. For writing composition topics, videotape is considered by El-Araby (El-Araby, 1974) as a useful medium for providing the learner with ideas and cultural content which he can make use of in writing.

As soon as the American University in Cairo purchased its first portable, half-inch, single camera videotape recorder, graduate students and their advisers began to explore means of producing programmes related to classwork. Mrs Judith Gould, a teacher in the Freshman Writing Clinic, a graduate student in the AV Resources class and one of the two authors of this paper, designed, wrote and produced a self-teaching videotaped programme to help students write controlled, well-organized compositions. The tape presents a systematic, precise description of the various parts of a 'shisha' (waterpipe) showing how they fit together to form a functional whole. During the second part of the tape, students are shown the process of smoking a 'shisha', from the time burning embers of coal are placed on washed tobacco to the final stage where the smoker inhales then exhales cooled tobacco smoke with evident pleasure.

When initial reaction to this programme from both teachers and students seemed encouraging, the authors started considering a systematic, rigorous way to measure the effects of the programme on composition writing. It was deemed necessary that as many variables as possible should be controlled in order to pin-point the possible advantage of this medium over any other.

PROCEDURES

Four groups of Liberal Arts students in the Freshman Writing Clinic were chosen as subjects for the experiment. The following controls were exercized to produce two groups (video and sound track) of 17 matched students. First, the four groups were classified according to their proficiency in the English language as determined by their scores on the Michigan Test and/or the number of semesters spent in the English Language Institute and the Freshman Writing Clinic. Second, their attitude towards English, their usage of the language and their experiences with a 'shisha' (waterpipe) were determined and seemed comparable as evidenced by their answers on the Student Data Sheet (Table 1). Due to these controls the two major groups of video and sound track were further subdivided to produce a 'HIGH VIDEO' (where high refers to level of English proficiency) and 'LOW VIDEO', 'HIGH SOUND TRACK' and 'LOW SOUND TRACK'. Before the test, a sound track of the videotape was prepared, to be administered to the second group of candidates. Second, identical instructions were typed and handed to the proctors of each group of students. Candidates were asked to view, or listen to a tape on the waterpipe describing its parts and explaining the processes for smoking it. Third, a diagram of a waterpipe was given to candidates of both groups so that they might take notes while viewing or listening to the programme. Fourth, both groups were given exactly 40 minutes to write the composition without asking for help from the proctors.

The authors agree with John Oller (Oller, 1973) that the major difficulty with using composition as a testing device is correction. Checklists and itemized evaluation sheets, such as Don Knapp's (Knapp, 1972) have been devised to guide the subjective judgement in marking composition. The authors, therefore, prepared a draft checklist of items graded according to a five-point scale from 1 fair to 5 excellent. A jury of five professors and eight language teachers at the American University reviewed the checklist and modified it into the final version shown in Table II. The evaluation form was divided, according to the presentation of the taped programme, into three major categories. The first was a check on the spatial order, or description of the major parts of the waterpipe. The second was concerned with the explanation and logical sequences of the processes involved in smoking it. The third category sought to evaluate students' performance and skill in presenting interesting, precise information within an integrated unified composition.

Four experienced teachers were selected to grade the student composition tests, so that each student composition was read and graded twice. Each pair was asked to grade one video set and one sound-track group without knowing the nature of the candidates. Whenever the discrepancy between the two markers was within 10% of the grade, the average of the two marks was

Table I. Student data sheet

Name: .... Age: ...... Class: ....

Please answer the following questions by checking (✓) only <u>one</u> answer.

ITEMS	Video 17 students			Soundtrack 17 students		
1. I attended a/an:						
Arabic School	3			1		
English School	11			12		
French School	5			6		
2. I was registered in ELI for:						
One Semester	4			4		
Two Semesters	4			7		
Three Semesters	1			–		
not at all	8			6		
3. I have been in the Freshman Writing Clinic for:						
One Semester	9			8		
Two Semesters	8			9		
4. I have had the following experience with a waterpipe:						
I've seen it used by others	13			17		
I've used one of them	4			3		
I own one	2			1		
A close friend/relative owns one	–			2		
I've never seen one	–			2		
I am familiar with all its parts	4			4		
I am familiar with all its processes	3			6		
5. I speak the following languages:	a	b	c	a	b	c
Arabic	8	3	2	9	3	2
English	9	8	3	4	9	4
French	1	9	8	4	3	7
6. I write (letters, stories, notes) in the following languages:						
Arabic	4	7	1	6	2	4
English	12	3	12	7	8	1
French	1	3	–	4	3	5
7. I am studying English at AUC to:						
pass exams in English and other subjects	4	–	–	4	1	–
learn more about English-speaking people	1	–	–	1	1	–
learn more about the culture of English-speaking people	2	–	1	–	–	1
explain Egyptian cultural features to others	1	1	1	–	–	–
secure a better job	14	1	–	1	2	2
please my parents	–	–	–	–	1	–
communicate better with native speakers	2	3	1	7	–	2
fulfil AUC requirements	4	5	1	5	2	–

248

Table II. Composition evaluation form

ITEMS	Poor	Fair	Good	V.Good	Exc
I. Spatial Order (Description)					
1. Topic sentence gives main idea of paragraph					
2. Description of each part clearly stated					
3. Relations between parts clearly given					
4. Relationship and transition between sentences clear					
II. Sequential Order (Process)					
1. Topic sentence gives main idea of paragraph					
2. Each process clearly explained					
3. Action and processes in correct order					
4. Relations among processes clear					
5. Conclusion draws all processes together					
III. Overall Evaluation					
1. The two paragraphs form an integrated and unified composition					
2. Ideas clearly expressed and easy to understand					
3. Presentation is interesting, precise and informative					

considered the final score for the paper. In seven cases the difference was beyond the limits specified. A third marker checked the compositions and an average of the two closer grades was recorded as the final grade for each of the seven papers. A meeting was held before the process of correction to help the four markers agree on similar interpretations of the twelve items on the evaluation sheet and the five-point credit scale for each.

LIMITATIONS OF THE EXPERIMENT

The constraints on this study are mainly due to practical considerations and technical limitations. University authorities encourage research studies as long as they do not unduly interfere with regular course proceedings or students' learning interests. The experiment had to be carried out within the existing structure of student classification and course progress. The authors had to wait until the classes had covered description and explanation in composition writing before administering the test. A further test to ensure reliability of the composition scores would have been frowned upon because it would have disturbed the same subjects while they were learning different skills.

Technical limitations have been imposed by the nature of the video equipment operated by semi-skilled, amateurish technicians. The portable, half-inch Sony AV 3670 CE set includes one fixed camera with a zoom lens and a fairly sensitive microphone. No television studio with proper acoustic treatment and stage props was available. Because facilities for editing the videotape were non-existent, a great deal of effort and time were spent in numerous rehearsals with the university custodians who played the leading parts in the video programme. Though the videotape was pedagogically satisfactory, it lacked many fine touches that better equipment could have realized.

RESULTS AND IMPLICATIONS

The most important limitation of the study is the small number of students in the matched groups tested. Although they constitute representative samples of the student population in the Freshman year at the American University in Cairo, the results of their performance on the video, audio composition test cannot be generalized to other groups performing under less rigid controls. In short, the results of this experiment should not be read as a conclusive indication of the relative effects of video aids and sound track in composition writing. A much larger sample of students, a third control group taught according to traditional methods and a re-test to check reliability would have given more strength to the results of the study. However, enough information was gathered after analysing the results to suggest the interaction between students' learning styles and the kinds of media used to present the composition theme.

As the scores of the four subgroups show in Table III, the high video group scored consistently higher than the low video, the high sound-track or the low

Table III. Scores master sheet

Bases	Video		Soundtrack	
	High	Low	High	Low
Scores	91.6	79.16	75.0	76.6
	80.0	68.3	72.5	73.3
	73.3	66.6	66.6	67.5
	69.2	61.6	57.5	62.5
	69.2	49.16	52.5	60.9
	60.8	47.5	45.0	47.5
	60.4	41.6	35.0	42.5
	57.5	33.3		41.6
	45.8			41.6
				30.8
Means	67.53	55.90	57.73	54.47
Standard Deviation	12.7	14.5	13.7	14.8
Mean Scores on Parts of Composition:				
Description	74.72	57.18	63.92	62.12
Process	69.44	58.50	54.85	53.90
Overall	62.21	53.34	57.61	46.50

sound-track groups. Although the difference is not statistically significant it is frequent enough to suggest that, according to the representative sample, higher proficiency students learn better when videotaped programmes are used to help them write controlled composition. Both individual percentage scores and means of the four groups (Table III) would support this notion. In general the scores of the two video subgroups are consistently higher than those of the two sound-track subgroups. It is interesting to note that while the 'high video' group was 9.80% higher than the 'high sound-track' group, the 'low video' group was only .43% higher than the 'low sound-track' group. This further reinforces the idea that students with a higher level of proficiency in English were able to benefit more from the multi-media presentation. Although the difference once more is not statistically significant, it does show a slight advantage for the video group at both levels.

A breakdown of the scores on the three parts of the composition was made to determine whether any one group has done consistently better than the others on spatial description, sequential order of process or overall evaluation. All subgroups, with the only exception of 'low video' have been much better on the description of parts of the waterpipe than on the other two categories, logical sequence and overall evaluation. It seems that the step-by-step description of the various parts of the waterpipe via video or sound track has been of significant help to the candidates. One possible explanation of the relatively low score of the 'low video' group is that they had too many things to cope with at the same time. They had to listen to the recorded voice, write down notes on the sketch given to them and watch the video image. However, within the limitations of the present study there is no sure way of determining the validity of this observation. The classroom teacher of this group has found similar difficulty when a film has been shown to the students for the purpose of controlling composition writing. It may also be worthy of mention that the 'high video' group has scored appreciably higher than all other groups on overall evaluation. One may cautiously assume, on the basis of the representative sample in the study, that students of higher proficiency in the language are more responsive to video media than those who are less competent in the language.

On the basis of this study the following conclusions can safely be stated:

1. That both video and sound-track programmes can be used with advantage to test controlled composition writing.
2. That according to the sample investigated there seems to be no significant difference between the use of the two media for the purpose stated.
3. That self-teaching can be achieved through the use of video and audio programmes.

Better-controlled experiments on a much larger number of subjects may give conclusive answers to many of the questions this limited pilot experiment has not dealt with.

ACKNOWLEDGEMENT

The authors are deeply indebted to the Ford Foundation and the Administration of the American University in Cairo whose financial and moral support made this study possible.

REFERENCES

El-Araby, Salah (1974) 'Audio Visual Aids in Teaching English: An Introduction to Materials and Methods'. Longman, London, p 141

Brown, James et al (1973) 'AV Instruction: Technology, Media and Methods'. McGraw Hill, New York, p 244

Knapp, Donald (1972) 'A focused, efficient method to relate composition correction to testing aims'. In 'Teaching English as a Second Language'. (Eds) Harold Allen and Russel Campbell. McGraw Hill, New York, pp 213 - 21

Oller, John and Richards, Jack (Eds) (1973) 'Focus on the Learner'. Newburry House

Factors affecting the programming and control of individualized systems of instruction (for the training of technical and science teachers in a developing country)

A J ROMISZOWSKI

ABSTRACT

Individualized or 'personalized' systems of instruction vary widely in structure and in the techniques used for presentation and control. They also vary in what aspects of a course are indeed 'personalized'; variable content, variable learning modes, individual evaluation and feedback, or simply self-pacing. The majority of systems in widespread use are only individualized in the last one or two of these aspects.

One such system which is gaining rapid acceptance at university level, in academic courses mainly, is the Keller Plan. Its popularity stems partly from the ease with which it can be implemented in the traditional structure of a long academic course, partly from the level of sophistication of the typical undergraduate.

Its applicability is less proven in short, intensive courses, with practical rather than academic objectives and with a target population with less experience of studying from the printed word.

After a brief summary of the Keller Plan, this paper discusses five experimental courses for technical and scince teachers which are based on a somewhat modified version. Each course consists of about 150 hours of study usually completed in a month. A total of 266 students were involved in the trials. Four courses taught basic subject matter (electrical and electronics procedures); the fifth also taught laboratory practice, lesson planning, materials and visual aids preparation and use, etc.

The philosophy underlying the use of individualized techniques in these courses is discussed and the rationale for modifying certain aspects of the original Keller Plan are examined.

Among the points discussed are:

> The overall effectiveness of the courses.
> The significant early drop-out rate.
> The use of the 'unitmeter' for group motivation.
> The role of the monitor/proctor in the system.
> Student reactions to continuous evaluation and to differences
>> in the severity of individual monitors.
> Programming factors - optimal length for study units
>>   - effect of units having varying levels of difficulty
>>   - techniques for rapid revision of the materials.

INDIVIDUALIZED INSTRUCTION - WHAT IS INDIVIDUALIZED?

'Individualization' is one of those catch-phrases of recent educational jargon which has been used to describe so many patently different systems of instruction that, unqualified by further definitions, it often confuses more than it communicates. At one extreme, individualization is deemed to have taken place if students are working alone at their own pace. At the other extreme the term may imply a system in which any or all of the following factors are adapted to the needs of each individual student - pace, medium of presentation, study style, content, evaluation techniques.

A simple classification is suggested by Edling (1970) which can be summarized in Table I.

Table I.

| | Objectives | |
Media	School Determined	Learner Selected
System Determined	'Individually diagnosed and prescribed (IPI) (PLAN) (Some CAI)	'Personalized' (many CAI systems)
Learner Selected	'Self-directed' (Learning resource centres) (Some multi-media kits)	'Independent study' (Project QUEST)

This classification, though useful, makes no direct mention of learner groupings or learning pace (often considered key factors in individualization), although all the examples quoted by Edling happen to involve self-instruction or small groups under self-paced learning conditions, as if this was an essential ingredient.

However, it is by no means clear whether a CAI course which allows the learner to select his objectives, is any more or less 'personalized' than the system at Summerhill (Neil, 1960) which also allows the student to select the lessons he attends. If there is a difference then surely it lies in what happens within the lesson. How does the lesson adapt to the learner? Which experience is more individualized, a linear programme in which all students read the same material (albeit at their own pace) or a traditional lesson where all the students have been selected by some diagnostic procedure so that the teacher has an inventory of their learning problems?

We might add a 'third dimension' to Edling's model by constructing a hierarchy of potential individualization among media, based on the degree to which a medium can adapt a presentation automatically to the needs of the individual learner. This is the degree to which a given instructional system is a cybernetic system.

Even in the majority of current CAI adaptive programmes now in existence, one sees only a limited level of adaptability. In highly specific subjects (tracking skills or Suppes' 'drill and practice' mathematics courses, for example) the adaptive machine may have the edge on the human teacher, but in most academic 'open-ended' disciplines the personal tutor, backed up by efficient diagnostic procedures, is still hard to beat. The more open-ended the subject and the more inquisitive and sophisticated the student, the greater the need for adaptive capability. Hence the relative lack of acceptance of 'traditional' programmed instruction at university level, and hence also the origins of the Keller plan.

THE KELLER PLAN AND DERIVATIVES

The main features of the Keller plan include (Keller, 1967, 1968):

(a) Individual study units, usually written matter, which may be (but need not be) specially produced for the course, and may (but certainly need not) be in programmed instruction form.

(b) Self-tests which the student attempts and then discusses with a proctor or monitor.

(c) Study guides in the form of detailed objectives, cross-referenced to the reading and practical assignments.

(d) Individual and/or group practical work and discussion controlled by specially written guide notes.

(e) The role of the teacher is mainly that of a manager of the system. He has monitors to help him in assessing and tutoring the students. The monitors may be special staff but are often more advanced students who are given the responsibility for the progress of the slower ones. They usually have a monitor's guide book to help them. The teacher evaluates overall progress and revises the course materials, but he does take on monitoring when necessary.

(f) The teacher also gives a certain amount of face-to-face classes, but these concentrate on enrichment of the course and students have to 'earn' the right to attend these classes by reaching proficiency in certain sets of objectives.

(g) Proficiency in most Keller courses is taken to mean 100% on each study unit test before moving on to the next one.

The system was first introduced experimentally in the psychology department of the University of Columbia in 1963, and in 1964 was installed at the University of Brasilia (Azzi, 1964, 1965). Since then, use of the plan has spread to other universities and institutions in the USA and also in Brazil, and has been applied to subjects other than psychology, for example, physics MIT (Green, 1971).

Although the Keller plan is the name now in vogue, other attempts were being made to overcome some of the shortcomings of early programmed instruction courses; for example in the UK, Croxton and Martin at the University of Aston were attempting to increase the adaptive nature of programmed courses by roughly similar methods, although also utilizing a computer as a diagnostic aid (Croxton and Martin, 1970). Other examples abound which have some, though not all, of the characteristics of the Keller plan listed above. In the last few years such 'personalized' courses have developed an enthusiastic following in American universities and in other countries including Brazil. At a recent conference/workshop on personalized instruction in São Paulo, Sherman (1974) estimated that in the USA "... more than 500 professors have developed their own PSI (personalized systems of instruction) courses and their own materials. At least twice that number have given PSI courses with commercially available materials ..."

WHY USE PSI COURSES?

The acceptance of PSI courses at university level is a result of:
  (a) relative ease and speed of materials preparation (not specially programmed and often available from existing sources);
  (b) relative ease of implementation within a traditional university course structure (no major timetable changes, irregular attendance problems minimized, slower students may put in extra time).

The relative success, as compared with other attempts at more rigid programming, is probably explained by:
  (a) familiarity of the style of the learning materials to students;
  (b) the discussion/assessment sessions with the monitors (i) allow for expansion/inquiry/criticism, (ii) ensure full mastery before progress to new materials, (iii) make up for any deficiencies in the quality of the materials, (iv) supply rapid feedback to the teacher, enabling him to revise or add to the course materials on a regular basis throughout the year.

These benefits are particularly marked in long, academic courses and especially in subjects demanding discussion and open-ended responses, involving 'sophisticated' learners.

There is less evidence which supports the use of Keller-type course structures (as opposed to other strategies) in short, intensive courses, or when the subject matter is rigid, or with students not well accustomed to self-study from written materials. These are the characteristics of the courses described below.

PSI USED FOR TECHNICAL TEACHER TRAINING

The following discussion is based on the results of a series of PSI courses given in Brazil during 1973/74. The course materials were prepared at the National Foundation for Technical Teacher Training, by a team of specialists trained for the purpose. The courses are intended for trainee technical teachers with generally limited entry experience. A full account of the courses is given elsewhere (Netto, 1974). Table II summarizes the details pertinent to the current discussion. The arguments for using a PSI structure for these courses ran as follows:
  (a) A crash programme of training is required to produce the technical teachers required by current rapid industrialization. Traditional facilities for effecting this training do not exist. Therefore a type of in-service scheme is planned whereby the National Foundation trains and equips a first cadre of teachers, who in turn become trainers of teachers in their locality (the chain-reaction principle).

Table II. Details of three individualized courses for technical teachers

Course Title	Low Tension Electrical Installation (Design)	Basic Electronics	Physics (Experimental)
Objectives (and the main types of Learning Tasks)	Plan, draw, calculate and price an installation for a given building and given needs, following norms laid down and administrative procedures. (Procedural Tasks)	Identify the type, analyse and test basic electronic circuits. Analyse systems into basic circuits and explain function of each. (Conceptual and Discriminatory Tasks – and Laboratory Procedures)	Use laboratory equipment, carry out, write up and criticize experiments. Make and use equipment and teaching aids. Plan a teaching unit based on an experiment. (Conceptual, Procedural and Creative Tasks)
Course Length (Maximum)	150 hours (3 weeks)	156 hours (3 weeks)	150 hours (3 weeks)
Trainees (Number and Background)	48 + 51 + 42 (3 courses) All experienced installers.	41 Low entry level of knowledge.	44 Generally low entry level of physics. Not used to learning through experiments.
Materials	39 obligatory units. 2 optional.	29 obligatory units.	42 obligatory units. 5 optional discussion/ demonstration.
Monitors	Five monitors per course, giving a teaching ratio of about 10:1. All monitors were specially trained staff.		

(b) Thus effective training systems and materials must be developed to enable relatively inexperienced teachers to instruct others. These 'multiplicators', as they are called, must get experience in teaching others during their course. Involving them as monitors will achieve this.

(c) The multiplicators may have to instruct groups or individuals. Individualized materials give the necessary flexibility.

(d) Finally the concepts of 'mastery learning', behavioural objectives and self-pacing are generally new to the Brazilian educational system. Here is a chance to propagate them 'by example'.

Thus the basic Keller plan seems ideal. However there are several differences between these courses and the classic Keller model:

(a) The courses as given so far have a fixed maximum time and are very intensive. This was an unavoidable administrative constraint during the experimental testing period. There is no reason why in future the multiplicators need to follow the same time-scale.

(b) So far the students have not acted as monitors, again due to the extra functions the monitors have during the testing period (evaluating and improving the materials). Most of the monitors were also authors of parts of the materials. This again should change with future courses.

(c) Only very few optional 'motivational' lectures and discussions were included (and then only to present materials which cannot be conveniently presented in print). They were not deemed so necessary in a short course, and probably would not be very motivational as 'extra work' at the end of an eight-hour day of study.

(d) However, to keep up the pace of work, and also to increase motivation, a pacing device in the form of a graphical display of all students' progress was used. This 'unitmeter' proved very popular in practice.

(e) One comment made by Sherman (1974) concerning the success of PSI courses, is that the teacher must be there, constantly involved, modifying, improving, discussing, motivating. In a sense the chain-reaction scheme will send fledgling ex-monitors out to repeat their training course without the presence of the teacher/author. A certain contact and feedback from the field is planned, but this will necessarily be sketchy as the scheme expands. How the course efficiency will stand in the second and subsequent phases of the scheme has yet to be seen.

(f) Finally, as mentioned above, the target populations and the course contents are also very different from the classic university applications of the Keller plan. We shall examine this aspect in detail later.

SOME RESULTS IN SUMMARY

Completion of course within time

Two of the courses seem to have been relatively well timed. The electronics course, however, fared badly. Analysis showed that the early units were much too difficult and much too long. Unit 5, for example, took a mean study time of 14 hours, and one student spent 27 hours of study on this unit. This was obviously a great error in programming, which showed up all the more when one noticed that the later units of the course were very easy and quick. The 30% or 40% of the group who managed to struggle through the first 14 units then romped through the remaining 15 units at the rate of 2 to 5 hours per unit with hardly any problems. These trends can be seen on the graphs. So much for the claim that it does not matter about the quality of the course materials. There is obviously a limit to the number of problems caused by poor material which can be left to the monitors to sort out.

Table III

	Electrical Installation	Basic Electronics	Physics
Per cent of students who finished the course within time	84	34	88
Per cent who did not finish or finished later	11	61	5
Per cent of drop-outs	5	5	7

A further interesting point concerned the drop-outs. These almost all dropped out in the first couple of days of the courses, often claiming to have 'prior appointments'. There appears to be a small group in the target population which just does not take to self-instructional techniques. It would have been interesting to analyse this group further, but it vanished so quickly that no one had the chance.

Motivation

It is encouraging that the majority, including those who did not finish all their course, worked systematically to the end. Progress was helped by the 'unitmeters'. Students generally took pride in keeping their position on the graph up-to-date. It was found more effective to allow the students rather than the monitors to mark the graph. This competitive 'wish to be graded', much stronger than would be found in similar target populations in Britain, is probably a culture factor. The author has noted the same phenomenon in other developing countries.

Role of the Monitors

On the assessment of practical assignments, where the monitor's judgement enters, it proved difficult to standardize assessment procedures. Regular assessment meetings proved necessary. These variations in severity, however, did not seem to be reflected in undue favouritism for the 'lax' monitor on the part of students (Neves, 1974). On the contrary, a student who was failed tended to stick with the same monitor to be re-tested. He might change monitors for another study unit, however.

A very useful function was played by the monitor/authors, in revising weak points in the materials at evening meetings on a more or less daily basis. Thus, by the end of the three weeks of a course all materials had already been re-written in draft, ready for the next course.

PROGRAMMING FACTORS AFFECTING EFFICIENCY

Length of the study unit

The three scatter graphs illustrated below relate the mean study time of the units in a course to the number of students failing to obtain a 100% assessment first time off. There appears to be a certain amount of correlation. Longer units are more likely to give problems (or conversely is it that units which give problems take longer)?

The correlation is not very strong, however. There are several examples of long units with low failure rates (mainly long chunks of descriptive material) but much fewer short units with high failure rates.

The general lesson to learn is to keep the units reasonably short, say, two to four hours of study.

Effect of the type of learning task

Clearly a unit is not difficult simply because it is long. A further factor is the content of the unit. There are other student-related factors too. To establish some kind of absolute difficulty factor may indeed be an impossible task. If we use the failure rate as a criterion we get the type of chicken-egg argument illustrated in the last section. However, it was felt that the mean failure rate on similar types of units may yield some 'relative difficulty' figures as between different types of learning task.

It so happens that certain groups of study units in certain courses deal with predominantly one type of learning task. An effort was therefore made to analyse the learning tasks within the units and to classify the units accordingly. For this purpose, both Bloom's taxonomy of cognitive objectives and Gagné's hierarchy of learning categories was used. The results of this analysis are shown in Table IV.

Whereas not very much significance can be attached to this data, for the analysis is very general and (as all task analyses) somewhat subjective, a few interesting points emerge.

(a) The electrical installations course appears to have the lowest levels of learning task, and yet the highest mean failure rate. This illustrates the point that when Gagné talks of learning hierarchies he is referring to prerequisites rather than to absolute difficulty. It is quite easy to learn (and understand) a simple rule of grammar (such as that in Portuguese the adjective agrees with the noun in both number and gender). However, to use the rule one must first know a few nouns and adjectives, and it is at this simple stimulus-response level that all the

261

sweat of language learning takes place (eg in Portuguese there are hardly any guidelines to help you decide if a particular noun is masculine or feminine - you just 'know').

(b) The electronics course is difficult to interpret as it was so badly programmed in terms of study unit length. However, the first 14 units (which most people completed) are analysed here. Despite their length the mean error rates are lower than on the electrical installations course. It seems that the programming quality of the electrical installations course, though uniform, is uniformly poor.

(c) The materials of the physics course would seem to be much better programmed, if mean error rates are a guide. A subjective reading of the various course materials confirms this view. Indeed, the physics programming team had much more extensive experience and training, and had better opportunities for pre-testing their materials. It would seem a sign of good programming too, that errors (and hence the need for monitor assistance) should occur in the conceptual material but should be almost completely eliminated from the simple procedural units.

CONCLUSIONS

1. PSI courses can be effectively used for short, intensive periods as well as for the more common applications on long courses.

2. The majority of students, although unaccustomed to this style of learning, showed themselves capable of studying for long periods at a much greater intensity than on courses of a traditional type.

3. For periods of up to several weeks, motivation can be maintained without use of motivational lectures. Simple progress records help to maintain motivation, through competition, even where adult students are concerned.

4. Programming factors are not as unimportant as some proponents of PSI would have us believe. Whereas it is true that weaknesses in the learning materials will 'come out in the wash' and that there is always the possibility of amplification or correction by the monitors, this is always wasteful of monitor time and of student time. In extreme cases (as the basic electronics course, for example) few students may finish the course in reasonable time (or before they lose all motivation), or alternatively monitors may lower standards or start 'expounding' in traditional teacher fashion in an attempt to speed things up.

5. The length of time necessary to complete a study unit should be kept short. Lengthy units should be split or re-written with more self-tests and monitorial interventions.

6. The course producer should be aware of the type of learning task he is setting his student and of its probable difficulty and necessary prerequisites. For this he needs to develop task analysis (preferably behavioural analysis) skills.

7. Thus, whatever the case at university level, Keller-type courses for use at lower levels need careful programming and should therefore be prepared by trained programmers.

SCATTER GRAPHS FOR THREE PSI COURSES

ELECTRICAL INSTALLATIONS

Results for course involving 42 students.
Each '•' represents a study unit of the course.
Vertical axis: Mean study time to complete first attempt (hours).
Horizontal axis: Number of students failing to obtain a satisfactory
                 assessment (100%) on first attempt

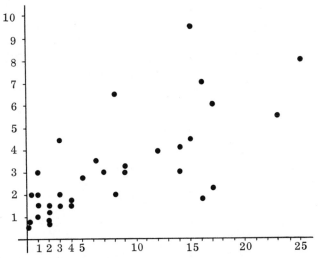

In general, longer study units have higher failure rates.

PHYSICS

Results of course involving 44 students.
Axes of graph as above.

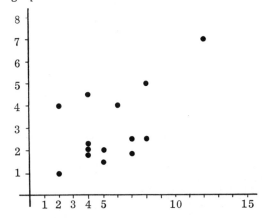

Note: Only the 14 units teaching theory are plotted here. The 14 laboratory and the 14 materials constructions units, being step-by-step instructions on how to perform self-checking procedures, produced no unsatisfactory assessments whatever the length of the unit involved.

ELECTRONICS

Results of course involving 41 students.
Axes of graph as above.

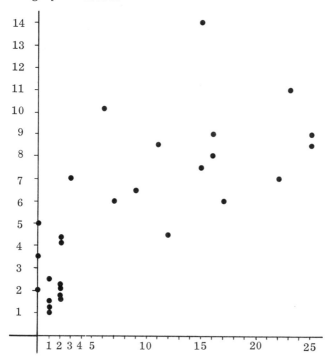

In general this graph supports the evidence of the earlier two graphs that the length of the study unit is an important factor controlling its difficulty.

However, the results shown here are distorted by the large number of students who did not complete the course.

The cluster of 'low difficulty' is exaggerated. All the shorter units were in the later part of the course, so a diminished number of students attempted the final tests on these units.

All students attempted the final tests on the initial, long study units of the course.

Table IV. A comparison of the relative success of the PSI courses in teaching different learning tasks

Course	Electrical Installations		Basic Electronics		Physics		
Commentary on Content of Study Units Analysed	As the trainees all had experience of installation work, they had to learn few new concepts. Mainly use of reference books, calculations, drawing conventions.		(Analysis of first 14 study units only.) Basically new material involving new ideas and relationships. Having learnt, student uses his information in intellectual tasks of analysing and identifying.		New information, followed by routine experiments to verify it. Also guided instruction on visual aid preparation, lesson planning, etc.		
	7 units theory	18 units practice	7 units theory	7 units practice	14 units basic physics theory	14 of laboratory experiments	14 on visual aids preparation
Main Class of Objectives (Bloom)	Knowledge	Application	Comprehension	Analysis	Comprehension	Application	Application
Main Categories of Learning (Gagné)	Multiple Discriminations	Chains	Concepts + Principles	Discrimination (some problem solving)	Concepts + Principles	Chains + Multiple Discriminations	Chains + Multiple Discriminations
Mean Initial Failure Rate per Study Unit	23.4	23.5	17	14	5.6	0	0

REFERENCES

Azzi, R, Bori, C M and Keller, F S (1964) 'Um curso Moderno de Psicologia'. 'Ciencia e Cultura' Vol 16, No 4

Azzi, R (1965) 'A Personalized Course - Second Report'. Paper delivered at the American Psychological Association

Croxton, P C L and Martin, L H (1970) 'The application of programmed learning in higher education'. In 'Aspects of Educational Technology IV'. (Ed) Leedham, J F, Bajpai, A. Pitman, London

Edling, J V (1970) 'Individualized Instruction - A Manual for Administrators'. DCE Publications, Oregon State University

Green, B A (jnr) (1971) 'Teaching of physics at the MIT by Keller Plan'. 'American Journal of Physics' Vol 39, No 7

Keller, F S (1967) 'Engineering personalized instruction in the classroom'. 'Revista Interamericana de Psicologia' No 1

Keller, F S (1968) 'Goodbye teacher'. 'Journal of Applied Behavioural Analysis' No 1

Neil, A S (1960) 'Summerhill'. Hart Publishing Company, New York

Netto, W W (1974) 'Analise de alguns cursos em PSI desenvolvidos pela Fundação CENAFOR'. Paper delivered at the UNESCO/CLAF/MEC/DAU seminar on personalized systems of instruction. CENAFOR, São Paulo

Neves, L P (1974) 'A preferencia de Alunos por Monitores em um curso Programado Individualizado'. Paper delivered at the UNESCO/CLAF/MEC/DAU seminar on personalized systems of instruction. CENAFOR, São Paulo

Sherman, J G (1974) 'Comments on Personalized Systems of Instruction'. Paper delivered at the UNESCO/CLAF/MEC/DAU seminar on personalized systems of instruction. CENAFOR, São Paulo

Self-teaching
in university courses

P J HILLS

Traditionally, most universities have followed a pattern of teaching and learning suited to the kind of student who was able to pursue learning for its own sake. Now the role of the university has changed and the doors are open for all who wish, for any reason, to pursue higher education. As a result, students' attitudes to learning are changing and becoming more career oriented. Learning is now for the student a means to an end and no longer an end in itself.

In spite of this, many traditional university methods have remained virtually unchanged even in science and engineering courses where the rapid change in the mass of knowledge and the greater number of students participating in courses demands that the university should adapt its methods to these new requirements.

In addition, one of the important aims of a university education is to help an individual not only to learn while at university, but also to help him continue to learn throughout his life. It is necessary therefore to evolve methods which help the student adapt to continuous change and which help him to become a self-directing individual. This theme runs through many of the writings on higher education, as for example, Brook writing in 'The Modern University' says "among the aims of a university education must be included the acquisition of knowledge, but of far greater importance are the development of intellectual curiosity and the realization that the acquisition of knowledge is pleasurable, for the development of these qualities is a guarantee that the acquisition of knowledge will continue after the student has left university." (Brook, 1965).

Sir James Mountford goes further in his book 'British Universities' when he says that we need to "...provide the student with a body of positive knowledge which enhances his store of learning ... To the limits of his capacity he is trained to collect evidence for himself and form a balanced judgment about it. He fortifies his ability to think for himself." (Mountford, 1966).

Let us extract three statements from this so that we may consider them in relation to some of the points later in this paper. These three statements

are, the need to:
- (a) provide a body of knowledge
- (b) train a student to collect evidence for himself and form balanced judgements and
- (c) to help a student to think for himself.

Whatever techniques have to be developed in order that the student should achieve these aims depends ultimately on the individual student himself and it is the task of the teacher to help him with this.

Concern for the student as an individual is particularly important at the time of entry to a university. At school the student is subjected to comparatively strict discipline and control, but once having entered university he is virtually thrown on his own devices. Many students need help and guidance in their first year until they become familiar with their environment and the methods of a university. O'Connell, studying the problem of transition of students from school to university at the University of Surrey, concluded that this first year at university should be an intermediate stage between school and university. (O'Connell, 1970).

Many first-year students, finding the gap between school and university too great, need help in two main ways: firstly with personal problems in adjusting to their environment and secondly with teaching and learning problems arising from course material. Problems of this kind can effectively block a student in his first year at university and perhaps decrease his chances of becoming a self-directing individual.

The University of Surrey, in common with other universities, attempts to help with the personal problems of a student by assigning a personal tutor to each one to whom they may go if they need help. A student counsellor is also available to the students at all times, and a full-time student health service is maintained by the University.

The research to which this paper makes reference is concerned with the second of these problems, namely those specifically concerned with teaching and learning - although it is obviously not always possible to separate these from the personal problems of the student. Implicit in this work is the belief that in the first year at university students should be given some degree of direction and should be encouraged to seek solutions to their own problems which gives us an indication of the role of the teacher in promoting self-teaching in the student.

Accounts of the self-teaching methods developed during this work have appeared in papers given at previous APLET conferences and at a conference of the Chemical Society. (Davis and Hills, 1972; Hills and Stace, 1974). Details will therefore only be given here where it is necessary to clarify any results quoted.

TEACHING METHODS IN UNIVERSITY COURSES

Teaching methods in traditional university courses have relied heavily on the lecture method and its demerits and merits have been widely discussed elsewhere, for example in Bligh's book 'What's the use of lectures?' (Bligh, 1972) and Costin's article "Lecturing vs other methods of teaching: a review of the research' (Costin, 1972).

The results of my own work suggest that lectures have considerable appeal for students since they continue to attend them even though outline notes were available for the course studies (and bought by all of the students). They also continued to attend them when taperecordings of the lectures were placed in the library.

In a questionnaire given after an experiment concerned with the replacement of lectures by group showing of tape/slide material, both the lecturer involved and the students tended to agree with statements like:
"I prefer lectures or tutorials given by members of staff as they give personal contact."
"I did not get the same amount of involvement as with an ordinary lecture."

SELF-TEACHING SYSTEMS

The lecture has often been viewed as a method which stands on its own, but my own work suggests that it is possible to use the lecture as one facet of a systematic approach which is designed to help and guide the student. The effectiveness of such a systematic approach does not of course necessarily confirm the effectiveness of the lecture.

The particular system which evolved from my work provided information on a student's progress to the individual student throughout the course and provided library-based help with any difficulties that he might be having.

Two of the main hypotheses in the evaluation of the system were that:
(a) Students who regularly receive information on their progress would use reference material to obtain further help with their difficulties.
(b) Students who regularly receive information on their progress do better than those who do not.

In terms of the first hypothesis, the pattern of use of the reference material did not coincide with the need for use and students' comments indicate that they found the self-tests which provided them with knowledge of their progress useful just to make them aware of that progress even if they did not follow this up by using the reference material provided.

Another point which emerges from this is that there was a certain disparity between staff opinion and student opinion on the usefulness of the self-test material and the references provided. It appears that although the provision of information on their progress was appreciated by the students, the details on group performance circulated to the tutors on the course was little used.

The second hypothesis, that students who regularly receive information do better than those who do not, was investigated mainly in relation to normal end-of-course examination performance and was found to hold as has been reported in a previous paper (Davis and Hills, 1972). In addition to this, other factors emerge and these can be summarized broadly under headings of students with differences in:
  (a) career motivation
  (b) end of course examination performance.
Let us look first at career motivation.

Career motivation

Students from the three departments separate themselves by their performance in the end of course examinations into two main classes:
  (a) students taking electrical engineering as a career choice
  (b) students taking the subject as part of their course but with the
      specialization in chemical physics or physics.
This difference manifests itself throughout the study in many ways from the greater use of the revision material by electrical engineering students, to a superior performance in the tests and their superior performance in end-of-course examinations as compared with the other students.

End of course examination performance

Again, it is obvious from the results obtained that two main types of student are being separated out in the examination of end-of-course examination performances. It would appear also that these students can be identified by their behaviour on tests early in the course and that this might be used as an indication of a student's need for more individual staff attention.

THE USE OF THE LIBRARY AS A RESOURCES CENTRE FOR NON-BOOK MATERIAL

The use of the library to hold and issue books, tapes and tape/slide material was central to the study. The problems of classification, storage and issue of material other than books were tackled by library staff as they arose and resulted in the preparation of a special catalogue for non-book material. There is a growing realization of this new role of the library which MacIntyre describes as follows:

"The library of the future will cease to be a place for the collection of printed materials only and will become instead an instructional resource centre reflecting the fact that information is now regularly maintained and disseminated in print, sound, films, other pictorial and electronic modes." (MacIntyre, 1970).

Mackenzie, Eraut and Jones stress this role in terms of the learner and his needs:

"From the standpoint of the learner, what matters most is not the formal instruction he is given, but the kind of learning resources to which he has access." (Mackenzie, Eraut and Jones, 1970).

One of the learning resources to which the student had access in this study was tape/slide material which consisted of short recorded tutorials explaining difficult areas of the course, or which went through a set of typical problems for the course.

THE USE OF TAPE/SLIDE MATERIAL

As I have already indicated, students did not appear to like the use of tape/slide material when it was given to a large group as a lecture substitute, but when used for individual work in the university library students generally found it more acceptable.

Dunn and his co-workers in a study to compare the effectiveness of individually used tape/slide programmes with conventional mass instruction for students of the Western Infirmary, Glasgow, found student opinion 'highly favourable' to the use of the tape/slide material and report high scores for the tape/slide group compared with the group which took part in the conventional instruction.

The attitude of dislike for group showings of tape/slide material as a lecture substitute reflects the attitude of students when television is used in the same mode, for example, Maclaine in a study where education students at the University of Sidney attended lectures and watched televised demonstrations found a non-significant difference in students' ability to recall information, but students were critical of the impersonal nature of the televised lecture (Maclaine, 1965).

One important feature of tape/slide material placed in the library for individual use during experimental work at the University of Surrey, was that the presentation was under the control of the student since he could stop it at any point or replay it as many times as he wished. The facility of repeated replay can be used to review parts of a tape/slide programme which does not sink in first time without any sense of embarrassment on the part of the student. This has also been commented on in terms of its usefulness for overseas students in the study previously cited (Harden et al, 1969) but was not noted particularly in my own work.

In this work it also emerged that the tape/slide material can be presented in a shorter time than the normal lecture and the findings of other workers support this (Kenshole, 1968; Bligh, 1970). However, for students who do replay the material, the time taken may well exceed the time taken for normal lectures. In the study by Harden, he found that the average time spent by the tape/slide group was thirteen hours and twenty minutes, the same material being covered in conventional lectures in nine hours but this again throws no light on the relative effectiveness of the two methods.

STAFF AND STUDENT NEEDS

In considering the behaviour and needs of both staff and students in relation to the course, it emerged that there is a need to make staff more aware of the implications of student perception of the teaching/learning process as well as the process itself. That this need exists appears in various points in my study and the disparity in staff/student opinion with regard to the usefulness of self-test material has already been referred to. Indications of this kind also lead to the conclusion that staff need greater experience of a number of methods other than the lecture, as for example, an awareness of and experience in the variety of methods and techniques that can be used in the small group type of situation. As Broadley says in his article on the conduct of seminars, the lack of response from the student in a small group teaching situation often leads a member of staff to fill 'the gap of silence' with a mini-lecture (Broadley, 1970), but with greater experience of group techniques he would know better how to handle the situation.

The promotion of thought amongst staff on both the wide aims of a university education and the methods and techniques available to help students attain these should perhaps be a desirable feature of the induction courses for new teachers in higher education which are at present multiplying rapidly.

Students usually see their needs in terms of short term aims, for example, the need to pass the end of course examination, the need to organize their work, the need to write and hand in essays on time etc. Staff need to look beyond these short term aims to both the wider aims of a university education and look at the needs of the learner in terms of practical applications of psychological learning theories. Four of these main practical applications are as follows:
(a) the need to provide the student with suitable motivation
(b) the need for the student to be actively involved in the work
(c) the need to relate new work to existing knowledge
(d) the need for the student to be able to evaluate his progress continuously.

In relation to the work described at the University of Surrey, students' needs seem difficult to interpret for although students said that they felt a need to write lecture notes and all students bought copies of the printed outline lecture notes provided for this course, only relatively few students added to their lecture notes or rewrote them afterwards. Similarly, many students stated that they did not feel the need to consult books and in the main study under half of the students taking the course indicated that they used more than one book for the course.

This pattern is reflected by the low use of reference material and the clue comes perhaps in students' comments that it was useful for them to be

272

informed of their progress by self-test material regardless of whether the reference materials were used or not. Students appeared to apply the very practical criteria of supposed usefulness in terms of the end-of-course examination to the use of any course materials or the performance of any tasks although this is obviously an oversimplification of the actual situation.

In this study students showed a liking for methods which involve them with the course material. Motivation appears to have been both an important factor both in terms of behaviour on a course and in performance in end-of-course examinations. The importance of motivation is shown in this study mainly by the behaviour and performance of groups of students from the Electrical Engineering Department when compared with students from the departments of Chemical Physics and Physics on both trials of the main experiment.

ALTERNATIVE METHODS OF TEACHING AND LEARNING

A variety of alternative methods of teaching and learning are now being used in institutions of higher education throughout America and Great Britain, as for example, the Open University in Great Britain and the Keller Plan and Postlethwaite Audio Tutorial method in both countries. A number of descriptions of these exist (Keller, 1969; Postlethwaite, Novak and Murray, 1971; Haynes, Hills, Palmer and Trickey, 1974).

Many differences, defects and strengths exist within each method, but like programmed learning these alternative methods are based on principles which recognize the need to motivate the student, to involve him actively in his work, to relate new work to existing knowledge and to allow the student to evaluate his progress throughout the course. These are I believe important principles to be taken account of in the design of any course of instruction.

THE SELF-DIRECTING INDIVIDUAL

The research which has been the subject of this paper largely confirms, in the particular situation to which it was applied, the importance of these factors, but it goes further in stressing the need to consider the individual in terms of a variety of factors which impinge on the teaching/learning process when we are considering it with a view to innovation and improvement.

If our aim is to produce a self-directing individual, then obviously the individual student is central to this process. The student himself needs to be shown how he can operate with greater efficiency in the university environment and his teachers' need to consider ways of helping him to achieve self-direction.

CONCLUSION

In conclusion, I should like to refer again to my title 'Self-teaching in University Courses' for as educational technologists we are often accused of using unnecessary jargon and it may appear to some that 'self-teaching' can be equated to 'learning'.

I believe the use of the term 'self-teaching' is very appropriate in the context of a realization of the learner as central to the teaching/learning process since it clearly indicates the change from a largely teacher-based process to one where the student actively takes responsibility for his own progress, that is, progress towards becoming a self-directing individual.

REFERENCES

Bligh, D A (1970) 'An experiment to compare the teaching effectiveness of a tape-recorded lecture at three speeds of delivery'. Unpublished report, University Teaching Methods Unit, London

Bligh, D A (1972) 'What's the use ot lectures?' Penguin, London

Broadley, M (1970) 'The Conduct of Seminars'. Universities Quarterly, Summer 1970, pp 274-275

Brook, G L (1965) 'The Modern University'. Andre Deutsch, London

Costin, F (1972) 'Lecturing vs other methods of teaching: a review of the research'. 'Journal of Educational Technology', 1.3. pp 4-31

Davis, Q V and Hills, P J (1972) 'The application of a systematic approach to an electrical engineering course'. In 'Aspects of Educational Technology', Vol VI, Pitman Publishing, London

Dunn, W R, Harden, M C G, Holroyd, C, Lover, R and Lindsay, A (1969) 'Investigations of Self-instructional Materials in Medical Education'. In 'Aspects of Educational Technology III' (Ed) Mann & Branstöm, Pitman Publishing, London

Haynes, L, Hills, P J, Palmer, C and Trickey, S (1974) 'Alternatives to the Lecture in Chemistry'. Proceedings of a meeting of the Educational Techniques Subject Group of the Chemical Society, Norwich, 1973. Chemical Society, London

Hills, P J (1974) 'An investigation of some applications of self-teaching systems in the University of Surrey'. PhD Thesis, University of Surrey

Hills, P J and Stace, B C (1974) 'Use of structured booklets in a Structure of Molecules Course'. In 'Alternatives to the Lecture in Chemistry'. (Ed) Haynes, L, Hills, P J, Palmer, C R and Trickey, D S. Chemical Society (Ed Techniques Subject Group), London

Keller, F S, 'Goodbye Teacher'. 'Journal of Applied Behaviour Analysis'. 1.1. pp 79-89

Kenshole, G E (1969) 'An experiment in undergraduate teaching using audiovisual aids'. 'Physics Education', Vol 4, pp 157-160

Mackenzie, N, Eraut, M and Jones, H C (1970) 'Teaching and Learning. An introduction to New Methods and Resources in Higher Education'. UNESCO, Paris

Maclaine, B (1965) 'A programme for improving teaching and learning in Australian Universities'. 'The Australian University', 3.3. pp 235-266

McIntyre, C J (1970) 'The Structure, Aims and Basis of Educational Technology'. Paper presented to a conference on Educational Technology for Principals of Colleges of Education in Scotland, May 1970

Mountford, J (1966) 'British Universities'. Oxford University Press

O'Connell, S (1970) 'From School to University'. Universities Quarterly, Spring 1970, pp 177-188

Postlethwaite, S N, Novak, J and Murray, H (1971) 'An Audio-Tutorial Approach to Learning'. Burgess Publishing Co, Minneapolis

Construct lesson plan

DANNY G LANGDON

For the past four years the author has been researching, developing, and evaluating a new approach to classroom instruction. This approach is called the Construct Lesson Plan. It means that the teacher puts together (constructs) a lesson for classroom presentation which meets the immediate learning needs of the students.

The prevailing manner in which students prepare for and receive instruction may be summarized as follows. Students are generally assigned preparatory study in advance of a lesson that will be given by the teacher. The teacher then assumes that the students have completed their preparatory study and embarks on the presentation of a lesson in the classroom, using whatever instructional method (ie lecture, discussion, discovery, etc) he chooses to employ. The assumptions that the teacher makes in regard to the preparatory study are many and quite varied. It can generally be agreed that the teacher does not, however, know exactly which objectives the students have or have not learned as a result of such preparatory study. Since, as teachers, we do not know exactly which objectives have been achieved, and by how many students or which students, then the conclusion must be made that classroom instruction is, at least to some degree, inefficient. It is inefficient in that our presentation may very well be on objectives which the students have already learned. Such inefficiency then takes away from the use of time that could more efficiently be devoted to improving on the effectiveness with which we deal with those objectives the students have not mastered.

The author suggests two basic methods by which the teacher can assess student-entry-level knowledge relative to the preparatory study that the students have undertaken. Before describing these methods, it would be well to note that in not accounting for what the students have learned on their own, there is a tendency on the part of students to conclude that preparatory study is not really all that necessary - at least not until testing time. If the teacher could show the students <u>directly</u> that preparatory study is worthwhile, then students' preparatory study is more likely to occur, and occur at a more effective level. In effect, we should provide a positive contingency for doing preparatory study.

The most objective and easily administered method for determining entry-level knowledge from preparatory study is by means of testing. However, this is not testing for grading purposes, but rather testing for knowledge gain only. It is diagnostic testing. It is testing all the objectives of a lesson that is about to occur in the classroom. This testing has many aspects to it. For one, it must adequately test each and every objective. We must be able to conclude that satisfactory performance on the test item means that the student has really achieved the objective. Secondly, the test must be capable of being easily 'scored' by the teacher, so that an inordinate amount of time is not required to determine how all students performed. Thirdly, completion of the test by the students will have to be somewhere other than in the classroom, due to the fact that there simply is not enough time to have the students complete the test in the classroom and have enough time remaining for instruction itself. So how do we meet these requirements for reliability, ease of assessment, and where and when the students will complete the test?

Reliability of test items is rather involved and although important not all that germane to the procedure involved in utilizing the Construct Lesson Plan approach. Suffice it to be said that adequate validation procedures and the use of good test item writing principles will take care of this need.

In terms of when and where the test will be completed, in most situations students can be counted on to complete the test on their own, outside the classroom, just after completing their preparatory study and just prior to, (say the night before) entering the classroom. But can the students be trusted to complete the test without cheating? Yes! Student trust, even in those situations in which trust cannot be assured, can be promoted. This is because the test is not an achievement test for grading purposes. Rather, it is a diagnostic test. If it is used for grading, then students will cheat.

Now, how do you score the test? Before you are, say, thirty students who have completed their tests. You cannot sit down and attempt to go over each test individually and then compile the results. There is not enough time for this and classroom instruction as well. The solution is the use of some type of response device. At The American College we use a coloured wheel responder. A six-inch, cardboard wheel, divided into six, pie-shaped pieces - with each pie having a different colour - is attached to a cardboard frame that is masked so that one of the colours can be dialled by the student and seen through the mask. On the back of each colour is printed a distinguishing letter, number or word. For example, the colour yellow means yes, true, response a, or response 1. Orange means no, false, response b, or response 2. The test questions are usually multiple-choice questions or short-answered, constructed responses. Thus, the teacher simply says, 'What is your answer to question 1?' and each student dials his or her response on the coloured wheel. The teacher sees the colours and makes an assessment of how many students, and which students, answered correctly or incorrectly. For correct answers the teacher tells the group what the correct answer is. For example, if 80% of the students get the correct answer to question 1, the teacher tells the students what the correct answer is. The teacher has in advance selected a criteria of group performance for each test item. For any test item on which the group criteria is not reached, the teacher does not give the correct answer. Rather, he informs the students that the objective which relates to that test item or items will be covered in the class lesson which is to follow. By proceeding through the entire test in this manner, the teacher ends with a listing of which objectives have been achieved and have not been achieved as a result of preparatory study. Before moving on to what the teacher does with these results, what would you do in a situation where there is no way in the world in which the students could be trusted to complete such a test on their own, outside the classroom?

A second method, which I have chosen to call the Screening Pattern, for determining entry-level knowledge relative to preparatory study, involves the use of five basic sources of information. It will be the combination of these five sources together which indicate which objectives the students have learned on their own, and not any one source in and of itself. Let me emphasize again that it is the combination of these five sources which are used to determine entry-level knowledge. They are: (1) teacher experience, (2) achievement test results, (3) practice needs, (4) student indications, and (5) limited testing. A chronological run-through of how each of these is used will serve to tell how each source contributes to the final end of determining student entry-level knowledge on an objective by objective basis.

Year after year as we, as teachers, go about the process of bringing instruction to the classroom, we find that there are certain concept and skill objectives of our courses which continue to be problem areas of learning for our students. We often indicate these to fellow teachers when we say things like, 'You know, students never seem to get this idea or that one' or 'I don't know why students have such difficulty with such and such'. Such areas of difficulty are also indicated by the amount of time spent on student inquiry during classroom instruction regarding certain objectives. It would do us well to keep accurate records, on an objective by objective basis, year after year, on such objectives. This becomes the first of five basic sources indicating potential problem objectives for the current students in our classroom. I emphasize that this source is an 'indicator' in that it will need to be further validated for accuracy.

The second source is that of past achievement tests. In reality this source may be even more reliable as an indicator than teaching experience itself. Since we do periodically give a variety of achievement tests, which sample certain objectives of our courses, it would be well to carefully analyze these test results and record which objectives are the ones of continuing difficulty. In part, past achievement test results, like teaching experience, is an indicator of potential problem objectives for our current students. Together, they may help to reaffirm each other as sources of problem objectives.

A third source, somewhat like teaching experience but slightly different, is that of determining group practice needs. Practice is basically a means for sharpening concepts and skills that have already been learned to some degree. Sometimes, but not always, we can analyze the objectives for a class session that is about to take place and find that some of our classroom activity should centre on group practice needs. Thus, while this source is not one of potential major problem objectives, it is useful, along with teaching experience and achievement test results, as a further indicator of classroom instructional activity.

It will be noted that three of the five sources described thus far for the Screening Pattern can all be completed by the teacher prior to entering the

278

classroom. In effect, the teacher can come to class with a list of objectives indicating which are potential problem areas. As the teacher, we will now need to affirm that these objectives are indeed problem objectives for the current class of students. This reaffirming process is where the two final sources come into play within the classroom itself at the beginning of the class session.

The fourth source of the Screening Pattern is student indications. Since it is the students who have just completed their preparatory study, they are in a good position to indicate to the teacher which objectives they believe they have and have not learned. We, as teachers, need only take the time to ask them. It really does not take that much time. In the course of a few minutes a list of the objectives numbered on the blackboard can be put together. It is simply a matter of requesting the students to come to the class with a list of those objectives they personally feel they need additional help with. The teacher then need only poll the students as a group. Then, by matching the students' list with the teacher's list ascertained through the three previous sources discussed, you now have a pretty fair idea of which objectives need the greater amount of in-class attention and instructional activity. By the way, do not be surprised to find that what the students select and what you, as the teacher, have selected are at odds. The point is that through these four sources you have a good idea of the problem objectives. How can you confirm these 'indicators'?

The fifth and final source of the Screening Pattern is where we bring to bear the most objective source for indicating problem objectives and the source which can validate the indications of problem objectives ascertained through the four previous, more subjective means. This source is limited, in-class testing. Whay do I say, 'Limited Testing'? Well, the teacher simply does not have enough time to test all the objectives in the classroom itself. So, which objectives do we test? There are two options. One, we can test those objectives selected by the four sources described previously so as to make sure those objectives are indeed really problem areas. Or, two, we could test the objectives not otherwise selected by the four sources to make sure we have not bypassed an objective that is really a problem objective. Whichever of these two the teacher choses to test will, by experience, be determined by the validity or lack of validity in the reliability of the four other sources. If the four sources continue to indicate the real problem objectives, then we need only test the non-problem objectives to make sure we have not bypassed a problem objective; or we might not have to do any testing at all. Thus, such testing not only indicates the presence or lack of problem objectives, but at the same time tests out the reliability of the Screening Pattern itself. One question to be resolved is how to do the testing itself?

The easiest manner in which to control and administer such in-class testing is to put the test items on overhead transparencies. You can then select out the test items for the objectives you want to test and project them on a screen or the wall and solicit student responses by use of the wheel responders previously mentioned. If overhead transparencies are not possible or are too expensive, then flipcharts or preprinted test booklets can be used.

For the latter, you simply refer the student to the questions to be answered and they use their response devices.

As a closing remark on the Screening Pattern, it may appear to be over-complicated and time-consuming as a procedure to administer. In reality, the discussion of the procedure is much more complicated than its implementation. Relative to the Testing Pattern described earlier, the Screening Pattern is more difficult to administer. I suspect that only actual use will convince you that both are possible. Our experience has shown that they are.

Okay, let us presuppose that you, as the teacher, have used either the Testing or Screening Pattern and have arrived at a list of learner objectives representing those which the students have and have not learned as a result of their preparatory study. Let us say that for a particular lesson there are ten objectives. Our analysis reveals that the students have learned four objectives on their own and they still need in-class instructional assists on the remaining six objectives. What does a teacher do with this knowledge?

Any teacher, given this knowledge, may proceed with the style and manner of presentation and related classroom activities that they are used to, and find most effective. This may be a lecture, discussion, discovery or whatever. Certainly, with this knowledge of existing student entry level, whatever instructional method is used, it should concentrate on those objectives that the students need the most help with. Two things should be kept in mind: first, most of the instructional time should be devoted to the problem objectives, and second, we need to maintain a continuity of instructional presentation. What does the latter - 'continuity' - mean?

Nearly every classroom presentation is structured around a conceptual idea, topic, theme, skill area or so forth. Thus, while we may determine that certain objectives for a given topic for an intended classroom presentation are known by the students, we cannot simply devote our time in class to only the objectives the students have yet to master. If we did, instruction might be fragmented. The question is, 'How do we maintain instruction efficiency and continuity in learning effectiveness?' The answer is rather simple. For those objectives the students have yet to learn, we use what we call instruction - the detailed presentation of content, involvement in learning activities, media support, and that all-important aspect of student-teacher interaction. For the objectives the students have already mastered on their own we use an informational approach - meaning the presentation of content on a generic; overview basis. However, in so presenting ourselves, as teachers, towards either instruction or information, we do not mean to discourage the more spontaneous interaction which is often generated by the students' own questions.

Where are we, therefore, in this approach to classroom instruction based on the Construct Lesson Plan? Nothing has really been said about that which we normally think of when we say 'lesson plan'. What is the structure of the 'notes', so to speak, for the teacher's presentation which can be built around the knowledge gained from using either a Testing or Screening Pattern which isolates student entry-level knowledge? How can we organize this lesson plan to assure both efficiency and continuity?

Well, even if we decided to present a pure lecture to the students we could put down our notes and continually remind ourselves to present very little content on the objectives the students have already learned, and a lot of content on those objectives they have yet to learn. I would like, however, to present a design (format) for a lesson plan which, while it would allow a lecture approach, also allows the use of nearly any other approach you can think of and has many additional benefits to it, including, amongst others:

1. Flexibility in sequencing instruction to meet the needs of a variety of potential student audiences from year to year or class to class.

2. A design that can be easily tailored by many different teachers to the style of teaching they prefer to use and have found successful.

3. A design that allows the teacher to 'personalize' the lesson plan to those content reminders so that he alone needs to remind himself of what to present, activities to occur, media to use, etc.

4. And a design that can be easily revised to reflect the new concepts, changes of emphasis and improvements for learning effectiveness that the teacher strives to build into his instruction on a continual basis, year after year, from class to class period.

There are two major components to the 'lesson plan' of the Construct Lesson Plan Approach. These are (1) a 'content outline', and (2) a series of 'lesson plan cards'.

The purpose of the content outline is threefold:

1. It assures the continuity of a classroom presentation as a whole.

2. It serves the teacher as a continuing overview of the presentation topic and subtopics.

3. It can serve as the source from which an informational approach by the teacher can be taken towards those objectives already mastered by the students in their preparatory study.

As Figure 1 illustrates, a content outline is simply a listing of major and minor topics. The only distinguishing feature of this outline is the numbers which appear in the left-hand column. These are the numbers which match the objective numbers for this lesson and they are placed in the outline wherein they relate to the content. More can be said about the outline once the lesson plan cards are described.

As Figure 2 illustrates, lesson plan cards are laid out to organize instructional activities around individual learner objectives. Each card contains six basic features:

1. A statement of the learner objective. Because the diagnostic test is organized to test each objective, in like manner each card is organized around a separate objective so that the cards may be divided as a whole into those achieved by the students as a result of their preparatory study and those which will need in-class attention.

2. Major and minor topic headings. These are given to show the relationship to the teacher and student as to where the objective lies in relation to the complete assignment or lesson. Such headings are drawn directly from the previously mentioned content outline.

3. A card number is placed in the upper right-hand corner. This number is for organizational purposes. The number matches both a list of objectives

Objective Key	Outline of Subject Matter
	1. Monetary and fiscal policy (Samuelson, pp 334-345)
1,2	(a) Liquidity preference and marginal-efficiency-of-investment
3	(b) Fiscal policy and income determination
4,5	(c) Interaction between fiscal and monetary policy
	2. Fiscal policy (Samuelson, pp 355-360)
6	(a) Goals of fiscal policy
7	(b) Automatic stabilizers
8	(c) Weapons of discretionary fiscal policy
	3. The budget (Samuelson, pp 360-363)
9	(a) Surplus and deficit financing
10	(b) the 'new' economics
11	(c) Full-employment budget surplus or deficit
	4. The public debt (Samuelson, pp 364-371)
12	(a) Burdens
13	(b) External debt and internal debt
14	(c) Measuring the public debt

Figure 1. A content outline

which the student studies from and the corresponding test item which is used in the pre-test to measure it.

4. A rectangular box in the centre of the lesson plan card is used by the teacher to write special notes regarding content that must be recalled for presentation to the students. Content reminders may also include visual materials to be used, special student activities, exercises, and so forth. When preparing lesson plan cards for another teacher to use, this area is usually left blank so that the teacher may personalize the lesson plan card to his own needs.

5. The answer to the pre-test item which was used to assess the student's knowledge or mastery of this objective is specified on the lesson plan card. At some point during instruction, the teacher will want to assess again the student's mastery of the objective after giving clarifying instruction. In many instances it is often recommended that a new test item and answer be available for this purpose and it can be specified in this section of the lesson plan card.

CLU COURSE 8
ECONOMICS

Assignment   9 SYNTHESIS OF MONETARY AND FISCAL POLICY

Topic   MONETARY AND FISCAL POLICY

Subtopic

Objective   Given a liquidity-preference schedule, explain how
                  monetary policy is used to effect a change in interest
                  rates. Samuelson pages 334-335 and Assignment 7
                  Objective 3

Pre-test
Answer   Blue, C

Notes (Content reminders, visuals, exercises, activities)

Enabling Questions

Figure 2. A lesson plan card

6. Finally, there is a section on the lesson plan card to specify any enabling questions. These questions can be used by the teacher to assess student progress along the way towards final achievement of an objective.

The value of lesson plan cards as the means to construct a lesson plan is in their flexibility. By organizing each card around a separate learner objective, the cards can easily be selected out to organize for each particular class session relative to pre-test results. The sequence can, in like manner, be easily changed. Necessary revisions and additions can be made. Just as importantly, the lesson plan cards can be used by a variety of teachers and personalized by each to their own needs.

Now we can come full circle to the use and practicality of the Construct Lesson Plan approach. By using either the Testing or Screening Pattern, the teacher can ascertain accurately and easily the specific learner objectives which the students have mastered on their own, and those which the students require attention on within the classroom. As the teacher goes over the test results at the beginning of the class period, a process that takes less than ten minutes, he divides his lesson plan cards into two stacks: those representing the objectives that the students have already mastered, and those with which the students need help. Taking the cards in the latter stack, the teacher then coordinates these cards with the content outline. On the outline, the teacher circles the objectives with which the students need in-class help. This is easily done, in that the card numbers tell which objective numbers on the outline to circle. Then, in implementing the lesson, the teacher simply presents any objectives already mastered in an overview, informational manner, using the content outline as a guide. Whenever the outline indicates an objective requiring more detailed instruction - the objectives circled on the outline - the teacher makes use of the lesson plan card for that objective. The card contains the specifications for specific content reminders, activities, media use, enabling questions and, finally, a test item for measuring student learning following classroom instruction. Thus, it can be seen that the continuity of instruction is maintained by the content outline and the concentration of instruction on the immediate learning needs of the students is assured by use of the lesson plan cards. This is the Construct Lesson Plan Approach to efficient and effective classroom instruction.

Organizing experience: structuring objectives in the military career[*]

ROBERT H KERR

INTRODUCTION

In contrast to many other types of careers, the military career affords the educational and training technologist a unique opportunity to study the effects of many factors which impinge on learning. The goals of the military organization can be quite clearly defined, the career progression of individuals identified, and changes can be introduced using the formal lines of communication which discipline provides.

Two developments which have been particularly interesting to the educational and training technologist are the strides which have been made towards defining the careers of individual service persons and the analysis developed in formulating relevant behavioural (or learning) objectives. Strong interdependencies between these developments have been established because of the timing of their implementation (1965-75) by various military organizations throughout the world. For example, the definition of careers expressed in terms of the behaviours required in the working environment is policy in the Canadian Military today, and takes the form of tasks (or groupings of tasks) to be performed by job incumbents. In the Royal Navy, job definition is accomplished by formulating Operational Behavioural Objectives, which specify in detail the job requirements (see Mager, 1962; a different format is used in Kerr, 1973). Both these services have implemented as policy the establishment of Learning Objectives in behavioural form in order to stipulate their course learner requirements. The United States Armed Forces are also committed to the behavioural approach in both areas and have provided much of the initial research into this approach and have pioneered its implementation. This paper discusses the relationships between these two developments as experienced in the military career structure.

THE MILITARY CAREER STRUCTURE

In order to study the behavioural relationship between careers and training it

---

[*] The opinions expressed in this paper are those of the author and do not necessarily express the official policy of the Canadian Armed Forces. Copyright Canadian Armed Forces.

is first necessary to examine the patterns within which service persons can proceed in their careers.

Service persons attain ranks in their careers which in most instances are related to functions of responsibility allocated to them in the job environment. To simplify this discussion I will use a numerical coding to indicate increasing rank, (1) being lowest and (9) being the highest. In many cases, rank attainment (4 to 9) is achieved through a performance-rating system which is based on such factors as ability to lead juniors, flexibility in handling novel situations, communicative skills (writing and speaking), loyalty, etc. These types of general factors are applied individually but are assessed service-wide using identical reporting formats, and are considered the critical factors for any service person to be a service person per se. The second set of variables in a career pattern involve a serviceman's proficiency in accomplishing the tasks specifically allocated to his particular career. These categories are akin to apprentice, journeyman, semi-skilled worker, highly-skilled worker or craftsman, etc, in civilian occupations.

In the military career structure, these two parameters (rank and trade proficiency) can be either contingent upon one another or they can be only loosely related. Figure 1 shows the possibilities with increasing trade proficiency indicated as A through G with G being the 'most proficient'. A contingent career requires promotion to be accompanied by a corresponding increase in trade proficiency.

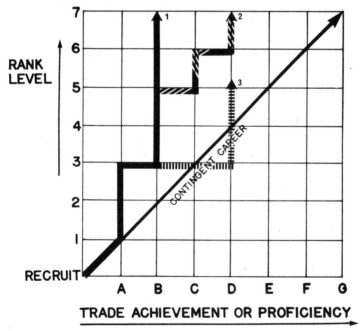

Figure 1. Military career structures

286

In Canada, the contingent career plan strategy is currently being utilized to a large extent. In the Royal Navy certain careers (1974) were being made contingent whereas other careers could follow the semi-contingent route, which allows for personnel to attain higher-rank levels, ie 5 to 9, with only trade-profiency gradings of B or C; the semi-contingent career pattern (currently being discussed as a possibility in Canada) also allows specified personnel who are trade proficient to work within job settings that utilize their skills as tradesmen while not over-burdening them with leadership or managerial tasks for which they may or may not be suited. On the other hand, certain personnel may not require the in-depth trade proficiency in order to lead in specified areas. Because everyone cannot be Generals or Admirals there may be substance in this approach! Of course, career progression is influenced by many other parameters such as pay, service conditions, time of service and the intrinsic nature of some career areas, but these considerations are not the subject of this paper.

To the military educational and training technologist, the previously mentioned two parameters (rank and trade proficiency), have demanded that different approaches be made when formulating objectives. In rank-oriented training, the training designer is stressing the learning of leadership qualities, managerial functions and decision-making skills (or divergent skills). In trade-proficiency-type training, the learning of specific (or convergent) skills is usually involved. These two training areas, however, are interrelated in many later stages of a service person's career when, for example, he may be thrust into the situation of managing a group of maintainers or operators, where both qualities are involved. In each case, the military has written learning objectives which, because of the differing behaviours involved, have demanded different objectives and, most important, different teaching and evaluative strategies to be tried (see section on predicted behaviour and learning, below).

The learning objective has been entrenched as a stepping-stone to promotion and trade proficiency as well. Figure 2 shows a sample progression with Learning Objective Packages (LOPs) in the contingent-career case. An LOP determines whether a recruit graduates to the job environment. This indoctrination phase ensures he/she exhibits the basic behaviours required for a service person; these behaviours are different in degree if not in kind to the civilian situation. As the service person progresses, learning objective packages for Course and On-Job Training are required; some LOPs are trade proficiency (specific) oriented, some are rank (or generally) oriented. In some cases, achievement of an LOP may be the deciding factor for promotion, which may follow immediately after course termination - these points are circled on Figure 2. In the Canadian Armed Forces, there are roughly 120 separate career structures for a forces' population of approximately 80,000. Not counting specialty courses, there are about 500 LOPs which are determinants in career progression.

In the Canadian Forces Training System, the achievement of learning

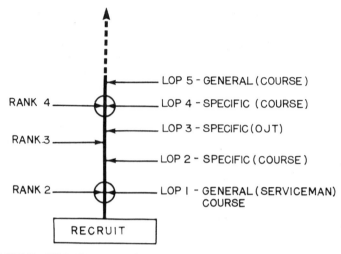

SAMPLE PROGRESSION (CONTINGENT)

✳ LOP — LEARNING OBJECTIVE PACKAGE

⊖ POINTS WHERE LOs LARGELY DETERMINE ADVANCEMENT

Figure 2. Relationships between learning objectives and career progression

objectives requires the manifestation of overt behaviour (Mager, 1962; Kerr, 1973) on the part of the student, and consequently the student's experience is considered effective and accountable if the behaviour learnt is realistic and required for the predicted experience to be encountered on the job. If a direct link can be established between the two 'experiences' then any training given is considered relevant. This philosophy is dependant upon predicting the tasking requirements for specific careers in order to organize the training experience (more simply the accomplishment of learning tasks). Two methods which have proved useful in predicting career tasks are now described and discussed.

OCCUPATIONAL ANALYSIS

"We don't know where we're going 'til we're there" - WWI military song.

In order to avoid the obvious implications of the above, it was considered that an analysis of the current tasks performed by job incumbents as well as other factors could lead to better prediction of what personnel should be doing. This analysis is termed occupational analysis. The implications are obvious: by analysing what is going on now (in terms of tasks performed and opinions regarding those tasks) the service will be in a better position to stipulate what should transpire in future - the predicted tasks, in part, should govern the training given. This paper discusses only some of the training implications of this approach, as these analyses are carried out for non-training purposes as well.

Anyone involved in these analyses processes is indebted to the pioneering work done by the United States Air Force Human Resources Laboratory, at Lackland Air Force Base, San Antonio, Texas, and particularly Dr R E Christal and his associates in developing the Task Inventory Technique for application and computer analysis. A thumbnail sketch of the procedures used in Canada* will now be described in terms of the phases of the analysis (Figure 3).

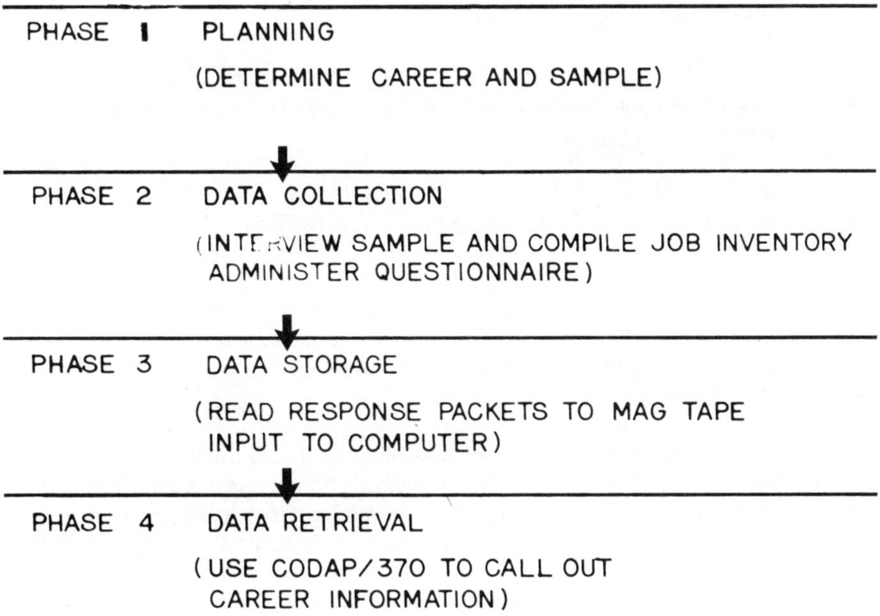

PHASE 1   PLANNING

             (DETERMINE CAREER AND SAMPLE)

↓

PHASE 2   DATA COLLECTION

             (INTERVIEW SAMPLE AND COMPILE JOB INVENTORY ADMINISTER QUESTIONNAIRE)

↓

PHASE 3   DATA STORAGE

             (READ RESPONSE PACKETS TO MAG TAPE INPUT TO COMPUTER)

↓

PHASE 4   DATA RETRIEVAL

             (USE CODAP/370 TO CALL OUT CAREER INFORMATION)

Figure 3. Phases of occupational analysis in the Canadian Forces

In the first or planning phase, one of the discrete trades or classifications is selected for analysis and a representative sample of this population is identified. In phase two, the Data Collection Phase, these personnel are interviewed and a task inventory is compiled which contains the tasks .which this sample state they perform, or are seen performing. The inventories could contain up to 1000 statements of tasks, examples:

        190 - Request coroner services.
        249 - Recommend approval of security clearance.

All the task statements are embodied in a questionnaire format. The responses to the task statements are designed to determine:

(a) the proportion of time spent by each job incumbent performing the task (relative to other tasks).

---

* The basic version was developed at Lackland Air Force Base, Texas. It was updated for use on an IBM 360 computer by the Office of Manpower and Utilization HQ, US Marine Corps, Quantico, Virginia.

(b) the degree of involvement of job incumbents in performing each task, ie, whether they assist in, do, do and supervise or only supervise each task.

Questions on job satisfaction are also added, to gauge the job-enrichment status of invidivual incumbents, example:

Q.12   'I AM ALLOWED ENOUGH FREEDOM IN MY JOB TO EXERCISE
(of 20) SOME PERSONAL INITIATIVE.
         (Respond: STRONGLY AGREE/AGREE/DISAGREE/STRONGLY
         DISAGREE)

Questions (termed variables) to assist the analysts in determining the job incumbent's opinions about various subjects involving their trade, position and career are also formulated, example:

Q.104   'DO YOU BELIEVE YOUR UNIT/COMMAND HAS AN EFFECTIVE
(of 119) ON-JOB TRAINING PROGRAM FOR YOUR TRADE?'
         (Respond: YES or NO)

The above examples are all taken from the task inventory of 'Security' (1974). The questionnaires are then group-administered (to ensure optimum reliability) to as large a sample of the population as possible - 80% to 90% of the career population is usual in Canada.

Phase three (DATA STORAGE) is accomplished by machine-reading of questionnaire response sheets followed by storage on magnetic tape. The last phase (Data Retrieval) involves the use of a special computer programme called CODAP/370 (Comprehensive Occupational Data Analysis Program).* By providing some readouts which aid in formulating objectives, this extremely versatile programme allows in-depth analyses which impinge on training in the services to be undertaken. Only a few of these are discussed now.

One useful readout has been the job description readout which for any rank, lists the tasks performed in such a manner as to indicate the percentage of members performing each task and average percent time spent by members performing each task. This particular readout settles many arguments concerning which learning objectives should be formulated, by displaying the relative relevance of particular tasks in the job environment as measured by the proportion of time filled by these tasks. The resulting information from this type of readout cannot be rejected as being questionable - the readout

---

* Under the direction of Cdr B Cormack, CF, Section Head, Occupational Analysis, National Defence Headquarters, Ottawa, Canada.

gives an objective picture of the situation. The only fault may be that not all the tasks were identified initially. This is unlikely considering the effort used to produce the job inventory. Tasks which the readout indicates that few personnel do, or a very small percentage of time is spent forming them, are scrutinized closely by job experts in order to determine whether training is necessary, and if so, where, or how it should be carried out.

The degree of involvement in performing a task has a major bearing on training for the task and prescribes the nature of the performance required at differing ranks/proficiency levels. Figure 4 shows a graph of two sample tasks in a study ('Study Report of Marine Engineering Technician', 1974) of 800 discrete tasks. Using a scale, the number of responses by rank level were summed and the mean calculated. From the job descriptions for each rank which corresponded to each task, the percentage of the population by rank who responded to each task was found – this percentage is shown by the numbers in each graph. By using this type of display, the training designer can identify the type of performance predominant at each rank level.

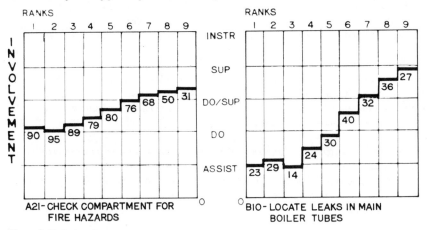

Figure 4. Task structure

In the same study the Canadian Forces Personnel Applied Research Unit, Toronto, correlated job involvement reported by personnel having from 0 - 5 years' service with the same group's response to career intent and found that the factors correlated highly. The Unit's recommendation was: "Positive steps to upgrade the caliber of the jobs which people hold during their first tour is most important if re-engagement rates are to be improved." Apart from changing employment attitudes, the training designer in this case may be forced to 'upgrade' his learning objectives to provide graduates who are more immediately operationally competent. This may involve coursing that strengthens the behavioural similarity between course and job activities. An undue emphasis placed on theoretical approaches (as opposed to application) in early training may not prove coextensive with retention in the forces.

The ultimate decision regarding the placement of tasks within operational career patterns is not made by the training designer, but by those who control the personnel system, ie, it is a Headquarters' function. There appears to be an increasing trend towards consulting Training Designers in this important process.

INTRINSIC ANALYSIS

This form of analysis involves the functional prediction of tasks for the purpose of the formulation of behavioural objectives. In many cases, the tasks involved may not yet have been performed, eg, when a new procedure or equipment is to be introduced in the future. Commencement of training design in these cases must pre-date the actual introduction of these 'new tasks' by a considerable time. Depending upon the situation, many military occupations with existing tasking workloads also must be analysed in this way when occupational analyses teams are not available. Because Canadian military training must be based upon behaviourally stated goals, the designer is faced with a formidable undertaking.

Intrinsic analysis is an orderly development of tasks on a functional basis. Morse (1971), and Hawkins (1972) in previous APLET submissions have described this process in considerable detail. Extensive work in this area (which has also been systematically applied) has taken place in the Canadian Forces Fleet School, Halifax, Nova Scotia, and in the Royal Navy (under the tutelage of the Royal Naval School of Education and Training Technology). The results of intrinsic analysis have provided for specific tasks to be identified as well as allocations of those tasks to specific rank/trade proficiency levels within a career structure to be made.

An example of this process, as applied to the maintenance of an electronic apparatus, is shown here in order to show how certain behavioural aspects are applied. There appears to be a finite number of task 'operatives' (verbs) which can be applied to any machine, ie, it must be repaired, calibrated, tested, etc. This list is finite and forms the action parts of operational task statements and ultimately, training objectives. These operatives can then be applied to a finite list of parts of the machine (or the machine as a whole) which are dictated by the designer. A matrix is developed as shown in Figure 5. The linking between the equipment parts and their operatives are established by a study of the equipment literature and by consultations with experts in the field - many times a maintenance philosophy dictates the exact relationship (repair or fit the spare, etc). Once the tasks are listed, the operational and Headquarters authorities are consulted and eventually decide:

(a) what trade will carry out the tasks;
(b) which rank/trade proficiency level will do specific tasks.

Whatever the outcome of these decisions, an analysis of the tasks themselves to determine the required skill/knowledge levels is conducted and training objectives are written.

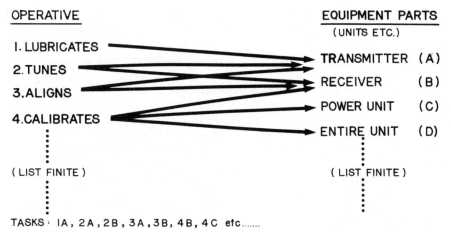

OPERATIVE

I. LUBRICATES
2. TUNES
3. ALIGNS
4. CALIBRATES
:
:
(LIST FINITE)

EQUIPMENT PARTS
(UNITS ETC.)

TRANSMITTER (A)
RECEIVER (B)
POWER UNIT (C)
ENTIRE UNIT (D)
:
(LIST FINITE)

TASKS : IA , 2A , 2B , 3A , 3B , 4B , 4C etc.......

Figure 5. Intrinsic task matrix

Training parameters have influenced the allocation of tasks to rank in some cases. Providing the student with the necessary skills/knowledge for fault-finding requires lengthy courses. In some cases a decision has been made to allocate these tasks only to personnel who have made their career decision. The involvement of lower-rank levels has been emphasized by formulating training objectives which ensure relevant task mastery in related areas - the intention being that both the individual and the service will realize benefits from that stage of their careers. There are dangers in the above approach since some complex behaviours have been found to require a major portion of a career to develop, and consequently must be nurtured early.

Intrinsic analyses for careers which involve the management and operation of equipment or those involving interpersonal relationships to a high degree are much more difficult to carry out and in the author's view are being done on an 'as needed' basis with limited efforts being made to attempt to clarify, substantiate or even formulate principles or guidelines on which to base objectives in these complex behavioural areas. Military training designers have been faced with predicting behaviours for a decade now, with some success, but it is obvious that continuing reasearch and correlation of experience in these areas are necessary. Sporadic validation programmes are rarely compared with underlying intrinsic analyses.

PREDICTED BEHAVIOUR AND LEARNING

Many people in the field may be disturbed by attempts to predict tasks which are to be accomplished by learners - such feelings are prevalent in the military as well. This disillusionment has been based, in my experience, on the belief that certain divergent behaviours will never be specified adequately and precisely. Let me tell you about a personal training experience which hopefully may clarify some of these doubts.

In formulating training objectives for an electronic trade, a predicted task

293

involving judgement and theory was identified as : locates faults in a complex computer. The next step was difficult - what was the achievable learning objective to be? How many faults, among the million possible ones? The job experts resisted all attempts to stipulate the number of faults required, and insisted that to pass or fail a student on a finite number of faults which were to be located in the time allowed would be unfair - they just would not gain the required experience in that short a time. It was discovered through analysis, that the real benefit of this training experience was garnered if the student followed a general, logical procedure in locating faults which (it was hoped) in the long run would eventually provide him with the ability to locate any fault. The standard of these objectives contained the general procedure to be followed while being tested, ie, objectives which call for a process, rather than a product.

When assessing students using these objectives they were required to note each step taken as the individuals proceeded to locate the faults placed on the computer. After the test, the student was debriefed on what he had done, with errors in judgement, logical-thought processes, theory and use of test equipment identified.

The training designer's triumph in this process was not perceived as being merely the achievement by students of a pass or fail learning goal, but in providing the students with a realization of their own capabilities, limitations, strong and weak points, within the framework of the forced experience of that learning objective.

The derivation of objectives based upon the life tasks of 'making effective decisions' or 'exercising critical thought' may be looked upon in the same light. If students in any discipline leave courses with a realization of their own strong points, weak points or biases without the Damoclean Sword of 'get the right answer or else' hanging above their heads, specific learning objectives could be formulated, provided they are assessed with this feature in mind. The keys for formulating objectives in these cases probably lie in the prediction and analysis of only a representative number of tasks. The resulting objectives would thrust students into life-related experiences that are conducive to self-evaluation. The types of standards (of objectives) which would lend themselves to this approach are those which call for a process to be enacted, for process standards facilitate psychomotor, affective and complex cognitive behaviours to be identified (Bloom et al, 1956). (There is much in the literature concerning the processes involved in decision-making - their intrinsic learning value may lie in the degree that they enable students to realize for themselves their own biases, strong and weak points, etc). Knowledge of results may be seen to be the 'real learning objectives' in divergent behavioural situations in preparation for those 'unspecifiable real-life tasks'. There is no doubt that further research in this area would enable the influence of presently assumed learning requirements concerning divergent task accomplishment in later life to be substantiated or alternative strategies to be identified.

Whatever the instructional system employed, it appears that students achieve learning objectives whether or not they are written down. It may be time for us to consider giving these learning experiences more direction than in the past, and when the goals involved are difficult to specify, perhaps we should allow our students the opportunity learn about themselves – is not this one of the prime tenets in the student-oriented philosophy?

CONCLUSION

The behavioural link between operational task accomplishment and the use of behavioural objectives is thoroughly established in many military career structures. Because of the information available through development and implementation, there is little doubt that the present criteria can operate within the Systems Concept of Education and Training to provide for effective and rewarding careers for service persons.

REFERENCES

Bloom et al (1956) 'Taxonomy of Educational Objectives' Vols 1 and 2. Longmans, London

Hawkins (1972) unpublished paper delivered at APLET International Conference, 1972

Kerr, R H (1973) 'The instructional objective'. 'Services Education' Vol 1, No 1. Ministry of Defence, London, p 17

Mager, R F (1962) 'Preparing Instructional Objectives'. Fearon Publications, Belmont, California

Morse, S L (1971) 'Implications of instructional technology as applied to the training of personnel in the Canadian Armed Forces'. In 'Aspects of Educational Technology V'. (Ed) D Packham, A Cleary and T Mayes, Pitman, London

'Security (81)' (August 1974). Task inventory. Ottawa, Ontario

'The Study Report of Marine Engineering Technician' (February 1974). Ottawa, Ontario

Educational technology in health education

W D CLARKE, B C JOLLY

COMMUNICATION IN HEALTH EDUCATION:
A THEORETICAL INTRODUCTION

By way of introduction I want to mention some of the work and ideas of Dr Robert Snowdon of the Family Planning Research Unit at Exeter University. There is little point in becoming too entangled in the specific area of population control, or what he calls 'fertility regulating behaviour', because this area has certain connotations and implications which the area of health education has not. Nor do I want to go into great detail about the development of his arguments, simply because there is not time. What I want to show is that a model of the relationships between the methods of fertility regulating behaviour and the providers and users of those methods, has implications for the development of health education and the involvement of psychologists and educational technologists in that development. The model will also put our small pilot experiment within a frame of reference, albeit a very broad one.

The model can usefully be viewed as a triangle of relationships (Figure 1), where the lines stand for possible interactions between the three elements. As we will see those interactions are not always this straightforward.

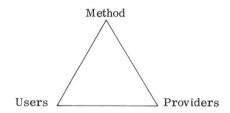

Figure 1. Basic model of health education

The overall objective of fertility regulating behaviour, if you like to use that term, is to stabilize world population. But to concentrate our attention on, say, broad divisions of users at the national or social-class level, and to analyse the success or failure of contraceptives accordingly, is not going to isolate those variables which may be crucial to successful fertility regulating

296

behaviour (Snowdon, 1975). Far more important are the characteristics of the different methods available, since these are likely to influence behaviour in specific situations. These characteristics, for example, can be based on the specific nature of the user - Male/Female, or the route of administration. Is is oral, vaginal, etc? As an example of a situation where such considerations are helpful, consider the programme for implementing the use of contraceptives amongst the Brazilian Indians (Snowdon, 1975). This programme encountered great difficulties and it might have been thought that it had failed for any number of reasons. An analysis in terms of this model, ie the characteristics of the pill and of Brazilian Indian society, would have shown differently. In Brazil taking white pills is regarded as a sign of sickness, so in order to avoid the stigma associated with this Brazilian women stopped taking them. Someone with the knowledge and foresight to have used red pills, or put them in the form of sweets, might have avoided the waste of a large allocation of resources. In a nutshell then, an analysis of the characteristics of the methods of contraception, and their interaction with the attributes of the user, will be much more helpful in successfully promoting fertility regulating behaviour than trying to fit what is available into a global, national or class structure.

The most interesting factors in this model are the relationships between the providers - doctors and nurses - and the other two elements - users and methods. Often the providers are responsible for 'advising' patients on what 'method' would suit them best; sometimes on medical grounds, sometimes for what may be purely arbitrary reasons. (See, for example, Green, 1971.) The implications of a taxonomy of contraceptive methods and a subsequent study of the interactions between methods, users and providers are that you can eventually prescribe, to use a metaphor, the 'perfect pill'.

Certain assumptions have to be made before the model becomes useful. The most important is the assumption that people are aware of the need for fertility regulation, whether or not this need conflicts with their personal characteristics, mores, values, status, and so on. This is certainly not always the case. In the field of health education how many people are still of the opinion that there is no need to give up smoking, so that the question of means does not arise? Alternatively "it should be remembered that the almost universal recognition by women that a lump in the breast might mean cancer has not, of itself, done anything to foster a great willingness among women with breast cancer to seek medical advice early." (Davidson, 1969; also see Legge, 1969). However, that the need is not perceived may be the result of some particular force (apprehensions, values) operating within the model, and it would be as well to consider this possibility before assuming that the situation could be remedied simply by providing more information.

Now it can be argued that this model generalizes equally well to 'health education'. Not to put too fine a point on it, the question arises as to whether the idea of fertility control could even be subsumed under the genus 'health education'. As well as encouraging well-established practices like brushing teeth, buying reasonable shoes, care of the skin, etc, rapid advances have been made towards the possibilities of self-care, for example in self-examination of the breast.

All these examples, firmly placed within the compass of health educators, require some activity to take place on the part of the patient. Moreover they are all behaviours which to a certain extent must take place regularly. Other behaviours, for example some of those we have concentrated on in our experiment, may only need to be used infrequently. But whatever the case, we could still go some way towards a systematic analysis of the best way to present information or promoting such behaviour by looking at what each particular method of ensuring health involves. This does not mean that what is proposed is a set of 'objectives' for, say, self-examination of the breast. What is of concern is, in Snowdon's model, the attributes of things people can do, or use, to regulate their fertility, and in the generalized model the attributes of things people can do or use to regulate their own health. The model has much more affinity, I would say, with an aptitude-treatment interaction process than with any type of hierarchial behaviour structuring.

So going back to the model one might construct a whole list of characteristics for self-examination of the breast. The model is useful because if one were not talking about English middle-class women, it is quite possible that problems would be encountered in teaching the skill (Green, 1973; Wood, 1968). Moreover, such interactions of methods with user-characteristics, which of course will need study, suggest that when it comes down to stimulating and preserving health-maintaining behaviour 'doctor doesn't always know best' (Snowdon, 1975).

There may be important distinctions to be made between what the doctor perceives as the behaviour involved and what the patient perceives as the behaviour involved in any particular method of controlling health. The situation with health education is notoriously 'paternalistic' in terms of the model (Figure 2). Any interaction which takes place is usually one-sided and is in a direction away from the providers and towards users and methods (Green, 1971). The influence of users on methods and providers is conspicuously lacking.

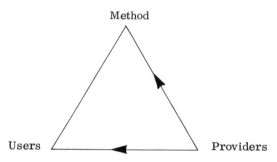

Figure 2. Actual model of health education

It is apparent how psychologists and educational technologists could make their presence felt in this field. By initiating studies of the social and psychological factors bearing on the maintenance of health-promoting behaviour, they can contribute positively towards the effectiveness of health education. But it should be pointed out, if it is not already evident, that the results of such work may have just as much bearing on 'doctor behaviour' as on 'patient behaviour'.

How does all this fit in with what we did? Essentially what we are doing maps onto the 'user' corner of the model quite well. We were concerned to know what it was patients would like to know. But we may have been at odds with the model in terms of the methods apex. We never really attempted a detailed analysis of the individual health-maintaining behaviours we were trying to promote. Indeed, the amount of behaviour involved varied considerably and in some cases we were only trying to provide information. But one thing we had hoped to do was to cross what might be called the user-provider interface. In retrospect we should have approached the problem in a much more analytical frame of mind, and used more explicitly the terms of the model. Had we done so we might have been very much more effective.

REFERENCES

Davidson, R L (1969) 'Knowledge and opinion: implications for health education'. 'Journal of Institute of Health Education' Vol 7, No 2, pp 3 - 6

Green, L W (1971) 'Identifying and overcoming barriers to the diffusion of knowledge about family planning'. 'Journal of Institute of Health Education' Vol 9, No 1, pp 2 - 10

Green, W J (1973) 'The health educator's responsibilities in a multicultural society'. 'Journal of Institute of Health Education' Vol 11, No 1, pp 7 - 12

Legge, C D (1969) 'The individual: barriers to learning'. 'Journal of Institute of Health Education' Vol 7, No 4, pp 3 - 5

Snowdon, R (1975) British Psychological Society Annual Conference. University of Nottingham

Wood, A J (1968) 'Selling health education'. 'Journal of Institute of Health Education' Vol 6, No 4, pp 17 - 20

From a slide-tape presentation

One of the most important requirements of
the medical service today is to find a way to
promote health education. In the field of
health education there are plenty of ideas
about what people ought to know, but very
few ideas about the way in which this should
be taught.

Doctors are often asked to give reassurance
on health problems but few have the time
when patients are coming for appointments.
One of the ideas which presented itself to us
was to use tape telephone messages in a
doctor's waiting room. We wanted to look at
the problems and the practicability of
supplying this information in a doctors
surgery

We approached a group practice in Catford,
South East London. The practice has a list
of 8,000 and draws upon a cross-section of
society. The actual building is fairly modern,
its spacious, its pleasantly equipped, and its
well furnished. What was the kind of
information which would interest patients in
this particular setting?

As one of the authors had been involved in
a Radio London phone-in programme it was
possible to get access to all the questions
that had been asked. When we had actually
collected these questions we found ourselves
faced with quite a large amount of
information. We concentrated on those
questions likely to be of general interest,

which we gradually whittled down, put into
script form and recorded, so that finally we
had 20 short messages which lasted between
90 seconds and 240 seconds each. They tended
to be on different aspects of health care, for
example, on how to treat an earache,
whether to put butter on a burn, where to
get information on ante-natal care; the things
that most people would ask their doctor from
time to time anyway.

Now we wanted to give patients access to this taped information, but at the same time we did not want to upset the normal routine of the surgery. In fact the system we used took up very little space and only a small amount of the receptionist's time. Five telephones were mounted around the walls of the surgery. Small leaflets placed on the centre table advertised what tapes were available and gave instructions on how to use the phones.

So a patient coming into the surgery could obtain a tape by picking up a phone and asking the receptionist for the tape number he wanted. The receptionist then inserted the correct cassette into a player and if the patient had asked for the tape about earache he would have heard: "What should I do about earache? Well that would depend on whether it's an adult or a child in pain..."

That was the situation as we first designed it, and we left it for what we thought was a reasonable period-3 months- to see how many patients would take advantage of the system. Well we soon got an answer. The answer was that the use of these tapes did not exactly measure up to our expectations.

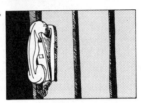

The tapes were being used about 12 times a week, and bearing in mind that 20 titles were available, each tape was being used rather less than once a week. So why weren't people using the facilities? The only practical way to answer this question was to distribute a questionnaire to about 200 of the people who had attended the health centre during the three-month period. About 90% of the people replying hadn't used a tape at all.

The replies also suggested that from our point of view there were two types of people visiting the surgery. One group hadn't used the tapes but given another oppotunity would. And the other group hadn't used them and didn't intend to.

Those people who'd have liked to use a tape either said that they were unsure of what to do, or they were too shy. We reasoned that both these difficulties could be overcome. First the patient's uncertainty about how to use the phones was tackled by designing new leaflets. Instead of placing these on the centre table we put them next to the phones within easy reach.

Second we thought that we could make people feel happier about using the phones by putting up light-hearted posters and by offering 4 tapes with music on. The music tapes were an immediate success, but although there was some early improvement in the number of health tapes being used, as the weeks passed by this improvement gradually fell away.

After a second period of 3 months we were back to square one. During that time the 4 music tapes were used a total of 355 times altogether compared with a total of 123 uses of the 20 health tapes. Tapes with a broader interest seemed to attract more attention. For example, the tape "Should I put butter on a burn" was used 11 times during the 3-months period whereas the tape on "Family Planning" was used only twice.

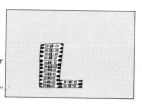

Perhaps then there were other reasons for such a low response. Could it have been that people weren't sitting near the phones, or just that people didn't have to wait long enough to get interested in the tapes? Answers to these questions could only be found by placing an observer in the waiting room. Our observer spent two days, a month apart, at the surgery.

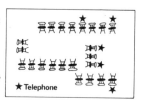

Out of an average of 117 patients using the surgery each day, only 20 had easy access to a phone. This meant that the number of people who might use the system was bound to be considerably less than the total number of people using the surgery. This was encouraging, perhaps our expectations had been too high after all.

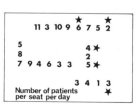

What about the amount of time they had to wait? About 70% of the patients waited long enough, say over 10 minutes, to listen to a message. So it is likely that most of the people who sat near a phone had the time to use it. If we estimate from these figures the number of people for whom picking up a phone was a practical proposition, our actual figures of usage still come no where near our estimates.

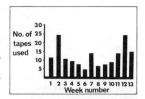

Was the soft sell approach then the right way of attracting attention to the facilities we had taken so much trouble to provide? Our last effort was to introduce yet another new set of posters to publicise the tapes. This time we contrived a much starker approach which included yet another re-designed leaflet.

At the same time we withdrew those tapes that had been used infrequently, and which were aimed at a fairly limited audience. In place of these specific tapes we substituted new subjects which would interest almost everybody. For example, "Acne",

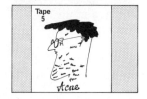

"Tonsilitis", "Depression", and "Glandular Fever".

We also wanted to transfer some of the interest in music tapes to the more serious aspect of the project. Out went "Mozart Horn Concerto" and "Onedin Line" and in came "Migraine" and "Cervical Erosion",

So now there were only 2 music tapes and
22 health tapes. Over the next 6 weeks
interest in the music tapes certainly did wain
but it can hardly be said that interest in the
health tapes waxed. The 22 health tapes were
used a total of 69 times in this period. Well
what can we say about the project as a
whole? Looked at one way, our figures are
certainly not very encouraging.

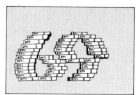

But I suppose it could be argued that getting
patients to listen to around 350 short health
messages represents some degree of success.
Perhaps in another setting, for example a
hospital waiting room, patients would not be
quite so reluctant to listen to tapes. However,
using a doctor's surgery to educate patients
still seems a valid idea. We are at present
trying another approach, which relies on the
visual rather than the auditory channel.

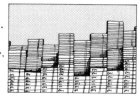

ACKNOWLEDGEMENTS

The second half of this presentation was based on work done in conjunction with
Mr C E Engel, and DR R Ll Meyrick. The slide-tape was a co-production
between the authors and Mick Devine.

The 'members marathon': a summary of contributions

The concept of a 'members' marathon' represented an innovation in APLET International Conferences. Deriving from the practice in recent academic conferences in North America, and the 'open room' sessions arranged by the local section at the Brighton Conference, the intention was to offer a forum for communication and discussion to any participant who did not wish to go through the rigours of submitting a paper beforehand and making a formal presentation.

In the event, relatively few members availed themselves of the opportunity largely, it would seem, due to the attraction of the scheduled presentations and a wish to hear and contribute to discussion.

By the second day, however, contributions were forthcoming, and all those who took part in this experiment felt that it had been worthwhile, although it was recognized that greater prior publicity would have increased the number participants.

Papers, or presentations for the generation of discussion, were contributed by the following:

Robert Quinot, Office Francais des Techniques modernes d'education
G Slamy, OFRATEME, Division d'Etude
M J Sleight, Cybernetic Teaching Systems Ltd
Hans Oosthoek, University of Utrecht
E C J Cuppens, Philips Research Laboratories, Holland

Concluding address: 'educational technology with a human face'

L F EVANS

The word 'technology' seems, inevitably, to conjure up in people's minds an image of dials and flashing lights, inexorably continuous processes, and a concern with products rather than people. When the word 'educational' precedes 'technology', the public image still seems to be of soulless teaching machines producing dalek-like pupils.

The conference theme, 'l'Education Permanente', 'continuous', or 'life-long' education was chosen to enable a truer picture of the purpose, possibilities and practice of educational technology to be presented and developed.

The concept of continuous development as an individual, initiated by appropriate provision at school age, and continued with the support of every sector of our educational and training system throughout life, has seized the imagination in the way that the hope of universal free primary education did a century ago.

If the concept is to become reality, educational technology must play a very important part. A systematic approach to teaching and learning, the design of systems, and the planning and provision of their components and processes encompass the real nature of educational technology, and its employment will be vital in providing the re-orientation, re-cycling and re-training which is becoming increasingly vital if we are to develop as individuals in our rapidly changing society. Educational technology must plan and provide for the aspirations of the mature, seeking in an Open University course the cultural opportunities denied them in their youth; it must train the young, untrained and unemployed in the skills that will bring employment and enrichment of life. With the wealth of resources available to the educational technologist, individualized learning can be provided for the non-vocational, as well as vocational and academic students, to enable their achievement of their goals in personal development.

The provision of individualized learning resources can and should liberate the teacher and the learner for more extensive personal contact, and there have been examples of this, here in this conference; in fact the pleasant, very human face of educational technology has been shown to great effect by many of its practitioners.

Lewis Elton added tactile sensation to an interesting and stimulating presentation, John Cowan enabled an absent colleague to discuss his topic

307

with his audience through an adept use of video-recording, Leo Evans provided a 'crash course' to develop the olfactory and gustatory senses and Sid Connell persuaded participants to produce joyful noise from laboratory tubing. In weather apposite to the occasion we have heard from Gary Coldevin how educational technology has brought undreamt-of opportunities for study and cultural development to the Eskimos in Canada, and, in an effective participatory exercise, Rien Buter has ensured that everyone's heart is in the right place.

All have shown that educational technology is for, and about, people, and that its practitioners are involved in continuously developing that technology, and themselves, the better to help others.

The world-wide appeal of the conference theme has, clearly, been great. We have among us visitors from all five continents, representing forty-three different countries. We welcome particularly the delegates from Thailand, paying their first visit to APLET's Annual International Conference, and our friends from just across the water in the Netherlands who have taken part in every conference since their inception ten years ago. We have all worked together, happily and fruitfully, and have surely continued our education.

The success of the conference has been due to this amicable spirit among all attending, in addition to the efforts of the many individuals who have worked so hard over the past year or more to ensure its achievement. Among them, special mention must be made of Ron Britton, Robert Matkin, Clive Neville and John Leedham as consultants and planners, the members of the Council of the Association for Programmed Learning, under whose aegis the conference is held, many of whom chaired the working sessions and gave support in other ways, the staff and students of the City University who provided the services and facilities and formed the core of the conference organization, Mrs Wynn Ghouse and Mrs Peggy Day, Miss Jeannie Swann, Messrs Peter Brown, Peter Aprile, James Chant and J Knight, and the many others who gave so freely of time and effort.

To all of them our thanks.